Project-Based Language Learning and CALL

Advances in CALL Research and Practice
Series Editor: Greg Kessler, Ohio University

This series is published in cooperation with the Computer Assisted Language Instruction Consortium (CALICO). Each Spring just prior to the CALICO annual conference the series publishes one volume comprised of original studies on a specific topic.

Published:

2016
Landmarks in CALL Research
Edited by Greg Kessler

2017
Learner Autonomy and Web 2.0
Edited by Marco Cappellini, Tim Lewis, and Annick Rivens Mompean

2018
Assessment Across Online Language Education
Edited by Stephanie Link and Jinrong Li

2019
Engaging Language Learners through CALL
Edited by Nike Arnold and Lara Ducate

2020
Understanding Attitude in Intercultural Virtual Communication
Edited by Ana Oskoz and Margarita Vinagre

Project-Based Language Learning and CALL

From Virtual Exchange to Social Justice

Edited by
Michael Thomas and Kasumi Yamazaki

SHEFFIELD UK BRISTOL CT

Published by Equinox Publishing Ltd.

UK: Office 415, The Workstation, 15 Paternoster Row, Sheffield, South Yorkshire S1 2BX
USA: ISD, 70 Enterprise Drive, Bristol, CT 06010

www.equinoxpub.com

First published 2021

British Library Cataloguing-in-Publication Data
A catalogue record for this book is available from the British Library.

ISBN-13 978 1 80050 024 2 (paperback)
978 1 80050 025 9 (ePDF)
978 1 80050 046 4 (ePub)

Library of Congress Cataloging-in-Publication Data
Names: Thomas, Michael, 1969- editor. | Yamazaki, Kasumi, editor.
Title: Project-based language learning and CALL : from virtual exchange to social justice / edited by Michael Thomas and Kasumi Yamazaki.
Description: Sheffield, South Yorkshire ; Bristol, CT : Equinox Publishing Ltd, 2021. | Series: Advances in CALL research and practice | Includes bibliographical references and index. | Summary: "This book is the first substantive scholarly book on project-based and cross-curricular language learning using digital technologies"-- Provided by publisher.
Identifiers: LCCN 2020046883 (print) | LCCN 2020046884 (ebook) | ISBN 9781800500242 (paperback) | ISBN 9781800500259 (pdf) | ISBN 9781800500464 (epub)
Subjects: LCSH: Project method in teaching. | Language and languages--Study and teaching--Computer-assisted instruction.
Classification: LCC P53.67 .P74 2021 (print) | LCC P53.67 (ebook) | DDC 371.3/6--dc23
LC record available at https://lccn.loc.gov/2020046883
LC ebook record available at https://lccn.loc.gov/2020046884

Typeset by S.J.I. Services, New Delhi, India

Contents

1 Introduction: Projects, Pandemics and the Re-Positioning of Digital Language Learning

Michael Thomas and Kasumi Yamazaki

1 Background

It is difficult to ignore the fact that this volume has been completed during the six months from March to September 2020, a period of unprecedented social and economic flux around the world that has profoundly influenced all levels and aspects of education (Bates, 2020). Across the developed and developing world, the Corona virus (COVID-19) crisis has amplified inequalities inextricably linked to existing education and health systems and forced policymakers and educators to question inherited models of teaching, learning, literacy and the role of digital technologies and online learning (Jandrić, 2020). While online education has occupied a steadily increasing role and profile over the last two decades, especially since the emergence of Massive Open Online Courses (MOOCs) in 2012, the widescale adoption of web-based instruction within a matter of weeks in March and April was swift and unforeseen.

As time has passed since the initial move online, it has been acknowledged that the forms of 'emergency remote learning' that have emerged require us to reflect more deeply on appropriate forms of pedagogy, curricula, and teacher training for the post-COVID-19 digital age (Cahapay, 2020). And while many teachers have come to grips with online and blended learning for the first time during the last six months, the new 'phygital' environment (a neologism mixing the 'physical' and 'digital') has brought to prominence deep-seated concerns about the potential consequences of an even more dramatic consolidation of this direction of travel: the increasing casualization of teachers, the growing use of analytics and performance indicators, the role of internationalization, the implications of an unpredictable global educational marketplace, and the sustainability of models of growth in education (Macgilchrist, Allert, & Bruch, 2020). As Zhao (2020: 1) has pointed out, "The massive damages of COVID-19 may be incalculable. But in the spirit of never wasting a good crisis, COVID-19 represents an opportunity to rethink education." In this vein, when we look back on the pandemic of 2020 from a future vantage point, will educators be able to say that it precipitated a profound rethinking and progressive reorganization of education? Or will it be seen as an event that continued and perhaps even deepened and extended recent trends related to the de-skilling of teachers, resulting in greater casualization, increased uptake of instructivist remote learning, and more reliance on digital technologies, sometimes under the guise of disruptive learning, in post-pandemic educational institutions? (Selwyn et al., 2020). These are questions that confront us all as academics, teachers, and researchers, particularly in the area of second language acquisition and the niche subfield of computer-assisted language learning (CALL), which is often at the forefront of developments in the rapidly changing local, national, and global marketplace for students and new educational technologies.

Pre-dating the pandemic, numerous research studies over the last two decades have explored these key questions from a variety of perspectives (Gray, 2019). Foreign language education has often found itself deeply entangled with these debates because of the rapidly changing macro-policy landscape (O'Regan, Gray, & Wallace, 2018). It is no longer the case, if indeed it ever was, that these are simple questions of pedagogy or curricula. Across all disciplines from STEM (science, technology, engineering, and mathematics) to the Arts and Humanities, teaching and learning are increasingly shaped by global as well as local sociopolitical factors as educational institutions respond to their role in the global economy and network society. Technology has been a key driver of these socioeconomic changes in the workplace but increasingly also in the field of education and training. The role of education in increasingly wholly or partly privatized systems in which teachers and learners have become consumers has turned learning into a product and challenged the notion that it is concerned merely with humanistic goals (Giroux, 2014). In its place, driven by the culture of the marketplace and increasing student fees, in many educational systems learning has become a commodity, positioned primarily as service industry that prepares students for employment and the world of work (O'Regan & Gray, 2018). In UK higher education, as an example, the government's Teaching Excellence Framework, or TEF, evaluates the success of teaching based on statistics related to the employability of graduates six months after the completion of their course of study and no classroom observation of actual teaching practice is included in the review process. The TEF is a symbol of the increasing use of evaluation frameworks, metrics, and analytics, borrowed predominantly from the world of business and marketing, that have been imported into the field of education (Block & Gray, 2016).

Since the emergence of neoliberal forms of education in the late 1970s and early 1980s, humanistic disciplines such as foreign language learning have often been caught in the crosshairs of this debate about the use value of the liberal and creative arts versus the sciences or STEM and more directly vocational forms of education. In its defense, advocates have responded to the challenge by identifying the value of language learning in economic or strategic terms, noting its cultural importance for developing transferable skills. Following this line of argument, languages are central to cross-cultural communication and multiculturalism, and important areas of the economy such as the military and intelligence services prioritize less commonly taught languages such as Chinese, Russian, and Arabic, as well as the strategic fields of translation and interpreting. From the egalitarian perspective, foreign language learning is also strategically important in dealing with the integration of increasingly large flows of refugees and migrants. In the UK, for example, English as a Second Language (ESL) is worth an estimated £2 billion annually to the local and regional economy, a figure that places it above the national fisheries industry by comparison. In line with the growth of instrumental approaches to education over the last four decades, it is perhaps no accident that we have also seen the rise and mainstreaming of digital educational technologies (Torsani, 2016). These technologies have moved from providing individual tools aimed at helping language learners and teachers, often through autonomous and increasingly mobile learning platforms via smartphones and tablets, to giving learners opportunities for social interaction and collaboration through the use of games and immersive environments, thus supporting the social turn in learning theories that we have also seen since the early 1980s (Block, 2003).

It is important, then, to consider the strategic, historical, and socioeconomic factors shaping foreign language education policy and practice in any particular national context, as they are often overlooked in favor of less overtly ideological concerns in the research literature. The growing turn towards more instrumental forms of language learning at the beginning of the 1980s in the form of task-based language teaching (TBLT), a natural outgrowth of dissatisfaction with communicative forms of language teaching, reflects this functional approach in some respects (González-Lloret & Ortega, 2014; González-Lloret, 2017). In the intervening period, task-based language teaching has led to an extensive and wide-ranging body of research, with research on task types, task sequencing, and the efficacy of the task approach across different levels, in different cultural, proficiency, and skills contexts, among many areas of enquiry (Van den Branden, Bygate, & Norris, 2009). From the early 2000s, research on TBLT also started to consider the role of digital technologies in overcoming some of its perceived misconceptions and limitations (Thomas & Reinders, 2010). Indeed, research and practice on TBLT has clearly breathed new life into communicative language teaching, giving it a role to play in teaching students the skills they may need in the world outside the classroom and beyond the kind of "drill and kill" rote learning that characterized the generation before CLT in the shape of grammar translation and audiolingualism (Van den Branden, 2006). While research on TBLT has addressed specific aspects of linguistic concern, the types of tasks have often been limited and pedagogical in nature and TBLT has rarely been cited as contributing to the wider repositioning of language learning required by the economic critique.

Arising from and related to task-based learning, project-based learning derives from similar origins but has often wider and larger, cross-disciplinary aims and objectives. Projects are naturally longer in duration than individual discrete tasks and, crucially, require a diverse range of skills and disciplinary knowledge from students to complete them (Beckett & Slater, 2019). They are typically collaborative and the range of different skillsets underlines the importance of multimodality in terms of datasets, disciplines, and perspectives. Several countries have pioneered approaches to project-based learning under a variety of names and descriptors. For example, in Finland, long-renowned for its radical educational ideas, it is called phenomenon-based learning, while elsewhere it draws on theme-based approaches to learning which we might see integrated into learning approaches typical of primary schools. Another name for project-based learning is cross-curricular learning, which reflects the integration of several disciplines to enable learners to solve a common problem or achieve a common goal (Barnes, 2015; Ward-Penny, 2010). While it appears to continue the instrumentalist, task-based approach on a larger scale in terms of the number of participants, the size of the tasks, and the duration of the activities, initiatives that have harnessed project-based or cross-curricular learning also include an emphasis on engaging learners in "grand challenges" or "wicked problems" alongside a more recent focus on raising awareness about social justice, environmentalism, sustainability, and civic engagement (Macgilchrist, Allert, & Bruch, 2020). Indeed, there is a growing body of work on project-based learning of this type that aims to engage learners in online-mediated "challenge-based learning" addressing specific questions of societal value and significance (Beckett & Slater, 2019).

2 Project-Based Language Learning

There are strong similarities and continuities between task-based and project-based language learning, principally in that they both share a common concern with activities or "real-world" tasks that engage learners in the world beyond the classroom. Like TBLT, advocates have argued that project-based learning (PBL) provides ample opportunities for interaction to enable meaningful second language learning. Moreover, as has been the case with defining the keyword "task," project-based approaches have suffered from ambiguity (Ellis, 2009). While the quantity of research on language learning has dramatically increased over the last four decades, the English language education industry has expanded dramatically. Less commonly taught foreign languages have seen a decline in the curriculum in many countries and where budgets are tight, these are often the first areas to be targeted for closure in an increasingly marketized and competitive system of higher education. Project-based learning is different in that it aims to appeal to a wider range of disciplines beyond merely language learning. In the context of PBL, the integration of different skills, activities, and tasks with different durations is a key principle. The last is important, as projects are longer than discrete activities and may be seen as several interconnected tasks. In terms of language learning theory, this extended notion of a project provides more opportunities for input and output as learners move towards a common target. In project-based learning, other skills are developed, including project management and problem-solving, prior to disseminating the solution in a concluding reporting stage. Projects can take place in a mixture of learners' L1 and L2 as well, and an emphasis on collaborative problem-solving can help to integrate many of the processes of interaction central to second language acquisition, such as negotiation of meaning (Beckett & Slater, 2019). The higher-order cognitive skills associated with the project approach are central to constructivist learning theories, including creating, evaluating, analyzing, applying, understanding, and remembering.

Several varieties of PBL have developed, mediated by cultural traditions of learning. In Finland, phenomenon-based learning has developed by interweaving multiple disciplines across the sciences and arts and humanities, including foreign language education without privileging it (Symeonidis & Schwarz, 2016). In Italian schools, Content and Language Integrated Learning or CLIL has been developed in a similar way, and has become an approach which enables students to study an area using the target language (see Cinganotto, this volume). Using "hard" CLIL, which is more subject-focused and relies less on communication, or "soft" CLIL which aims to use the target language most if not all of the time, content is also taught.

These cultural variants provide an indication of how PBL can require high levels of student engagement and cognitive skills. In opposition to transmission or delivery modes of pedagogy, what in Freire's terminology would be called the "banking" model, project-based learning is a type of social and experiential learning involving risk and interaction in place of rote and memorized forms of learning (Freire, 2000). Central to the projects are meaning-based tasks that encourage students to combine "learning by doing" with research skills. Unlike specific tasks that may be required within relatively short timescales, the longer project durations involved suggest that collaborative learning in this context may lead to lower levels of learner anxiety and stress, and higher levels of student engagement and creativity, as students occupy a range of changing positions in a collaborative team and thus develop diverse skillsets.

There are inevitable similarities between project-based approaches and constructivism given the focus on high levels of student engagement, the importance of designing authentic tasks, and the role of collaboration and mutual discovery rather than individual forms of learning, as well as a recognition of multiliteracies including information and communication technology literacy. In online environments, collaboration can also involve language learners or groups of learners in different geographical locations working together, code-switching between their L1 and L2 as is the case with telecollaboration or virtual exchange (O'Dowd, 2016). Accumulatively these skills are harnessed to address problem-based forms of learning. The teacher or instructor is often seen as a facilitator in this type of collaborative learning rather than an expert, though s/he may also be called upon not merely to enable learning as a facilitator would, but to question and problematize learning and normalized assumptions as per a "difficultator" (Bax, 2011).

While TBLT has attracted a range of criticisms such as its appropriateness for non-western learning cultures, the same applies to projects, which continue the same emphasis on soft skills rather than traditional linguistic form, and it is clear that not all learners will find the collaborative or group-based approach appealing or meaningful (Thomas & Reinders, 2015). Learning cultures may also lead to challenges owing to the types of leadership often required by learners in projects, as well as their cognitive skills. The same challenges may also apply to teachers who may prefer to maintain close control over their classrooms, as collaborative projects often lead to noisy environments in which instructors are required to play a range of positions and different roles. In addition, meaningful forms of project-based learning may impact on the type of learning environment required and influence the physical design and layout of classrooms as well as the cultural context and the wider goals of the educational sector within a particular system, especially when it is more outcome- or performance- and therefore examination-focused (Thomas, 2017).

3 Projects and Digital Technologies

The role of digital technologies has become increasingly prominent in education over the last twenty years, as technologies have moved from being viewed as tools to help individual learning, to networks that facilitate and support social interaction and collaboration. A major spur for these developments was the emergence of Web 2.0 technologies from around the year 2005 onwards, and their emphasis on user-generated content and user agency. There has been a strong emphasis on technology as liberatory, democratic, and aligned with the agency within the Web 2.0 paradigm, building on the ability of end-users no longer simply to consume content but also to produce and disseminate it. Indeed, the technologies and applications associated with Web 2.0 reinforce these ideas, such as wikis and blogs, as well as more creative use of media literacy in photo- and video-sharing websites such as YouTube and via social networking such as Twitter and Facebook, as well 3D immersive virtual and game worlds (Yamazaki, 2019). These online communities promote social learning, peer-to-peer learning, and the sharing of expertise, while also empowering individual learners (Thomas & Schneider, 2018).

Research on these collaborative environments suggests that they promote new forms of multimedia literacy, presenting opportunities for multimodal forms of communication in settings that would prove difficult in traditional classrooms. Undertaking projects in these immersive environments can lower risks, both psychological and physical, for participants, particularly those with learning difficulties or who are less extrovert (Thomas & Schneider, 2020). The act of making and creating is central to these types of constructivist environments and this helps to produce agency in the language classroom. Such projects draw on students' higher-order critical thinking skills and they can participate with others in communicative activities such as role-plays, discussion and other forms of collaborative dialogue and interaction, thus presenting opportunities for target language use.

On the other hand, the use of social media of this kind has also brought significant challenges to educators. Online forms of education promote communication but can also present obstacles to effective communication as a result of the lack of nonverbal cues and abbreviated forms of language use. Discourses promoting the use of digital technologies in education have become pervasive, but technology usage may not suit all learners or may include bias towards particular types of learners. This understanding undermines the notion of "digital natives" or any attempt to homogenize learners in a generational sense, though more research is still needed on the digital skillsets of language learners in this respect in particular (Thomas, 2011).

While it is clear that there are several challenges presented by the use of digital technologies, there is no denying that it has become increasingly prominent in language learning in the first world and more central to task- and latterly project-based learning. Both task- and project-based learning have turned to technology to plug perceived gaps and weaknesses in their approach (González-Lloret & Ortega, 2014). Digital technologies have been primarily of value in language learning to stimulate motivation and engagement by offering opportunities for communicative interaction, or developing other skills such as intercultural communication or digital literacy. The move from simple tasks to larger projects brings the potential for the extension of broader skillsets, with less structure but more focused on learner agency and L2 identity development and strategies aligned with enquiry, problem-solving, and investigation (Savery, 2015).

Research in the field has tended to be perceptions-driven and more research utilizing relevant theory is necessary to move the field forwards. Consideration of the effect on learning outcomes is important but an exclusive focus on measurable outcomes would risk reinstating a testing-focused agenda which project-based learning was actively established to reconsider. Indeed project-based learning aims to pivot instructed learning towards a more holistic notion of second language learning that engages with a wider range of subject disciplines and multiple skillsets, particularly those not typically represented in classroom learning. Projects involve an emphasis on the unmeasurable and the productive nature of meaningful play. Nevertheless, more research is needed to understand how learners process tasks within a project-based approach, and to examine the structure and sequence of task completion, as well as the roles students adopt as they grapple with complex tasks in a project context. How and which types of learners are capable of problem-solving are important questions to address within the learner-centered context of projects. Likewise, we need to understand more about the responsibility and role of teachers in facilitating and challenging students, as well as their changing instructor profile at different stages within the process. Related to these are the skills required to manage complex multidisciplinary learning contexts, and how learners and teachers deal with different types of profiles and disciplines in which they will typically not be experts. Project-based teaching places a heavier cognitive load on students as well as teachers, and researchers need to grapple with how to collect data effectively from these complex "phygital" learning contexts following their verbal and nonverbal interactions as they complete physical tasks over extended periods of time and as they move around the physical and virtual spaces and landscapes. This requires a multimodal approach to data collection involving several approaches and real-time data collection such as video, learning analytics, observation, and other forms of screen capture (Zheng, Newgarden, & Young, 2012).

In the context of project-based learning and digital technologies, several approaches to the blend of content and communicative skills have emerged, with CLIL being perhaps the most important. In the context of CLIL an immersive approach to language learning is coupled with subject knowledge and expertise (Dalton-Puffer, Nikula, & Smit, 2010). CLIL approaches have developed to the extent that they can best be envisaged as a continuum from hard to soft varieties, though the typical approach adopted in a particular context will depend on local factors and a hybrid approach. Within a CLIL project-based approach, students also have opportunities to use both L1 and L2 and there is a desire to effectively integrate a range of other skills and competencies such as intercultural communication. Like other varieties of task- and project-based learning, CLIL also places a heavier cognitive load on teachers and students and training is essential to bolster the specific knowledge and skills required by the approach. Teachers need to consider the importance of materials design and students need to be aware of the extra emphasis placed on cultivating their analytical, predictive, and comprehension skills (Torsani, 2016). Culturally the benefits appear potentially significant, with opportunities that draw on research in virtual exchange to investigate multiculturalism, intercultural awareness, and cross-disciplinary approaches to knowledge and skills development. In the research on virtual exchange and language learning, as technologies have improved opportunities for reliable video streaming and online collaboration, we have seen a transition from tasks and projects focused primarily on linguistic outcomes, to those which have a wider social and values-based dimension as well. The latter show significant potential for reconceptualizing foreign language learning using (where appropriate) digital technologies to address problems related to inclusivity, social justice, and environmentalism, and other "wicked problems" and "grand challenges" of importance to teachers, students, and researchers across the humanities and sciences.

4 An Overview of the Book

Following this introductory chapter, the book is divided into three parts. Part I on "Project-Based Language Learning and Virtual Exchange" consists of two chapters which each explore telecollaboration from different perspectives. Part II on "Project-Based Language Learning in Pedagogical Contexts" contains five chapters, each dealing with a variety of learning environments and languages including French, Italian, English, and Japanese. Finally, Part III on "Project-Based Language Learning and Social Justice" looks towards the future of project-based approaches by exploring its potential for a wider social impact agenda in the form of social justice, equality, and diversity.

In "Project-Based Language Learning, Virtual Exchange, and 3D Virtual Environments: A Critical Review of the Research," Benini and Thomas provide an overview of current research trends and issues in project-based learning with specific focus on the contexts of telecollaborative and 3D virtual learning. Through the lens of a connectivist framework, the authors identify the changing roles of teachers and students arising from the ongoing advancement of technology, highlighting the potentialities as well as the need for creating interactive, immersive, and collaborative teaching and learning environments. With a theory grounded in student-centered pedagogy and the acquisition of 21st-century skills, the authors explore the ways in which the multimodal approaches can enhance student learning with regard to motivation, autonomy, collaboration, and digital skills, as well as sociolinguistic and pragmatic competences. Based on the systemic review of PBL, telecollaboration, and 3D virtual learning research, Benini and Thomas conclude the chapter by addressing the advantages and challenges to the proposed PBL environments afforded by technology.

In "Business English Telecollaboration in Project-Based Learning: Indonesian and Saudi Arabian Contexts," Bangun and Alfaifi investigate the use of technology-mediated PBL approaches in the context of EFL Business English classrooms. In particular, the authors provide a systematic review of literature aiming to identify the trends and issues of telecollaboration in PBL with a special focus on two teaching and learning environments in Indonesia and Saudi Arabia. With reference to the cultural and pedagogical foundations specific to these environments, Bangun and Alfaifi point out the importance of technology-mediated PBL, not only for the purpose of fostering English language proficiency, but also to promote cross-cultural understanding among the participants through the implementation of social entrepreneurship projects. In the theoretical review of technology-mediated PBL in Business English, Bangun and Alfaifi lay out a summary of current research with regard to its theoretical frameworks, PBL processes, various telecollaboration PBL tools, and modelled PBL studies' outcomes. Based on the critical review of literature, the authors present a practice-theory-practice approach guided by sociocultural theory, and discuss how the effective implementation of Computer-Assisted Language Learning (CALL) and PBL approaches may shed light on the cross-curricular development of social entrepreneurship projects in an English for Business course in the two countries. The authors conclude the chapter by calling for future research involving mixed-method approaches to better understand the complex nature of telecollaboration and PBL research.

In the first chapter in Part II of the book, "Project-Based English Language Learning through Multimodal Videos: An Online Learning Case Study," Valentina Morgana describes the use of multimodal video projects with secondary school EFL learners in an online learning context during the COVID-19 pandemic in Italy. The study investigates the implementation of PBL as a response to learners' needs, and describes its effects on learners' English language and digital literacy skills. Findings suggest that PBL can influence the development of autonomous learning and language awareness. Although the learners were isolated as a result of COVID-19 measures, the collaborative aspects of PBL helped them to feel part of an online community and develop their agency.

"Project-Based Learning in Online Synchronous Writing Classrooms: Enhancing EFL Learners' Awareness of the Ethics of Writing" examines PBL in the context of an online synchronous writing course with a particular emphasis on the ethics of writing. Through a quasi-experimental case study among EFL graduate students, Nami explores how PBL-based online writing environment may contribute to the development of student technical writing, namely, skills and knowledge pertaining to plagiarism, patchwriting, paraphrasing, in-text direct citation, end-of-text referencing, and in-text referencing. In the review of recent PBL literature in the context of language learning classrooms, there is a general consensus of research favoring PBL on L2 learners' literacy development, particularly because of the problem-solving, contextualized, and meaningful nature of the learning involved. However, Nami also points out the general limitations in the field, arguing that there is a lack of empirical evidence surrounding the effectiveness of PBL in CALL and, in particular, the issue of how online PBL instruction may enhance the development of student writing proficiency. To respond to this, Nami examines the effectiveness of a synchronous PBL writing course compared to the control group which received the conventional treatment. Based on the pre- and post-PBL writing analyses in two different contexts, the findings suggest that there was an overall improvement of writing quality among both groups of students. However, when looking specifically at the technical writing skills, the PBL group performed better at appropriately using strategies pertaining to referencing and paraphrasing to avoid plagiarism and patchwriting issues. These findings suggest the effectiveness of PBL-based online synchronous writing courses.

In Chapter 6, "Incorporating Digital Projects into an Advanced Japanese Course: Effectiveness and Implementation," Xie explores how the use of digital storytelling can play an important role in acquiring not only the content-specific knowledge related to Japanese culture but also language proficiency in speaking, writing, reading, and research, as well as translation. In her primary study involving ten undergraduate students in an advanced Japanese language course, Xie draws attention to technology-enhanced project-based language learning as a theoretical framework, aiming to create an integrative learning environment for students. In the study participants took part in a semester-long content-based advanced Japanese course with learning objectives related to the acquisition of contemporary Japanese culture and society through various authentic media and literal sources. As part of the course assignment, the participants were assigned to undertake an anime voice-dubbing project for their mid-term, and a short-video project about Japanese culture for their final examinations. The participants' assignments were later assessed on content, comprehension, productivity, accuracy, and effort. Based on the comparative analysis of the student performance between the digital and non-digital projects, Xie found evidence supporting the effectiveness of digital storytelling projects. Students generally performed better on both projects in terms of linguistic and content skills, and particularly in the categories of comprehension, accuracy, and effort. The survey data also revealed positive perceptions and experiences among the participating students. Overall, Xie's findings suggest the potential of technology-enhanced PBL for more integrative forms of language teaching and learning.

The pedagogical dimension of PBL is also prevalent in Cinganotto's contribution in Chapter 7 entitled, "Project-Based Learning for Content and Language Integrated Learning and Pluriliteracies: Some Examples from Italian Schools." Cinganotto provides a thematic review of literature in PBL and Content and Language Integrated Learning (CLIL) as part of a broader attempt to conceptualize the characteristics of project-based CLIL. In particular, Cinganotto focuses on "pluriliteracies," a model defined by the Graz Group at the European Centre of Modern Language (ECML) which focuses on the integration of subject content and discipline specific communication. Through the theoretical interactions between PBL, CLIL and the "Pluriliteracies Teaching for Deeper Learning" (PTL) project, Cinganotto argues that the focus on pluriliteracies may promote deeper student learning and transferable skills both in languages and in subject content. The author further adds that the combined use of technologies in PBL and PTL play an important role in enhancing an integrative approach for teaching and learning. In the latter half of the chapter, Cinganotto provides a summary of several project-based CLIL case studies promoted by the Italian Ministry of Education in cooperation with INDIRE (National Institute for Innovation, Documentation, Educational Research). While some of the advantages and challenges of PBL for CLIL in Italy are considered to be linked to the level of digital literacy among teachers, overall the qualitative analysis of data retrieved from the participating teachers suggests several reasons for the effectiveness of technology enhanced project-based CLIL.

Drawing on sociocultural theories of learning, Chism and Faidley's contribution in Chapter 8, "Project-Based Learning via ePortfolios: Integrating Web 2.0 Tools into Higher Education World Language Classes," investigates the use of ePortfolios for PBL in the context of a university-level intermediate French course. The objectives of the study were to identify the implications of utilizing ePortfolios, particularly in terms of how ePortfolio tools like *Weenly* provide opportunities for linguistic and culture knowledge construction.

In the study, Chism and Faidley collected survey data from 18 undergraduate students to examine the student attitudes and perceptions toward the use of ePortfolios for PBL. The course consisted of four modules, with each centered around several cross-cultural topics such as family and friends, food, school and work, and leisure. After engaging with topics through various communicative activities in and outside the class, the participants were asked to create ePortfolios consisting of blog entries, Q&As, and vlogs, which were later used as qualitative data to examine the occurrence of any significant learning events. Based on the thematic and interpretative analysis of data, the major finding of the study was that the students using ePortfolios as a new tool for PBL generally perceived their experiences favorably compared to the traditional textbook approach. From an instructional point of view, the use of ePortfolios for PBL created an opportunity for peer-collaboration, learner autonomy, and effective open assessment, as well as supporting cost-efficient implementation, as opposed to the traditional textbook-based instruction.

Part III of the book contains three chapters. The first by Hernández Alvarado and Brinckwirth entitled, "Transcultural Language Learning through a Cinema and Social Justice Teletandem Program," explores the potential of telecollaboration for project-based language learning (PBLL) via a large, cross-national pilot study involving university students in the United States and Mexico. The purpose of the study was to provide opportunities for students to foster cross-cultural knowledge through guided teletandem exchanges, while at the same time evaluating the practical knowledge necessary to deliver successful teletandem interactions from the instructional point of view. In this study, Hernández Alvarado and Brinckwirth focused on the integration of social justice and institutionally integrated teletandem into a PBLL telecollaboration with the goal of optimizing the effective implementation of online telecollaborative exchanges for a large-sized class. By integrating cinema and social justice into a teletandem classroom, the authors aimed to provide more transformative and intercultural language learning experiences for their students. This pilot study followed structured and scheduled exchanges among the two participating universities, in which a group of students from each university participated in teletandem sessions in order to share perspectives on the different social issues between Mexico and the United States. During the study, various sources of data were collected, including an evaluation survey, journals, and *Voice Thread* reflections. Based on both the statistical and qualitative analysis of data, findings suggest that the participants, when engaged in the teletandem sessions, improved their language learning experience. Students generally favored the approach, with evidence supporting their increased confidence and performance in speaking the target language.

Chapter 10, "Stories, Communities, Voices: Revitalizing Language Learning through Digital Media within a Project-Based Pedagogical Framework," also focuses on the use of digital storytelling using a PBL framework. Anderson and Macelroy's aim was to examine the significance of multilingual digital storytelling by drawing on findings from an ongoing project called "Critical Connections: Multilingual Digital Storytelling" which was initiated in 2012. This translingual-transcultural project engages students between ages 6 and 18 in seven countries (England, Algeria, Cyprus, Luxembourg, Palestine, Taiwan, and the United States) to take part in the collaborative production and publication of multilingual digital storytelling in over 15 languages. To effectively theorize the framework, significance, and implications of the successful implementation of multilingual digital storytelling, Anderson and Macelroy revisit their previous critical ethnographic study (Anderson & Macleroy, 2016) to explore the claim that the use of digital media plays a critical role in transforming language learning into a dialogic, student-led, inquiry-based model, providing students with an opportunity to move beyond their classrooms to embrace critical and creative language learning experiences. To provide a better understanding of how multilingual digital storytelling with PBL are designed, integrated and executed, the authors analyze three sample cases of multilingual digital storytelling implementation. Despite some of the challenges discussed in the chapter, Anderson and Macelroy's findings provide major implications for both learning and pedagogical perspectives.

In the final chapter, "Epilogue: Critical Project-Based Learning and Moving Forwards in the Post-Pandemic University," Thomas reflects on the eleven chapters collected in the volume, and argues for a repositioning of both language learning and the subfield of computer-assisted language learning in light of the wider social turn in humanities teaching and research. In terms of research on CALL, the chapter argues for a "social" and "critical pedagogy" turn which moves beyond the narrow agenda of experimental research designs. It calls for a critical turn from purely pedagogical concerns to a wider, social and impact agenda, in the context of a cross-curricular approach to teaching and learning in which language learning plays a role alongside a multidisciplinary approach. Within the increasingly corporate approach to language learning adopted across school, college, and university curricula, this book aims to further stimulate discussion about its purpose and scope, and to re-examine the potential of language learning, and its associated aspect of promoting cross-cultural communication and understanding, through the lens of a project-based approach.

The book's eleven chapters investigate the potential of digital technologies to complement PBL but do not assume that their use is always appropriate, all of the time, for all teachers, all students, all languages, or all proficiency levels. Indeed, it is most likely the case that future research on PBL and CALL technologies will have to explore a hybridized approach to cross-curricular learning, as Ellis (2015) has argued elsewhere should apply to TBLT. Such an approach would involve a blend of synthetic and analytical syllabi, teachers as facilitators and difficultators, and learning theories that are constructivist as well as drill-based, as appropriate to the context. Such an approach would be comfortable with using digital technologies when relevant, while also critical enough to refrain from their use when not required. One constant limitation of CALL as a subfield of SLA is that the acronym rather assumes that technology must always be used to "assist" learning. Where PBL and other approaches to language learning are concerned, it is also important to involve activities in which digital technologies are not used, and to recognize that they are neither always beneficial to or even healthy for engaged, balanced, and worthwhile forms of student learning.

References

Anderson, J., & Macleroy, V. (Eds.). (2016). *Multilingual digital storytelling: Engaging creatively and critically with literacy*. Oxford: Routledge. https://doi.org/10.4324/9781315758220

Barnes, J. (2015). *Cross-curricular learning 3–14*. London: Sage.

Bates, T. (2020). Advice to those about to teach online because of the CORONA-virus. Retrieved from https://www.tonybates.ca/2020/03/09/advice-to-those-about-to-teach-online-because-of-the-corona-virus/

Bax, S. (2011). Digital education: Beyond the "wow" factor. In M. Thomas (Ed.), *Digital education: Opportunities for social collaboration* (pp. 239–256). London & New York: Palgrave. https://doi.org/10.1057/9780230118003_12

Beckett, G. H., & Slater, T. (2019). *Global perspectives on project-cased language learning, teaching, and assessment: Key approaches, technology tools, and frameworks*. London & New York: Routledge. https://doi.org/10.4324/9780429435096

Blin, F. (2012). Introducing cultural historical activity theory for researching CMC in foreign language education. In M. Dooly & R. O'Dowd (Eds.), *Researching online foreign language interaction and exchange: Theories, methods and challenges. Telecollaboration in education* (pp. 87–106). Berlin: Peter Lang.

Block, D., & Gray, J. (2016). "Just go away and do it and you get marks": The degradation of language teaching in neoliberal times. *Journal of Multilingual and Multicultural Development*, 37(5), 481–494. https://doi.org/10.1080/01434632.2015.1071826

Block, S. (2003). *The social turn in second language acquisition.* Washington: Georgetown University Press.

Cahapay, M. B. (2020). Rethinking education in the new normal post-COVID-19 era: A curriculum studies perspective. *Aquademia*, 4(2). https://doi.org/10.29333/aquademia/8315

Dalton-Puffer, C., Nikula, T., & Smit, U. (Eds.). (2010). *Language use and language learning in CLIL classrooms*. Amsterdam: John Benjamins. https://doi.org/10.1075/aals.7

Ellis, R. (2009). Task-based language teaching: Sorting out the misunderstandings. *International Journal of Applied Linguistics*, 19(3), 221–246. https://doi.org/10.1111/j.1473-4192.2009.00231.x

Ellis, R. (2015). Epilogue. In M. Thomas & H. Reinders (Eds.), *Contemporary task-based language teaching in Asia* (pp. 381–384). London & New York: Bloomsbury.

Freire, P. (2000). *Pedagogy of the oppressed*. New York: Continuum.

Giroux, H. (2014). *Neoliberalism's war on higher education*. Chicago: Haymarket.

González-Lloret (2017). Technology for task-based language teaching. In C. Chapelle & S. Sauro (Eds.), *The handbook of technology in second language teaching and learning* (pp. 234–247). Malden, MA: Wiley-Blackwell. https://doi.org/10.1002/9781118914069.ch16

González-Lloret, M., & Ortega, L. (Eds.). (2014). *Technology-mediated TBLT: Researching technology and tasks*. Amsterdam & Philadelphia: John Benjamins. https://doi.org/10.1075/tblt.6

Gray, J. (2019). Critical language teacher education? In S. Walsh & S. Mann (Eds.), *The Routledge handbook of English language teacher education*. Abingdon, UK: Routledge. https://doi.org/10.4324/9781315659824-6

Jandrić, P. (2020). Postdigital research in the time of Covid-19. *Postdigit Sci Educ*, 2, 233–238. https://doi.org/10.1007/s42438-020-00113-8

Macgilchrist, F., Allert, H., & Bruch, A. (2020). Students and society in the 2020s: Three future "histories" of education and technology. *Learning, Media and Technology*, 45(1), 76–89. https://doi.org/10.1080/17439884.2019.1656235

O'Dowd, R. (2016). Emerging trends and new directions in telecollaborative learning. *CALICO*, 33(3), 291–310. https://doi.org/10.1558/cj.v33i3.30747

O'Regan, J. P., & Gray, J. (2018). The bureaucratic distortion of academic work: A transdisciplinary analysis of the UK Research Excellence Framework in the age of neoliberalism. *Language and Intercultural Communication*, 18(5), 533–548. https://doi.org/10.1080/14708477.2018.1501847

O'Regan, J., Gray, J., & Wallace, C. (2018). Education and the discourse of global neoliberalism. *Language and Intercultural Communication*, 18(5), 471–477. https://doi.org/10.1080/14708477.2018.1501842

Savery, J. (2015). Overview of problem-based learning: Definitions and distinctions. In A. Walker, H. Leary, C. Hmelo-Silver, & P. Ertmer (Eds.), *Essential readings in problem-based learning* (pp. 5–16). West Lafayette: Purdue University Press. https://doi.org/10.2307/j.ctt6wq6fh.6

Selwyn, N., Hillman, T., Eynon, R., Ferreira, G., Knox, J., Macgilchrist, F., & Sancho-Gilet, J. M. (2020). What's next for Ed-Tech? Critical hopes and concerns for the 2020s. *Learning, Media and Technology*, 45(1), 1–6. https://doi.org/10.1080/17439884.2020.1694945

Symeonidis, V., & Schwarz, J. F. (2016). Phenomenon-based teaching and learning through the pedagogical lenses of phenomenology: The recent curriculum reform in Finland. *Forum Oświatowe*, 28(2), 31–47.

Thomas, M. (Ed.). (2011). *Deconstructing digital natives: Young people, technologies and the new literacies*. New York: Routledge. https://doi.org/10.4324/9780203818848

Thomas, M. (2017). *Project-based language learning with technology: Learner collaboration in an EFL classroom in Japan*. London: Routledge. https://doi.org/10.4324/9781315225418

Thomas, M., & Reinders, H. (Eds.). (2010). *Task-based language learning and teaching*. London: Continuum.

Thomas, M., & Reinders, H. (Eds.). (2015). *Contemporary task-based language teaching in Asia*. London & New York: Bloomsbury.

Thomas, M., & Schneider, C. (2018). Language learning with machinima: Video production in 3D immersive environments. In P. Hubbard & S. Ioannou-Georgiou (Eds.), *Teaching English reflectively with technology*. Canterbury: IATEFL.

Thomas, M., & Schneider, C. (2020). *Language teaching with video-based technologies: Creativity and CALL teacher education*. London & New York: Routledge. https://doi.org/10.4324/9781003003311

Torsani, S. (2016). *CALL teacher education: Language teachers and technology integration*. London: Springer. https://doi.org/10.1007/978-94-6300-477-0

Van den Branden, K. (Ed.). (2006). *Task-based language education: From theory to practice*. Cambridge: Cambridge University Press. https://doi.org/10.1017/CBO9780511667282

Van den Branden, K., Bygate, M., & Norris, J. M. (Eds.). (2009). *Task-based language teaching: A reader*. Amsterdam & Philadelphia: Benjamins. https://doi.org/10.1075/tblt.1

Ward-Penny, R. (2010). *Cross-curricular teaching and learning in the secondary school... Mathematics*. London: Routledge. https://doi.org/10.4324/9780203835630

Yamazaki, K. (2019). The effective use of a 3D virtual world in a JFL classroom: Evidence from discourse analysis. In E. Zimmerman & A. McMeekin (Eds.), *Technology supported learning in and out of the Japanese language classroom: Pedagogical, theoretical, and empirical developments* (pp. 227–251). Bristol, UK: Multilingual Matters. https://doi.org/10.21832/9781788923514-012

Zhao, Y. (2020). COVID-19 as a catalyst for educational change. *Prospects*. Retrieved from https://link.springer.com/article/10.1007%2Fs11125-020-09477-y. https://doi.org/10.1007/s11125-020-09477-y

Zheng, D., Newgarden, K., & Young, M. F. (2012). Multimodal analysis of language learning in World of Warcraft play: Languaging as values-realizing. *ReCALL*, 24(3), 339–360. https://doi.org/10.1017/S0958344012000183

About the Authors

Michael Thomas is Professor of Education and Chair of the Centre for Educational Research (CERES) at Liverpool John Moores University in the UK. He is the author or editor of over thirty books and peer-reviewed special editions and founding editor of four book series, including Advances in Digital Language Learning and Teaching (Bloomsbury), Digital Education and Learning (Palgrave), and Global Policy and Critical Futures in Education (Palgrave). Among his other books on CALL are *Project-Based Language Learning with Technology* (Routledge 2017) and *Language Teaching with Video-Based Technologies* (Routledge 2020).

Kasumi Yamazaki is Associate Professor of Japanese in the Department of World Languages & Cultures at the University of Toledo, where she teaches advanced-level courses of Japanese as a Foreign Language (JFL) and culture. Dr Yamazaki's research focuses on a wide range of contemporary Computer-Assisted Language Learning (CALL) pedagogy and integration, namely, the use of 3D simulation games and virtual realities (VRs), the development of intelligent CALL (ICALL) systems, and the effectiveness of technology-enhanced language learning curricula. Dr Yamazaki currently serves as Editor-in-Chief of *Technology in Language Teaching and Learning*.

PART I

Project-Based Language Learning and Virtual Exchange

2 Project-Based Language Learning, Virtual Exchange, and 3D Virtual Environments: A Critical Review of the Research

Silvia Benini and Michael Thomas

1 Introduction

This literature review aims to provide a critical evaluation of existing studies on project-based learning (PBL), virtual exchange learning, and learning in 3D virtual environments. It looks first at language learning and teaching in the 21st century, providing background information on the changing role of teachers and students arising from the role of technology both in their academic and personal lives. In the following sections, different types of learning which recognize a student-centered approach while addressing 21st-century competencies are outlined and analyzed, starting with PBL, moving then to virtual exchange learning and finally to learning in 3D virtual environments. The last section focuses on the relationship between these types of learning approaches, presenting current trends and some of the initiatives that aim to combine them.

2 Background and Description of the Research

The 21st century has been labelled in different ways by researchers operating in different fields, including the Creative Age (Florida, 2004), the Digital Age (Thomas & Brown, 2011), and the Conceptual Age (Pink, 2005). These terms reflect a shared acknowledgment that the third millennium has distinctive features that differentiate it from previous ages, being a time when the "*digital revolution* – embodied in personal, mobile, and networked technologies – has replaced manual and routine mental labour with ideas, innovation, and personalized services" (Pei-Lin Tan et al., 2017:

425). In work, personal, and academic spheres, people are now required to acquire and foster specific skills and competencies that allow them to engage proactively and productively with the digital environment they operate in – be they involved with political, social, economic, and/or cultural activity. Creativity, critical thinking, collaboration, communication, ICT literacy, critical and agentive digital literacy, productivity, social and cultural skills, problem-solving skills, flexibility, and adaptability are just some of the 21st-century competencies required to participate actively in local, global, and virtual societies (Murray, Giralt, & Benini, 2020). In this context lie the roots of different types of learning practices that we are now going to introduce: project-based learning, virtual exchange learning, and 3D virtual learning.

Project-based learning is a model of practice that organizes learning activities around projects. According to Jones, Rasmussen, & Moffitt (1997), projects can be described as a series of tasks based on challenging questions that involve students in design, problem-solving, decision-making, or investigative activities which give them the opportunity to work relatively autonomously over extended periods of time while producing – sometimes collaboratively – realistic products (see also, Thomas, 2000). As Markham, Larmer, & Ravitz point out (2003), project-based learning emerges from two important developments over the past 25 years. On the one hand, there has been a revolution in learning theory. Research in neuroscience and psychology (Goswami, 2004; Ochsner & Gross, 2008; Meltzer, 2018) has extended cognitive and behavioral models of learning to show that knowledge, thinking, doing, and the contexts for learning are inextricably linked. Moreover, it has been shown that learning is partly a social activity that takes place within the context of culture, community, and past experiences.

On the other hand, education urges us to respond to the needs of the 21st century. As Markham et al. (2003: 3–4) indicate, modern workplaces now demand "high-performance employees who can plan, collaborate, and communicate" as well as young people who can "learn civic responsibility and master their new roles as global citizens." In this scenario, technology occupies a crucial role, offering several possibilities among which is the chance to learn from and with experts from all around the world and have easier access to different and valuable resources. As Kineshanko & Jugdev (2018) have pointed out, technology integration in educational practices has been widely discussed in social constructivist and connectivist theories where the discussion has focused on how pedagogy can be incorporated "mindfully" and effectively into blended learning or digital education contexts (see also, Kop & Hill, 2008; Siemens, 2005). The need for education to adapt to a changing world is at the core of PBL in that it aims to create new instructional practices that reflect the environment in which students and educators now live, learn, and teach.

Above all, PBL means learning through experience. In PBL learning, students work in groups to solve challenging problems that are authentic, curriculum-based, and often interdisciplinary. Because students are engaged in hands-on, authentic experiences they are given opportunities to learn content in more in-depth ways, while taking responsibility for their learning, building confidence, working collaboratively, communicating ideas, and being creative innovators (Buck Institute for Education, 2010). Thus, PBL provides an effective way to address key 21st-century competencies.

When designing a solid PBL curriculum, research shows that eight essential criteria should be met: (1) the availability of significant content, (2) a need to know, (3) a driving question, (4) an emphasis on student voice and choice, (5) 21st-century skills, (6) inquiry and innovation, (7) feedback and revision, and (8) opportunities to publicly present the product created (Ravitz et al., 2012). Although not necessary for PBL, the role of digital technologies is becoming increasingly recognized. As will be discussed in more depth in Section 5, Solomon (2003) suggests that students can use and integrate digital tools (such as Web 2.0 tools, spreadsheets, word-processing, and databases) into learning practices, while engaging with specific tasks, whereas teachers, on the other hand, may employ technology to monitor, assess, and evaluate students' work in a more creative and proactive fashion.

Virtual exchange or telecollaboration is the second type of pedagogical practice analyzed here. According to Helm (2015), it can be defined as a systematic process of communicating and working with people from different locations through online or virtual means for the development of language and/or intercultural competence.

O'Dowd (2007) also refers to virtual exchange as a form of Online Intercultural Exchange (OIE) and internet-mediated Intercultural Foreign Language Education (ICFLE). For Helm (2015: 187), telecollaborative learning offers the opportunity for learners to engage in a productive dialogue with peers located in different parts of the world while also offering the opportunity for universities "to support their internationalization strategies by 'globalizing their curriculum'." In the education context, virtual exchange can be considered, as Makaramani (2015) suggests, a form of problem-based learning framed within a real context where telecommunication tools such as emails, chats, wikis, forums, or other types of web communication are used. Technology is the mediational tool in the virtual exchange; it is therefore central to telecollaborative pedagogy and has an impact on interaction, as Kern (2014) argues, as participants engage with the technical as well as the social layer of interaction. In terms of terminology, it is important to specify that while the term *telecollaboration* is sometimes questioned, the term *virtual exchange* appears to be used increasingly in a wide range of contexts including governmental and intergovernmental bodies such as the Bureau of Educational and the European Commission (O'Dowd, 2018).

The third type of pedagogical practice uses 3D virtual learning environments. Three-dimensional virtual words are platforms that were first developed for the purposes of entertainment and gaming, but are now also being used for educational purposes (Duncan, Miller, & Jiang, 2012; Schmidt et al., 2012). Such educational environments are called 3D virtual learning environments (3DVLE) (Zuiker, 2012). Numerous 3D learning environments have been developed using platforms such as Active Worlds, Second Life, Open-Sim, Minecraft, Traveler, Adobe Atmosphere, and There (Hew & Cheung, 2010). In 3DVLEs, students have the possibility of being fully engaged with the learning context; they can be anybody through avatar creation and they can experience different times and places as well as the learning environment in which they are immersed (Seo, 2012). Users can communicate via audio- or text-based tools (Dalgarno & Lee, 2010; Dickey, 2005). 3DVLEs offer the possibility for users to design interactive environments with their preferred content (Omale et al., 2009). They also provide the possibility to view a given problem from different perspectives, presenting activities that may be difficult to practice safely in real life. Users are able to access virtual content simultaneously, share information (Prasolova-Førland, 2008), receive feedback (Cheng & Wang, 2011), and complete activities by engaging with objects and individuals from different locations (De Lucia et al., 2009). Technology is of course central in 3D virtual learning as it is the tool that allows such communicative and pedagogical experience. As for the other pedagogical approaches described above, when users are immersed in and engaged with these digital and virtual learning contexts, they have the possibility to develop and foster 21st-century digital competencies.

3 Methodology

This study employed a review method in which concepts were built from data that had been previously analyzed and coded (Glaser & Strauss, 2017). Following Norris and Ortega (2000: 430), the process started by retrieving a body of relevant studies through a "principled, replicable, and exhaustive search of literature." The focus was on gathering relevant studies that were published as either peer-reviewed journal articles or book chapters, hence unpublished papers and dissertations were excluded. This is because the primary goals of the review were (1) to provide the reader with a sense on the current status of the research and projects that define the three areas under consideration, (2) to examine advances made in our knowledge and note areas to be improved, and (3) to stimulate future research and understanding of the areas. Given the broad coverage of issues over the last two decades, the researchers do not try to provide an exhaustive review of the areas of interest, instead they aim to present a selective and qualitative review of published research since roughly 2010.

In order to access the initial corpus of literature relevant to the subject area, appropriate books, chapters, and articles were selected via a keyword search in multiple databases such as Google Scholar, ERIC (Cambridge Scientific Abstracts), JSTOR Education, SAGE Full-Text Collection, SCOPUS, Web Science, Linguistics and Language Behaviour Abstracts, and MLA International Bibliography. Various topic keywords and subject headings and combinations of both were used to conduct the research including terms such as: *project-based language learning, virtual exchanges, telecollaboration, 3D virtual environments,* and *3D virtual learning.*

Bibliographies of all the retrieved studies were then analyzed for relevant research. After excluding duplicate study reports, the titles and abstracts of the retrieved studies were read and categorized accordingly. Following Morris's (2008) approach, categories were developed via inductive analysis of the data and the relationships between categories were investigated based on a process involving adjustment, integration or deletion according to the results of the analysis. The categories proposed were: (1) studies that were most relevant to the topics and (2) studies that were clearly irrelevant (i.e., studies on biology, business, etc.). This paper is organized around the overarching themes of reliability, validity, and construct breadth, within a social framework.

4 Teachers' and Students' Roles in the PBL, Virtual Exchange, and 3D Virtual Learning Contexts

The impact of new technologies in education fosters the vision of an open, global and flexible form of learning leading to radical shifts from "traditional" modes of instruction to a new current mode that is infused by new pedagogical ideas. Teachers are now required to develop suitable skills related to the new learning contexts and paradigms; their role has expanded to various challenging settings, allowing them to become a guide for the autonomous learning process, a researcher and a designer of suitable learning scenarios, an adapter and producer of new didactic materials in technology-based settings, a collaborator and contributor with other teachers and students from all over the world, an evaluator, and finally a life-long learner in technology among all the other professional fields (Stickler & Hampel, 2015).

PBL, virtual exchange, and 3D virtual learning environments offer teachers the opportunity to act as facilitators by being the program director or administrative e-moderator, the technical director or technical e-moderator, the instructor or academic e-moderator, and the social director or social e-moderator (Thomas, 2000; Bronack et al., 2008; Clavel-Arroitia & Pennock-Speck, 2015; Ensor, Kleban, & Rodrigues, 2017). O'Dowd (2015), focusing on telecollaborative learning, describes in detail teachers' roles and competencies; however, we feel that this suggested framework can be applied to both PBL and 3D virtual learning. He proposes that teachers' competencies can be divided into three categories: organizational, pedagogical, and digital. The first category refers to the organizer, facilitator, and course or task designer as well as reflective practitioner, including also the outcomes gathered from previous experiences. The second category focuses specifically on the role of a facilitator where teachers need to be able to provide adequate scaffolding and support for completing specific learning tasks, and also the role of the organizer, explaining the objectives and outcomes of the different learning approaches. The third category of competencies addresses the digital skills which teachers need to be equipped with. This requires teachers to be knowledgable in digital communication and responsible for specific technical aspects. Because of the often integrated use of digital and Web 2.0 tools in these three learning approaches, there is an opportunity for teachers to encourage the development of critical reflection skills in students. This refers to the skill to critically engage with, filter, collect, and evaluate online information (Cottrell, 2017; Dooly, 2010; Hockly, Dudeney, & Pegrum, 2014).

Technology is influencing and supporting what is being learned in institutions but also the way students are learning. Learners are moving from a passive stance and teacher-centered form of delivery to a more active and student-centered one; instead of taking in information from a unique source (the teacher), students have the chance to learn more independently and collaboratively, interacting, comparing interpretations, and working with teachers, fellow students, and peers in other parts of the world to achieve mutual understanding.

The role of the modern student is strictly related to learner-centered pedagogy which is also at the core of learning practices proposed here (PBL, telecollaboration, and 3D virtual learning). This new pedagogy needs to offer learners not only the technologies they are likely to use in the knowledge economy but also the apprenticeship for different kinds of critical knowledge practice, new processes of inquiry, dialogue, and connectivity (Beetham & Sharpe, 2013; Hourigan, Murray, & Riordan, 2011). Practices underpinning effective, innovative pedagogy will differ according to the subject areas but they are likely to include the following central elements (McLoughlin & Lee, 2008):

- Digital competencies that focus on creativity and performance;
- Strategies for meta-learning, including learner-designed learning;
- Inductive and creative modes of reasoning and problem-solving;
- Learner-driven content creation and collaborative knowledge-building;
- Horizontal (peer to peer) learning and contribution to communities of learning.

5 Project-Based Learning

Emerging from this context, project-based learning (PBL) has been defined by Markham et al. (2003: 4), as "a systematic teaching method that engages students in learning knowledge and skills through an extended inquiry process structured around complex, authentic questions and carefully designed projects and tasks." PBL focuses on activities in which students are actively involved in the planning, designing, and implementing of projects in real-life situations while collaborating with their peers and teachers who also provide scaffolding for their learning. PBL is therefore an inquiry-based instructional approach built around a learner-centered environment that focuses on students' use of subject-related concepts, tools, experiences, and technologies to answer questions and solve real-world problems (Krajcik & Blumenfeld, 2006; Markham et al., 2003). PBL has been adopted extensively by K-12 schools, however research shows that higher education institutions have been slow to integrate PBL into their practices (Lee et al., 2014). Because of the different approaches undertaken in educational settings, there is often a natural link to problem-based learning (PrBL) when referring to PBL. As a matter of fact, both PrBL and PBL are similar yet quite different in how they are conceptualized (Savin-Baden, 2000). PrBL and PBL are inquiry-focused learning approaches that encourage an action-oriented model to engage students in complex forms of critical thinking. Their similarity derives from the fact that the learning activities are organized around achieving a shared goal or project (Savery, 2015). It is important to say that in this context, PBL is presented as a specific method of PrBL, whereas PrBL represents a wider and more comprehensive context.

A dominant model for PBL learning is the one supported by the non-profit Buck Institute for Education (BIE). According to this model, originally developed in the K-12 setting, students go through an extended process of inquiry in response to complex questions or challenges proposed. Within this process, projects are designed, managed, and assessed carefully in order to help students learn academic content while fostering key skills such as collaboration, communication, critical thinking, and creating authentic and valuable products (Buck Institute for Education, 2010). The BIE model proposes specific criteria to implement PBL based on the so-called *Six A's* that allow projects to be structured and relevant. Specifically, the project has to meet the following criteria:

1. it is *authentic*: presenting a real-world challenge;
2. it is *academically rigorous*: structured, reliable and critically developed;
3. learners *apply learning* by using cognitive, communicative and digital skills;
4. learners engage in *active exploration* by gathering and filtering information from various resources;
5. learners *interact* making adult connections; and
6. various forms of both formal and informal *assessment practices* are integrated within the PBL approach.

These six features of the PBL approach show that, when integrated into the curriculum, students have the possibility to learn in a real, authentic context where they can foster their creativity and their critical, problem-solving, and collaborative competencies.

PBL learning is an inquiry-based instructional approach that aims to stimulate reform-based constructivist practices (Savery & Duffy, 1995). This approach challenges traditional pedagogical practices where teachers' roles shift from providers of knowledge to facilitators of learning. Research has shown that transitioning from a traditional instructional model to a PBL model can be challenging for both teachers and students. Specifically, Bradley-Levine et al. (2010) and Grant (2011) indicate that, despite the fact that teachers and students understand their new role in the PBL classroom, they struggle to find an appropriate and precise position. In Bradley-Levine et al.'s study it has been recognized that

> PBL teaching takes *more* time to plan, *more* curriculum and technology resources, *more* day-to-day problem solving about how to scaffold student growth and success in their project work, *more* effort to authentically assess student learning, *more* communication with persons in the community, *more* support from the administration in terms of suitable scheduling and curriculum alignment, and *more* opportunities to collaborate with their teaching colleagues. (2010: 19–20)

This aptly summarizes the benefits and challenges that teachers, students, and institutions may face in the PBL classroom.

There is an important link between PBL and language learning, and research has addressed this extensively. Following the PBL socio-constructivist approach proposed by BIE, various researchers have in fact promoted PBL for languages, referring specifically to Project-Based Language Learning (PBLL) (Beckett, 2006; Fried-Booth, 2002; Stoller, 2006). As indicated by Dooly (2013), PBLL fits easily within an approach consistent with communicative language teaching. In her study Dooly employed a blended approach using both CMC (Computer-Mediated Communication) and PBLL. Referring to PBLL in particular, she indicated that students participating in her study successfully gained new information about the topic proposed, and this information was then used to communicate face-to-face (with classmates) and online (with telecollaborative partners) in the target language in order to tackle and solve problems related to the topic.

5.1 Motivation and Benefits of PBL

Several authors have described the characteristics and features required for a successful PBL approach to instruction. Duch, Groh, & Allen (2001), for example, described the methods used in PBL and the specific skills developed, including the ability to think critically, analyze and solve complex, real-world problems, to find, evaluate, and use appropriate learning resources; to work cooperatively, to demonstrate effective communication skills, and to use content knowledge and intellectual skills to become continual learners. Torp & Sage (2002) described PBL as focused, experiential learning organized around the investigation and resolution of real-world problems. Hmelo-Silver (2004) described PBL as an instructional method in which students learn through facilitated problem-solving that centers on a complex problem that does not have a single correct answer. Stripling, Lovett, & Macko (2009) presented PBL as an instructional strategy that empowers learners to pursue content knowledge autonomously while demonstrating their new understandings through a variety of presentation modes. In the same year Grant said that PBL is a "learner-centered strategy that affords learners the opportunity for in-depth investigations of worthy topics and the learners are more autonomous" (2002: 1). As a matter of fact, the student participants in Grant's study saw PBL as engaging, giving them increased freedom and autonomy. Specifically, the study indicated that students understood the role of weighted grades in a PBL project, with grades assigned for work ethic, collaboration, and aesthetics. They understood also that PBL may take more time. Hence, according to the proposed literature, when employing PBL in the classroom, students have the possibility to plan, implement, and evaluate projects that have real-world applications beyond the classroom. Students also have the possibility to work collaboratively with other co-learners while sharing and constructing knowledge on their own. This is the ideal context where 21st-century skills such as communication and presentation skills, critical thinking, creativity, collaboration, research and technical skills, time management skills, etc. can be fostered and enhanced in order to engage effectively and successfully with today's globalized society.

5.2 Possible Problems and Difficulties in PBL

Various researches have addressed the challenges that teachers and students face when integrating PBL into their practices. It has been highlighted that possible problems in PBL implementation may refer to the teacher role and management of the classroom, to the control of student behavior, to the use of technology, and to the assessment and support of student learning. On a practitioner level, Mergendoller & Thomas (2000) in their qualitative study of K-12 teachers highlighted that one challenge characterizing PBL implementation is finding and incorporating community partners. Teachers, in fact, need to allocate time to select appropriate partners and assess the feasibility of the projects rigorously. Referring to a limitation of previous studies, the researchers stated also that "very little is known about the challenges by teachers in developing and enacting PBL on their own. Existing research on implementation is useful for identifying the kinds of training and support teachers need when using packaged or published materials ... but these findings may not generalize to or fully capture the challenges of teacher-initiated PBL" (Mergendoller & Thomas, 2000: 38). In addition, teachers integrating PBL approaches move from the role of knowledge providers to that of facilitators of learning, and specific teaching skills should be developed to support such scaffolding (Ertmer & Simons, 2006).

On a student level, some studies found that they may struggle to discern their roles in a PBL classroom, especially when it comes to accepting responsibility for their own learning (Ertmer & Simons, 2006). Learners who are new to PBL require significant instructional scaffolding to support the development of problem-solving skills, self-directed learning skills, teamwork and collaborative skills in order to achieve a level of autonomy where the scaffolds can be later removed. Finally, it is important to highlight, as Savery (2015) argues, that teaching institutions that have integrated a PBL approach into their curriculum have in parallel provided extensive tutor-training programs recognizing the critical importance of this element in facilitating and enhancing the PBL learning experience.

6 Telecollaborative Learning

Virtual exchange is an area of CALL (Computer-Assisted Language Learning) and CMC (Computer-Mediated Communication) which has been developed greatly over the last two decades. Telecollaboration has been defined by Belz (2003: 2), as: "institutionalized, electronically mediated intercultural communication under the guidance of a linguacultural expert (i.e., a teacher) for the purposes of foreign language learning and the development of intercultural competence." Similarly, Guth, Helm, & O'Dowd (2012: 42) proposed a definition of telecollaboration as "internet-based intercultural exchange between groups of learners of different cultural/national backgrounds set up in an institutional blended-learning context with the aim of developing both language skills and intercultural communicative competence." Hence, telecollaborative learning involves connecting teachers and learners from institutions located in different countries using internet-based communicative tools to enhance language, intercultural, communicative, and digital competences while fostering learners' autonomy. Within this context, virtual exchange also offers the opportunity, as Helm (2015) further suggests, for institutions to develop their internationalization strategies by globalizing their curriculum. Virtual exchange is characterized by the use of both asynchronous CMC (ACMC) tools (i.e., email, bulletin board/online forums, blogs, etc.) and synchronous CMC (SCMC) tools (i.e., videoconferencing tools, text chat tools, virtual learning platforms such as Second Life, OpenSim, etc.). Research studies, as will be outlined below, have integrated and combined these tools according to the most current technological developments.

Virtual exchange has been the subject of extensive research based mostly on individual projects and studies focusing on pedagogical design, technological tools being used, analysis of the interaction, linguistic and/or intercultural learning outcomes, and possible difficulties encountered (Dooly &

O'Dowd, 2012; Helm 2015). As indicated by Helm, a limitation in virtual exchange research concerns the fact that very "few studies offer a bigger picture of telecollaboration in terms of its implementation in higher education, other than a preliminary study carried out by O'Dowd (2011) which revealed that it is very much a peripheral or add-on activity that is not being fully integrated into foreign language programmes" (2015: 198). However, because of the existence of extensive literature on virtual exchange, the following paragraphs will briefly review the research related to the following domains: virtual exchange and educational environments; the languages in use in virtual exchange projects; the role of technology as a mediation tool; and tasks in virtual exchange projects.

Research on virtual exchange shows that very few studies have focused on the use of online collaborative learning with young (beginning) language learners (although see Gruson & Barnes, 2012; Kennedy & Miceli, 2013; Tolosa, Ordóñez, & Alfonso, 2015; Verdugo & Belmonte, 2007). Among the reasons why such telecollaborative methods are used mainly in secondary education or university levels include the limitations of interests and comprehensive topics, the fact that little or no written input can be provided (depending on the age and proficiency level), and the difficulties presented by oral interaction when telecollaborative tasks with other speakers are in place (Sadler & Dooly, 2016). Another issue may be the teacher's digital competence and understanding of the relevance of CMC platforms and CALL games for primary education. Virtual learning environments and serious games have been used in primary education for years; however, they seem to usually involve a more individual and linear form of computer interaction where learners advance from simpler to more complex tasks without consistent and effective interaction with their peers performing in the same virtual environments. In addition, according to Sadler & Dooly (2016), the tasks set in virtual worlds seem to be focused more on acquiring lexical, syntactic, and morphological knowledge and less on meaningful and authentic communication.

Literature on virtual exchange offers a significant number of studies that employ the most commonly taught languages in their exchange programs, with English being the most popular, followed by French, German, Spanish, and Italian (Helm, 2015). In 2003, Belz addressed the lack of research on virtual exchange involving the so-called less commonly taught languages (LCTL); however, more recently, several studies have been conducted employing such languages (Wang et al., 2013; Klimanova & Dembovskaya, 2013). Various virtual exchange projects (i.e., Cultura project, eTandem project) have been based on the bicultural/bilingual model where the "native speaker" is considered the "ideal interlocutor" who can "act as a cultural informant and/or language expert, providing error correction, feedback, and cultural information" (Helm, 2015: 199) However, more recently, research has focused on the use of a *lingua franca*, namely, the foreign language common to all the participants in the exchange programs. According to Lewis, Chanier, & Youngs (2011), this may be due to projects that involve multiple partners and also, as Helm suggests, to an acknowledgment reached mainly by English language teachers, that their students are more likely to communicate with non-native speakers (2015). In addition, when interacting with non-native speakers, learners seem to be more relaxed and more inclined to support each other in the interaction and completion of different tasks (Helm, 2015).

Virtual exchange experiences are always mediated by technology. Both synchronous and asynchronous tools may be employed during the telecollaborative interactions and, in this regard, it is important to underline that the majority of studies on telecollaborative exchange projects carried out in the 1990s investigated asynchronous CMC applications more regularly, whereas an increasing number of studies on virtual exchange have more recently utilized synchronous tools solely or in conjunction with asynchronous CMC tools to maximize technological affordances (Cunningham, 2018). Synchronous communication is argued to help participants to be more motivated and engaged with the task at hand while fostering effective collaboration among peers (Lee, 2006; Jauregi, Melchor-Couto, & Vilar Beltrán, 2013; Helm 2015; Çiftçi & Savaş, 2017).

On the other hand, asynchronous communication offers participants time to reflect upon their task while finding the best strategy to employ in order to complete the task, may that be through blogs, forums, or wikis (Lee, 2006; Dooly, 2008; Guth & Thomas, 2010). The mediational role of technology has also been analyzed by researchers from a social level of interaction focusing specifically on the role of social media networks (Lomicka & Lord, 2012; Chen, 2013; Guth & Thomas, 2010) and the opportunities these platforms may offer for what has been described as intercultural communication in the wild (Thorne, 2010). Social media offer opportunities situated in scenarios where in fact the social activity is "less controllable than classroom or organized online intercultural exchanges might be, but which present interesting, and perhaps even compelling, opportunities for intercultural exchange, agentive action and meaning making" (Thorne, 2010: 144). In this regard, it has been highlighted by various reports that this telecollaborative approach allows learners to negotiate new roles, identities, and meanings, overcoming possible limitations due to low-level proficiency, a process which shifts them from second language learners to active second language users (Lee, 2018; Thorne, Black, & Sykes, 2009; Thorne, Cornillie, & Piet, 2012).

Virtual exchange projects generally employ a task-based approach and, in this regard, an extensive range of research studies have explored the different types of tasks designed to foster meaning-making while integrating them into the development of communicative, intercultural, and digital competencies (Blake, 2000; Thomas & Reinders, 2010).

Information about the types of tasks used in telecollaborative exchanges can be gathered from project descriptions and few studies have examined in detail the outcomes of specific tasks and their impact on participants. Harris (2002), for example, suggested that telecollaboration can be divided into three genres of online activity:

1. *Interpersonal Exchanges:* activities that involve individuals talking electronically with other individuals, individuals talking with groups, or groups talking with other groups.
2. *Information Collection and Analysis:* activities that involve students collecting, compiling, and comparing different types of selected information.
3. *Problem-Solving:* activities that involve the promotion of critical thinking, collaboration, and problem-based learning.

A few years later, O'Dowd & Waire (2009) documented 12 different, frequently recurring tasks used by intercultural virtual exchange projects and synthesized them into three types:

1. *Information Exchange* tasks focus on students providing information to each other.
2. *Comparison and Analysis* tasks are usually classroom-embedded and focus generally on discussing similarities and differences on cultural products such as movies, books, articles. The model for this task type is the Cultura project (Furstenberg et al., 2001).
3. *Collaboration and Product Creation* tasks focus on the creation of a product through active collaboration. This may include but is not limited to a production of a presentation, joint translation, or essay. These types of tasks are considered the most challenging and demanding, especially for teachers with poor technology competency (O'Dowd & Waire, 2009).

Among the three types of tasks outlined above by O'Dowd & Ware, the most commonly used are the first two, as the third one requires teamwork, reciprocity among learners, a balanced workload, and mutual respect for deadlines (Guth & Helm, 2010) which make the task particularly complex for both teachers and students.

6.1 Affordances of Virtual Exchange

Over the years, different studies have shown enough evidence of how telecollaboration contributes to linguistic development (Belz, 2003; Guth & Helm, 2010; Chun, 2015), sociolinguistic and pragmatic competence (Guth & Helm, 2010; Chun, 2015), motivation (Jauregi, 2015), intercultural competence of the learner and practitioner (O'Dowd, 2011), as well as digital competence (Hauck, 2019; Guth & Helm, 2010). In addition, several studies suggest that student autonomy and collaborative interaction may both increase when students take part in telecollaborative practices (Belz, 2003; Dooly, 2008). As Kinginger (2016) states, virtual exchange has the potential to contribute to different aspects of a learner's development:

> In telecollaborative pedagogies, students can create social connections with their peers, see themselves through the eyes of others, be exposed to specific attitudes and discourses about foreigner identities, experience and analyze spoken or informal forms, and expand their discourse options beyond the strictly pedagogical. (p. 20)

When taking part in a virtual exchange, students from different cultures and in different locations can establish a virtual relationship; indeed, participants embrace a different kind of learning experience that provides them with opportunities to engage in international online communication in ways that are not typically enacted in a conventional language setting. As outlined above, in the virtual exchange scenario, participants can foster linguistic, cultural, and digital skills; however, it is important to highlight also that the curriculum can be positively affected. As a matter of fact, research conducted both at secondary (Ware & Kessler, 2016) and university level (Helm, 2015) shows that virtual exchange has the potential to globalize the curriculum while meeting and strengthening its established learning goals. This is perfectly in line with the increased demands for 21st-century paradigms and skills and, moreover, global communication.

6.2 Possible Challenges in Virtual Exchange

As for other models of instruction, the virtual exchange model presents challenges that can make communication between participants difficult or even, sometimes, unsuccessful. The literature has widely addressed those challenges. In particular, O'Dowd & Ritter's (2006) research proposed four levels at which the telecollaborative approach may result in a negative experience: the individual level, the classroom level, the socio-institutional level, and the interaction level. The individual level refers to the learners' attitudes, motivation, knowledge, and expectations as well as the stereotypes that they may have and bring into the classroom and virtual exchange contexts. The classroom level addresses several factors that may be crucial for an effective interaction such as the task design, the relationship between the teachers involved in the telecollaborative exchange, the balance between the students paired for the project, and the overall group dynamic. The social-institutional level refers to the technologies mediating the process, the general organization of the module that students are undertaking (e.g., including workload and assessment), the recognition of attendance to the telecollaborative experience, as well as more practical factors such as differences in timetable and contact hours. According to O'Dowd & Ritter (2006), this is the level that has been examined most by the research literature. Finally, the interaction level addresses the differences in communication and behavior referring, for example, to the use of humor, nonverbal communication, and being more or less open and/or direct during the virtual exchange. However, many studies agree on the fact that the greatest challenge on the interaction level is having participants engaged to a deeper degree where they move beyond an assumption of similarity and manage to reach a critical intercultural perspective (Belz 2003; Kramsch & Thorne, 2002; Ware, 2005; O'Dowd & Ritter, 2006; Helm, 2013). It is important to specify that, although the factors that may lead to failure of the virtual exchange communication have been identified and examined by several researchers, a combination of these factors is more likely to create a challenging environment for the virtual exchange experience.

When it comes to challenges that may be encountered during a virtual exchange project, the role and skills required for the teachers involved have often been discussed. According to Helm & Guth (2016) many issues can be avoided if teachers communicate prior to an exchange and discuss planning, task design, and specific course needs while trying to understand their respective contexts. In addition, Ware's (2005) research indicates that teachers may be prepared to support and facilitate discussions about generic cultural differences but they may not be as prepared to facilitate students at a deeper level of interaction, tackling issues that may also be of a sensitive nature. Students tend to "avoid deep engagement through probing questions on sensitive issues" (Helm & Guth, 2016: 249) and this avoidance strategy "can lead to missed communication or missed opportunities for approximating the kind of rich, meaningful intercultural learning that instructors often intend with telecollaborative projects" (Ware, 2005: 66). As indicated by O'Dowd (2013), it is therefore essential to include strategies to engage with and tackle such sensitive topics in the professional development of in-service teachers in order to overcome possible misunderstandings or tensions in communications and, more specifically, the failure of the virtual exchange experience.

7 Learning in 3DVLEs

Three-dimensional (3D) technologies have become a central feature in the vast majority of computer games, including massively multiplayer online games (MMOGs) such as World of Warcraft and immersive virtual environments (VEs) such as Second Life (SL), OpenSim (OS) and Minecraft (MC). Nowadays, video games and virtual worlds are viewed as relevant educational tools not just for their potential for entertainment, but also for promoting learning. VEs can be described as "environments that capitalize upon natural aspects of human perception by extending visual information in three spatial dimensions" (Wann & Mon-Williams, 1996: 833) whereas an Educational Virtual Environment (EVE) or Virtual Learning Environment (VLE) can be defined as an "environment that is based on a certain pedagogical model, and incorporates or implies one or more didactic objectives, provides users with experiences they would otherwise not be able to experience in the physical world and redounds specific learning outcomes" (Mikropoulos & Natsis, 2011: 769). In 3DVLEs, avatars represent the users' real presence (Seo, 2012) and they can communicate and interact via audio- and text-based tools (Dalgarno & Lee, 2010). In 2012, virtual learning environments attracted significant interest which was subsequently renewed by the rise of augmented reality applications such as Pokémon Go and SoundPacman in 2015 (Chatzidimitris et al., 2015). The potential of using 3D games and virtual environments for teaching and learning has been widely acknowledged among educators and educational institutions throughout the world (de Freitas, 2006; Dalgarno & Lee, 2010; Panichi & Deutschmann, 2012). Over the years, resources and financial support have been allocated to enhance the pedagogical potential of these technologies with "academia, industry and government working to develop new platforms, tools and resources to support these endeavors" (Dalgarno & Lee, 2010: 11). Indeed, these platforms provide a new range of educational opportunities. They offer users not only the unique possibility to explore and navigate a pre-existing three-dimensional environment, but also to extend the environment by creating and manipulating virtual objects while interacting and collaborating with others. Each virtual world provides a set of tools for recreating real-world objects and experiences that can be expanded as much as an individual's imagination and technology allow for. The game-like techniques employed in 3DVLEs as well as in the so-called serious games (games whose main purpose is to educate while entertaining their users) promote user engagement and motivation and, in recent years, the learning potential of games and virtual worlds has been increasingly recognized in the computer-assisted language learning field (Cornillie, Thorne, & Desmet, 2012; Jauregi et al., 2013; Panichi & Deutschmann, 2012; Reinders, 2012; Reinhardt & Sykes, 2012).

7.1 Affordances of 3DVLEs as Learning Spaces

According to Panichi & Deutschmann (2012), 3DVLEs are very effective learning spaces where formal and informal learning can be created and effectively employed (see also Thomas & Schneider, 2018). These multi-user environments offer teachers and students the unique opportunity to create and collaborate while experimenting with their creative competencies and fostering responsibility for their own learning (Ferguson, 2011). As widely confirmed by the research, 3DVLEs can also be more appealing and motivating for certain subjects and for certain types of learners than the use of traditional learning material; they may be in fact useful to simulate the effect of physical laws (Brown et al., 1999), to simulate social environments and allow people to practice social skills (Liu et al., 2010) or to learn about history (Ketelhut et al., 2017; Di Blas, Paolini, & Poggi, 2005).

Dalgarno & Lee (2010) identified a set of contributions that can potentially arise from tasks conducted in 3DVLEs. Specifically, the authors describe five unique affordances characterizing these educational settings (see Figure 2.1):

1. 3DVLEs can be used to facilitate learning tasks that lead to the development of enhanced spatial knowledge representations of the explored domain. This is the ability to move freely around a 3D virtual setting; interacting and manipulating objects allow also the development of spatial knowledge as well as using photographic or video technologies (such as QuickTime VR).
2. 3DVLEs can be used to facilitate experiential learning tasks that would be impractical or impossible to undertake in the real world. This is the opportunity for users, as confirmed also by Ortega & Falconer (2015), to attempt or complete tasks that may have been impossible or difficult in a real-world setting. For example, Wiecha

et al. (2010) describe a range of 3D web-based tools designed to support training in various medical procedures.

3. 3DVLEs can be used to facilitate learning tasks that lead to increased intrinsic motivation and engagement. Simulations and virtual worlds have the potential to simulate intrinsic learning as a result of the high degree of personalization that arises from learners' choices and achievements (Rieber, 2005). As indicated by Csikszentmihalyi (1990), some tasks can be so engaging that the user feels fully immersed and focused in the activity undertaken. The term "flow" proposed by Csikszentmihalyi describes learners' experience in these situations. The high degree of fidelity of 3DVLEs allows the users to become psychologically engaged with the virtual world and concentration or absorption, central concepts in flow theory, are strictly related to meaningful learning, deep cognitive processing, and academic performance (Corno & Mandinach, 1983; Csikszentmihalyi, 1990; Fullagar, Knight, & Sovern, 2013).
4. 3DVLEs can be used to facilitate learning tasks that lead to improved transfer of knowledge and skills to real situations through contextualization of learning. 3D technologies can offer realistic and interactive settings consistent with the real world, hence concepts learnt within a 3DVLE could be more readily recalled and applied to the corresponding real environment. This calls for a situated kind of learning as described by Ruzic (1999: 188) who stated that "[t]he advantages of VR-based teleteaching are individualized, interactive and realistic learning that makes virtual reality a tool for apprenticeship training, providing a unique opportunity for situated learning," which was later emphasized by several authors (Bronack et al., 2008; Chittaro & Ranon, 2007).
5. 3DVLEs can be used to facilitate tasks that lead to richer and/or more effective collaborative learning than is possible with 2D alternatives. In collaborative environments, such as Second Life or Minecraft, users can meet each other and collaborate or socialize. These environments provide users with the possibility to engage with each other and carry out tasks together while also collaborating in the creation of joint products. Mennecke et al. (2010) report on how students undertook a scavenger-hunt activity in Second Life, in which they explored the virtual world as they embarked on a mission to discover interesting places and practice basic virtual world skills. To complete the tasks, students had to retrieve information, decipher hints and 'teleport' to the location of the item they

were searching for. The activity required students to work in teams, while communicating and coordinating their activities throughout the process.

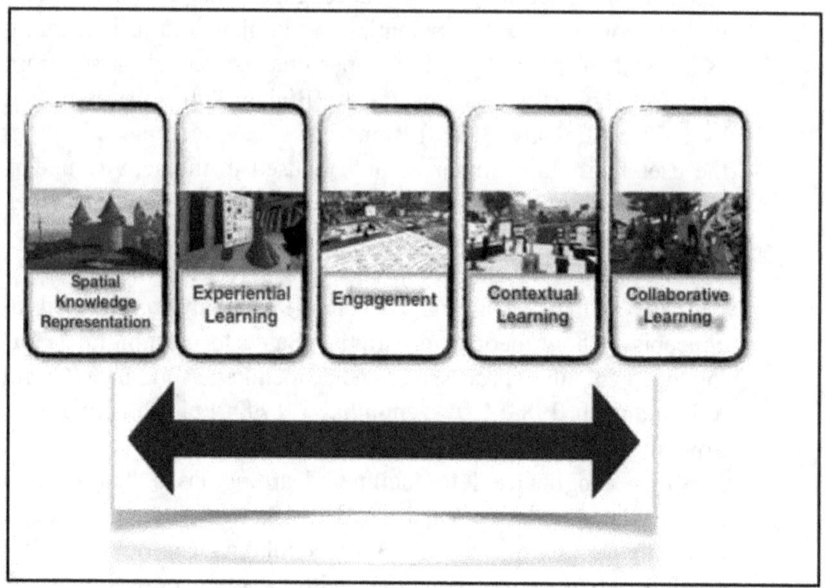

Figure 2.1. The Five Unique Affordances of 3DVLEs (Dalgarno & Lee, 2010)

In 3DVLEs a student-centered model of instruction can be fostered as constructivist and problem-based pedagogies can be easily implemented. According to Polka (2001: 55), learners can in fact "use their experiences to actively construct understanding that makes sense to them, rather than have understanding delivered to them in already organized form." Students are actively and regularly involved in the process of constructing meaning from their own experiences while also "interacting in a way that conveys a sense of presence lacking in other media" (New Media Consortium, 2008: 18). It is important also to note that in 3DVLEs learners use avatar representations, which might be extremely helpful to improve communicative, linguistic, and social skills as it provides presence which is positively associated with better learning outcomes in such environments (Dickey 2005; Duncan et al., 2012; Moreno & Mayer, 2007). 3DVLEs can be also adapted to integrate authentic learning material and strategies. As indicated by Lombardi (2007: 2):

> authentic learning typically focuses on real-world, complex problems and their solutions, using role-playing exercises, problem-based activities, case studies, and participating in virtual

> communities of practice. The learning environments are inherently multidisciplinary. They are not constructed in order to teach geometry or to teach philosophy. A learning environment is similar to some "real world" application or discipline: managing a city, building a house, flying an airplane, setting a budget, solving a crime, for example.

In this sense, 3DVLEs offer the unique opportunity to take part in simulations and activities that closely resemble real-world situations. In addition, Moore, Fowler, & Watson (2007: 463) indicate that 3DVLEs offer an exceptional setting where educators can prepare their learners for "the increasingly complex and interconnected global society in which they live and work." Indeed, across various virtual worlds such as Second Life or Minecraft, students can engage with people from different cultural and linguistic backgrounds, encounter and approach a given task from different perspectives, experience real life-like situations, create and share content (Prasolova-Førland, 2008), and receive multifaceted feedback (Cheng & Wang, 2011), while being in charge of their own learning. Finally, 3DVLEs are important for those universities that aim to a close collaboration in virtual interactive classrooms among students located in different places (Phuong & Shimakawa, 2015; Shah and Kitzie, 2012). As a consequence, several universities around the globe have implemented their own 3D virtual campus environments using the types of instructional approach described above (Cheryan, Meltzoff, & Kim, 2011; Prasolova-Førland, 2008).

7.2 Possible Challenges in 3DVLE Learning

Although 3DVLEs offer many opportunities for learning, there are also challenges that need to be addressed from an institutional, educator, and learner level. From an institutional perspective, virtual worlds require a fast and resilient internet connection and hardware infrastructure as well as support in terms of costs. Specifically, regarding the latter, Second Life offers, for example, different membership plans with the opportunity to create a basic account for free. However, an institution can create a presence on SL and have an area dedicated to pedagogical activities with a premium account. A premium account is required to purchase land which is necessary to have a safe learning environment for students. Minecraft offers, on the other hand, an annual membership that can be purchased at an affordable price. Second Life and most virtual worlds were not created for educational purposes, however, and they have had to be repurposed by educators for teaching and learning.

Teaching in virtual worlds has its own challenges. Creating classes in virtual environments requires specific digital competencies on educators' part as well as the ability to overcome possible technical problems. Indeed, educators interested in conducting their teaching in virtual environments need to gain confidence and skills regarding the possible interruption of pedagogical activities due to technical problems (Bower, Cram, & Groom, 2010). It may take time to overcome issues regarding accessibility of objects or the design of the environments, thus teachers should be equipped with a number of skills that allow them to design effective virtual environments while coping with such possible scenarios (Warburton, 2009). It is important to highlight, as indicated by Riley (2008), that developing and managing courses in these settings takes time and effort that may go beyond what is "normally" required in a traditional classroom based approach. Finally, liability issues may be in place in 3DVLEs. Students in public areas (not restricted to only authorized people as in privately owned land) may be subjected to disruptive behavior by other players (Riley, 2008). Teachers need to be aware of these risks and, in this respect, specific legal issues need to be discussed further and finally resolved (Bugeja, 2007; Riley, 2008). From the students' perspective, novice users may feel overwhelmed or get lost in the 3DVLEs (Bricken & Byrne, 1992), not knowing what to do first or next and how to deal with specific situations. They require more time to become acquainted with such environments and, as a consequence, their short-term satisfaction may be affected.

On the other hand, learners who are used to playing video games may spend their time engaged in activities not related to learning, especially if their motivation is low. In this case, there will be a negative impact on the effectiveness of 3D virtual pedagogy (Ketelhu et al., 2003; Virvou & Katsionis, 2008). Overall, it can be said that possible technological problems, the cost of the chosen virtual environments, liability and adaptation requirements for environments are reported to be among the biggest limitations affecting the more widespread use of 3DVLEs (Eschenbrenner, Nah, & Siau, 2008).

8 PBL, Telecollaboration, and 3DVLEs: Current Trends and Initiatives

This final section focuses on various projects in which multimodal approaches have been employed to learn and practice languages as well as digital and intercultural skills. The value of combining different pedagogical practices has been identified by Kohn & Hoffstaedter (2015) who stated that "a multi-modal telecollaboration approach offering tool options from virtual worlds and video communication to chat and forum is ideally suited for providing practice opportunities for all skills relevant in foreign language learning from reading and writing to listening and speaking" (p. 5). In addition to fostering language competencies, these specific multimodal approaches offer the opportunity to enhance digital and intercultural skills while allowing students and teachers from different locations and cultural backgrounds to collaborate and create content together. Specific projects where such methods of instruction have been employed, were selected and are described below.

The TILA project (Telecollaboration for Intercultural Language Acquisition) was funded by the European Commission Lifelong Learning Programme (http://www.tilaproject.eu). It explored how to innovate and enrich foreign language teaching programs by encouraging the use of telecollaboration activities among European secondary schools. It also investigated how to support teachers to integrate digital and telecollaborative tools and activities into their teaching practices while developing their digital, intercultural, and organizational competences, and examined the added value of telecollaboration for language learning in relation to intercultural awareness, motivation, and communication amongst young learners (Jauregi et al., 2013). TILA employed different telecollaborative tools for both synchronous and asynchronous modes of instruction. In the synchronous modes, digital activities and games in 3D virtual worlds were employed together with chat and video communications. In the asynchronous mode, wikis and discussion fora were used. One of the main areas of research was task-based learning and the relationship between the tasks developed by teachers and the activities that learners carried out in the telecollaborative sessions.

The second project is TeCoLa (Pedagogical Differentiation through Telecollaboration and Gaming for Intercultural and Content Integrated Language Teaching) (https://sites.google.com/site/tecolaproject/background/project-summary) which was funded by the European Erasmus+ program. Its aim was to develop and validate innovative gamified telecollaborative approaches for secondary schools. At the core of the TeCoLa project was the investigation and validation of authentic, task-based telecollaborative process among peers of different sociocultural, educational, and language backgrounds. The project proposed a multimodular approach for teachers' development around task-based gamified telecollaboration while offering open educational resources and support (Jauregi & Melchor-Couto, 2017). The project started in 2019 and lasts for three years. In the first year the basis for teacher training programs were created together with a model of meaningful gamified telecollaborative tasks to be applied in different educational contexts. During the following years, the proposed model will be employed and validated.

GUINEVERE (Games Used IN Engaging Virtual Environments for Real-time language Education) was a two-year European Commission project (https://guinevereproject.eu) that investigated the potential of digital game-based learning in 3D immersive environments focusing on foreign language learning. The project started in 2017 and lasted two years. GUINEVERE examined digital play in specific 3D virtual learning platforms, namely Second Life, OpenSim, and Minecraft, across primary and secondary level school environments. At the core of the project was the promotion of language learning through the use of digital technologies to develop play, creativity, and dialogical thinking while understanding new cultures (Thomas et al., 2018).

Another project that targeted both primary and secondary levels was the eTwinning project (https://www.etwinning.net). It was launched in 2005 as the main action of the European Commission's eLearning Programme and was then integrated into Erasmus+ in 2014. The eTwinning project aimed to promote and support collaboration between schools through technology, providing tools and services. Specifically, the project developed a portal to help schools find partners and to facilitate communication and collaboration between staff and pupils of partner schools while engaging in joint educational projects. In addition, it offered opportunities for free and continuing online professional development for educators (Papadakis, 2016).

More recently, the Erasmus+ Virtual Exchange (EVE) program was launched (https://europa.eu/youth/erasmusvirtual/about_en) which aimed to expand the scope of the Erasmus+ program via virtual exchanges. During 2018, the EVE program aimed to engage over 8,000 participants from Europe and the South-Mediterranean area to create a safe online community where young people could increase their linguistic, intercultural, digital, and communicative competences. This program, currently implemented by a consortium of organizations led by the Search for Common Ground includes UNI Collaboration, and offers learners the opportunity to participate in various engaging virtual exchange initiatives (O'Dowd, 2018).

The TILA, TeCoLa, GUINEVERE, eTwinning, and EVE projects share the common purpose of internationalizing education by integrating telecollaborative approaches in schools, diversifying teaching, and facilitating content integrated language learning (CLIL) by using digital tools (serious games and virtual worlds in the case of the TILA, TeCoLa, and GUINEVERE projects). These projects aim to create the conditions to foster intercultural communicative competences, experience real-life communication, develop collaborative and personalized learning, and exploit the possibilities of Web 2.0 applications. Furthermore, these projects aim to offer educational resources to practitioners, as well as to empower and support teachers on the use of telecollaboration and gamification in their practices. In this regard, it is important to highlight that in the case of the TeCoLa project, teachers showed little experience with the digital tools proposed by the project (video communication, chats, digital games), especially with virtual worlds, which indicated that video communication was the tool with which they were more familiar, as it was the most valuable for dealing with diversity, promoting intercultural awareness and communicative competence (Jauregi & Melchor-Couto, 2017). The GUINEVERE and eTwinning projects were the only ones targeting both primary and secondary schools; however, only the GUINEVERE, TILA, and TeCoLa projects made regular use of virtual environments and serious games.

9 Conclusion

This literature review has provided a critical overview of recent and current research on teaching and learning in the 21st century, with a specific focus on project-based learning (PBL), telecollaborative learning, and learning in 3D virtual environments, in order to explore the potential of interactive, immersive, and collaborative pedagogical settings. The review started by discussing the role and contribution of technology to the educational field, and addressed the features and skills required by both teachers and students to engage and work effectively in the current digital environment. According to the research, all the learning methods proposed allow learners to develop specific competencies including motivation, autonomy, collaboration with peers, digital skills, and sociolinguistic and pragmatic competences. However, some challenges were addressed by different studies, above all, the role and skills required for teachers to implement effectively those methods of instruction in their teaching practices. Teachers need in fact to take part in structured teacher training programs that allow them to develop specific teaching skills essential to support and guide their students in such educational models of instruction. It goes without saying that the support of educational institutions is crucial for the success of the proposed learning processes.

Finally, research shows that the current educational scenario in which PBL, telecollaboration, and 3DVLEs are integrated as models of instruction (e.g., the TILA, TeCoLa, eTwinning, and EVE projects), demonstrates some promise for future research. These projects have a common purpose:

to internationalize education by integrating these approaches in educational settings, diversifying teaching, and facilitating the use of digital tools. Such a direction of travel is in line with the requirements and the development of 21st-century learning paradigms and the skills needed for global communication.

References

Beckett, G. H. (2006). Beyond second language acquisition: Secondary school ESL teacher goals and actions for project-based instruction. In G. H. Beckett & P. C. Miller (Eds.), *Project-based second and foreign language education: Past, present, and future* (pp. 55–70). Charlotte, NC: Information Age Publishing.

Beetham, H., & Sharpe, R. (Eds.). (2013). *Rethinking pedagogy for a digital age: Designing for 21st century learning*. London & New York: Routledge.

Belz, J. (2003). Linguistic perspectives on the development of intercultural competence in telecollaboration. *Language Learning & Technology*, 7, 68–99.

Blake, R. (2000). Computer mediated communication: A window on L2 Spanish interlanguage. *Language Learning & Technology*, 4(1), 120–136.

Bower, M., Cram, A. & Groom, D. (2010). Blended reality: Issues and potentials in combining virtual worlds and face-to-face classes. In C. H. Steel, M. J. Keppell, P. Gerbic, & S. Housego (Eds.), *Curriculum, technology & transformation for an unknown future* (pp. 129–140). Proceedings ascilite, Sydney.

Bradley-Levine, J., Berghoff, B., Seybold, J., Sever, R., Blackwell, S., & Smiley, A. (2010). What teachers and administrators "need to know" about project-based learning implementation. In *Annual Meeting of the American Educational Research Association*, Denver, CO.

Bricken, M., & Byrne, C. M. (1992). *Summer student in virtual reality: A pilot study on educational applications of virtual real-ity technology*. University of Washington, HIT Lab. https://doi.org/10.1016/B978-0-12-745045-2.50019-2

Bronack, S., Sanders, R., Cheney, A., Riedl, R., Tashner, J., & Matzen, N. (2008). Presence pedagogy: Teaching and learning in a 3D virtual immersive world. *International Journal of Teaching and Learning in Higher Education*, 20(1), 59–69.

Brown, D. J., Neale, H., Cobb, S. V., & Reynolds, H. (1999). Development and evaluation of the virtual city. *International Journal of Virtual Reality*, 4(1), 28–41. https://doi.org/10.20870/IJVR.1999.4.1.2639

Buck Institute for Education (BIE). (2010). *Teaching with technology: A statewide professional development program*. Retrieved from http://www.bie.org/files/twtfinal.pdf

Bugeja, M. J. (2007). Distractions in the wireless classroom. *Chronicle of Higher Education*, 53(21), C1–C4.

Chatzidimitris, T., Gavalas, D., & Kasapakis, V. (2015). PacMap: Transferring PacMan to the physical realm. In *Internet of Things. User-Centric IoT: First*

International Summit. Revised Selected Papers, Part I. Rome, Italy, October 27–28 (pp. 139–144). London: Springer. https://doi.org/10.1007/978-3-319-19656-5_20

Chen, H. I. (2013). Identity practices of multilingual writers in social networking spaces. *Language Learning & Technology*, 17(2), 143–170.

Cheng, Y., & Wang, S. H. (2011). Applying a 3D virtual learning environment to facilitate student's application ability – The case of marketing. *Computers in Human Behavior*, 27(1), 576–584. https://doi.org/10.1016/j.chb.2010.10.008

Cheryan, S., Meltzoff, A. N., & Kim, S. (2011). Classrooms matter: The design of virtual classrooms influences gender disparities in computer science classes. *Computers & Education*, 57(2), 1825–1835. https://doi.org/10.1016/j.compedu.2011.02.004

Chittaro, L., & Ranon, R. (2007). Web3D technologies in learning, education and training: Motivations, issues, opportunities. *Computers & Education*, 49(1), 3–18. https://doi.org/10.1016/j.compedu.2005.06.002

Chun, D. M. (2015). Language and culture learning in higher education via telecollaboration. *Pedagogies: An International Journal*, 10(1), 5–21. https://doi.org/10.1080/1554480X.2014.999775

Çiftçi, E. Y., & Savaş, P. (2017). The role of telecollaboration in language and intercultural learning: A synthesis of studies published between 2010 and 2015. *ReCALL*, 30(3), 1–21. https://doi.org/10.1017/S0958344017000313

Clavel-Arroitia, B., & Pennock-Speck, B. (2015). Telecollaboration in a secondary school context: Negotiation of meaning in English as a lingua franca/Spanish tandem interactions. *@tic. revista d'innovació educativa*, 15, 74–81. https://doi.org/10.7203/attic.15.6411

Cornillie, F., Thorne, S. L., & Desmet, P. (2012). Editorial – Digital games for language learning: From hype to insight? *ReCALL*, 24(3), special issue *Digital games for language learning: Challenges and opportunities*, 243–256. https://doi.org/10.1017/S0958344012000134

Corno, L., & Mandinach, E. B. (1983). The role of cognitive engagement in classroom learning and motivation. *Educational Psychologist*, 18(2), 88–108. https://doi.org/10.1080/00461528309529266

Cottrell, S. (2017). *Critical thinking skills*. London: Macmillan Education. https://doi.org/10.1057/978-1-137-55052-1

Csikszentmihalyi, M. (1990). Literacy and intrinsic motivation. *Daedalus*, 115–140.

Cunningham, J. D. (2018). Synthesizing the practice of SCMC-based telecollaboration: A scoping review. *CALICO*, 35(1), 49–76. https://doi.org/10.1558/cj.33156

Dalgarno, B., & Lee, M. J. (2010). What are the learning affordances of 3-D virtual environments? *British Journal of Educational Technology*, 41(1), 10–32. https://doi.org/10.1111/j.1467-8535.2009.01038.x

de Freitas, S. (2006). *Learning in immersive worlds: A review of game-based learning*. Bristol, UK: JISC. Retrieved from http://www.jisc.ac.uk/media/documents/programmes/elearninginnovation/gamingreport_v3.pdf

De Lucia, A., Francese, R., Passero, I., & Tortora, G. (2009). Development and evaluation of a virtual campus on Second Life: The case of Second DMI. *Computers & Education*, 52(1), 220–233. https://doi.org/10.1016/j.compedu.2008.08.001

Di Blas, N., Paolini, P., & Poggi, C. (2005, March). 3D worlds for edutainment: Educational, relational and organizational principles. In *Pervasive Computing and Communications Workshops, 2005. PerCom 2005 Workshops. Third IEEE International Conference* (pp. 291–295).

Dickey, M. D. (2005). Brave new (interactive) worlds: A review of the design affordances and constraints of two 3D virtual worlds as interactive learning environments. *Interactive Learning Environments*, 13(1–2), 121–137. https://doi.org/10.1080/10494820500173714

Dooly, M. (2008). Constructing knowledge together. In *Telecollaborative language learning: A guidebook to moderating intercultural collaboration online* (pp. 21–45). Bern: Peter Lang.

Dooly, M. (2010). Teacher 2.0. *Telecollaboration*, 2, 277–303.

Dooly, M. (2013). Promoting competency-based language teaching through project-based language learning. In M. L. Pérez Cañado (Ed.), *Competency-based language teaching in higher education* (pp. 77–92). Dordrecht: Springer.

Dooly, M., & O'Dowd, R. (2012). *Researching online foreign language interaction and exchange: Theories, methods and challenges*. Berlin: Peter Lang Publishing. https://doi.org/10.3726/978-3-0351-0414-1

Duch, B. J., Groh, S. E., & Allen, D. E. (2001). Why problem-based learning? A case study of institutional change in undergraduate education. In B. Duch, S. Groh, & D. Allen (Eds.), *The power of problem-based learning* (pp. 3–11). Sterling, VA: Stylus.

Duncan, I., Miller, A., & Jiang, S. (2012). A taxonomy of virtual worlds usage in education. *British Journal of Educational Technology*, 43(6), 949–964. https://doi.org/10.1111/j.1467-8535.2011.01263.x

Ensor, S., Kleban, M., & Rodrigues, C. (2017). Telecollaboration: Foreign language teachers (re) defining their role. *Alsic. Apprentissage des Langues et Systèmes d'Information et de Communication*, 20(2). https://doi.org/10.4000/alsic.3140

Ertmer, P. A., & Simons, K. D. (2006). Jumping the PBL implementation hurdle: Supporting the efforts of K-12 teachers. *Interdisciplinary Journal of Problem-based learning*, 1(1), 5. https://doi.org/10.7771/1541-5015.1005

Eschenbrenner, B., Nah, F. F. H., & Siau, K. (2008). 3-D virtual worlds in education: Applications, benefits, issues, and opportunities. *Journal of Database Management (JDM)*, 19(4), 91–110. https://doi.org/10.4018/jdm.2008100106

Ferguson, R. (2011). Meaningful learning and creativity in virtual worlds. *Thinking Skills and Creativity*, 6(3), 169–178. https://doi.org/10.1016/j.tsc.2011.07.001

Florida, R. (2004). *The rise of the creative class: And how it's transforming work, leisure, community and everyday life*. New York: Basic Books.

Fried-Booth, D. L. (2002). *Project work*. New York: Oxford University Press.

Fullagar, C. J., Knight, P. A., & Sovern, H. S. (2013). Challenge/skill balance, flow, and performance anxiety. *Applied Psychology*, 62(2), 236–259. https://doi.org/10.1111/j.1464-0597.2012.00494.x

Furstenberg, G., Levet, S., English, K., & Maillet, K. (2001). Giving a virtual voice to the silent language of culture: The Cultura Project. *Language Learning & Technology*, 5(1), 55–102.

Glaser, B. G., & Strauss, A. L. (2017). *Discovery of grounded theory: Strategies for qualitative research*. London: Routledge. https://doi.org/10.4324/9780203793206

Goswami, U. (2004). Neuroscience and education. *British Journal of Educational Psychology*, 74(1), 1–14. https://doi.org/10.1348/000709904322848798

Grant, M. M. (2002, Winter). Getting a grip on project-based learning: Theory, cases, and recommendations. *Meridian: A Middle School Computer Technologies Journal*, 5(1). Retrieved from http://www.ncsu.edu/meridian/win2002/514

Grant, M. M. (2011). Learning, beliefs, and products: Students' perspectives with project-based learning. *Interdisciplinary Journal of Problem-based Learning*, 5(2), 6. https://doi.org/10.7771/1541-5015.1254

Gruson, B., & Barnes, F. (2012). Case study investigation of CMC with young language learners. *Journal of e-Learning and Knowledge Society*, 8(3), 79–90.

Guth, S., & Helm, F. (Eds.). (2010). *Telecollaboration 2.0*. Bern: Peter Lang.

Guth, S., Helm, F., & O'Dowd, R. (2012). *University language classes collaborating online: A report on the integration of telecollaborative networks in European universities*. Retrieved from http://citeseerx.ist.psu.edu/viewdoc/download?doi=10.1.1.457.9608&rep=rep1&type=pdf

Guth, S., & Thomas, M. (2010). Telecollaboration with web 2.0 tools. In S. Guth & F. Helm (Eds.), *Telecollaboration 2.0* (39–68). Bern: Peter Lang. https://doi.org/10.3726/978-3-0351-0013-6

Harris, J. (2002). Wherefore art thou, telecollaboration? *Learning & Leading with Technology*, 28(8), 46–49.

Hauck, M. (2019). Virtual exchange for (critical) digital literacy skills development. *European Journal of Language Policy*, 11(2), 187–210. https://doi.org/10.3828/ejlp.2019.12

Helm, F. (2013). A dialogic model for telecollaboration. *Bellaterra Journal of Teaching & Learning Language & Literature*, 6(2), 28–48. https://doi.org/10.5565/rev/jtl3.522

Helm, F. (2015). The practices and challenges of telecollaboration in higher education in Europe. *Language Learning & Technology*, 19(2), 197–217.

Helm, F., & Guth, S. (2016). Telecollaboration and language learning. *The Routledge handbook of language learning and technology* (pp. 241–254). London: Routledge.

Hew, K. F., & Cheung, W. S. (2010). Use of three-dimensional (3-D) immersive virtual worlds in K-12 and higher education settings: A review of the research. *British Journal of Educational Technology*, 41(1), 33–55. https://doi.org/10.1111/j.1467-8535.2008.00900.x

Hmelo-Silver, C. E. (2004). Problem-based learning: What and how do students learn? *Educational Psychology Review*, 16(3), 235–266. https://doi.org/10.1023/B:EDPR.0000034022.16470.f3

Hockly, N., Dudeney, G., & Pegrum, M. (2014). *Digital literacies*. London: Routledge. https://doi.org/10.4324/9781315832913

Hourigan, T., Murray, L., & Riordan, E. (Eds.). (2011). *Quality issues in ICT integration: Third level disciplines and learning contexts*. Newcastle: Cambridge Scholars Publishing.

Jauregi, M. K. (2015). Task development for telecollaboration among youngsters. In J. Colpaert, A. Aerts, M. Oberhofer & M. Gutiérrez-Colón (Eds.), *Task design and CALL* (pp. 312–322). Antwerp: Linguapolis.

Jauregi, K., & Melchor-Couto, S. (2017). The TeCoLa project: Pedagogical differentiation through telecollaboration and gaming for intercultural and content integrated language teaching. In *CALL in a climate of change: Adapting to turbulent global conditions – Short papers from EUROCALL 2017*, 163. https://doi.org/10.14705/rpnet.2017.eurocall2017.707

Jauregi, K., Melchor-Couto, S., & Vilar Beltrán, E. (2013). The European Project TILA. In L. Bradley & S. Thouësny (Eds.), *EUROCALL*, 20, 123–128. https://doi.org/10.14705/rpnet.2013.000149

Jones, B. F., Rasmussen, C. M., & Moffitt, M. C. (1997). *Real-life problem solving: A collaborative approach to interdisciplinary learning*. New York: American Psychological Association. https://doi.org/10.1037/10266-000

Kennedy, C., & Miceli, T. (2013). In piazza online: Exploring the use of wikis with beginner foreign language learners. *Computer Assisted Language Learning*, 26(5), 389–411. https://doi.org/10.1080/09588221.2013.770035

Kern, R. (2014). Technology as Pharmakon: The promise and perils of the internet for foreign language education. *The Modern Language Journal*, 98(1), 340–357. https://doi.org/10.1111/j.1540-4781.2014.12065.x

Ketelhut, D. J., Dede, C., Clarke, J., Nelson, B., & Bowman, C. (2017). Studying situated learning in a multiuser virtual environment. In *Assessment of problem solving using simulations* (pp. 47–68). London: Routledge. https://doi.org/10.4324/9781315096773-3

Kineshanko, M. K., & Jugdev, K. (2018). Enhancing digital intelligence through communities of learning. In B. Steward & A. Khare (Eds.), *On the line* (pp. 111–125). London: Springer. https://doi.org/10.1007/978-3-319-62776-2_10

Kinginger, C. (2016). Telecollaboration and student mobility for language learning. Paper presented at Telecollaboration in Higher Education, Dublin, Ireland, April 21–23.

Klimanova, L., & Dembovskaya, S. (2013). L2 identity, discourse and social networking in Russian. *Language Learning & Technology*, 17(1), 69–88.

Kohn, K., & Hoffstaedter, P. (2015). Flipping intercultural communication practice: Opportunities and challenges for the foreign language classroom. In *Task design & CALL. Proceedings of the seventeenth international CALL conference* (pp. 338–345).

Kop, R., & Hill, A. (2008). Connectivism: Learning theory of the future or vestige of the past? *The International Review of Research in Open and Distributed Learning*, 9(3), 1–13. https://doi.org/10.19173/irrodl.v9i3.523

Krajcik, J. S., & Blumenfeld, P. (2006). Project-based learning. In R. K. Sawyer (Ed.), *The Cambridge handbook of the learning sciences* (pp. 317–333). New York: Cambridge Universtiy Press. https://doi.org/10.1017/CBO9780511816833.020

Kramsch, C., & Thorne, S. (2002). Foreign language learning as global communicative practice. In D. Block & D. Cameron (Eds.), *Globalization and language teaching* (pp. 83–100). London: Routledge.

Lee, J. S., Blackwell, S., Drake, J., & Moran, K. A. (2014). Taking a leap of faith: Redefining teaching and learning in higher education through project-based learning. *Interdisciplinary Journal of Problem-Based Learning*, 8(2), 2. https://doi.org/10.7771/1541-5015.1426

Lee, L. (2006). A study of native and non-native speakers' feedback and responses in Spanish-American networked collaborative interaction. In J. A. Belz & S. L. Thorne (Eds.), *Internet-mediated intercultural foreign language education* (pp. 147–176). Boston, MA: Thomson Heinle.

Lee, L. (2018). Using telecollaboration 2.0 to build intercultural communicative competence: A Spanish-American exchange. In *Cross-cultural perspectives on technology-enhanced language learning* (pp. 303–321). Hershey, PA: IGI Global. https://doi.org/10.4018/978-1-5225-5463-9.ch017

Lewis, T., Chanier, T., & Youngs, B. (2011). Special issue commentary: Multilateral online exchanges for language and culture learning. *Language Learning & Technology*, 15(1), 3–9.

Liu, H., Bowman, M., Adams, R., Hurliman, J., & Lake, D. (2010). Scaling virtual worlds: Simulation requirements and challenges. In *Proceedings of the Winter Simulation Conference* (pp. 778–790). https://doi.org/10.1109/WSC.2010.5679112

Lombardi, M. M. (2007). Authentic learning for the 21st century: An overview. *Educause Learning Initiative*, 1, 1–12.

Lomicka, L., & Lord, G. (2012). A tale of tweets: Analyzing microblogging among language learners. *System* 40(1), 48–63. https://doi.org/10.1016/j.system.2011.11.001

Makaramani, R. (2015). 21st century learning design for a telecollaboration project. *Procedia – Social and Behavioral Sciences*, 191, 622–627. https://doi.org/10.1016/j.sbspro.2015.04.567

Markham, T., Larmer, J., & Ravitz, J. (2003). *Project based learning handbook: A guide to standards-focused project based learning*, 2nd edition. Novato, CA: Buck Institute for Education.

McLoughlin, C., & Lee, M. J. W. (2008). Mapping the digital terrain: New media and social software as catalysts for pedagogical change. In *Proceedings ascilite*, November 30–December 3, 2008. Melbourne, Australia. Retrieved from http://www.ascilite. org.au/conferences/melbourne08/procs/mcloughlin.pdf

Meltzer, L. (Ed.). (2018). *Executive function in education: From theory to practice*. London: Guilford Publications.

Mennecke, B. E., Triplett, J. L., Hassall, L. M., & Conde, Z. J. (2010). Embodied social presence theory. In *System Sciences (HICSS), 2010. 43rd Hawaii International Conference* (pp. 1–10). https://doi.org/10.1109/HICSS.2010.179

Mergendoller, J. R., & Thomas, J. W. (2000). Managing project-based learning: Principles from the field. Novato, CA: Buck Institute for Education.

Mikropoulos, T. A., & Natsis, A. (2011). Educational virtual environments: A ten-year review of empirical research (1999–2009). *Computers & Education*, 56(3), 769–780. https://doi.org/10.1016/j.compedu.2010.10.020

Moore, A. H., Fowler, S. B., & Watson, C. E. (2007). Active learning and technology: Designing change for faculty, students, and institutions. *Educause Review*, 42(5), 42–44.

Moreno, R., & Mayer, R. (2007). Interactive multimodal learning environments. *Educational Psychology Review*, 19(3), 309–326. https://doi.org/10.1007/s10648-007-9047-2

Morris, S. B. (2008). Book Review: Hunter, JE, & Schmidt, FL (2004). Methods of Meta-Analysis: Correcting Error and Bias in Research Findings. Thousand Oaks, CA: Sage. *Organizational Research Methods*, 11(1), 184–187. https://doi.org/10.1177/1094428106295494

Murray, L., Giralt, M., & Benini, S. (2020). Extending digital literacies: Proposing an agentive literacy to tackle the problems of distractive technologies in language learning. *ReCALL*, 1–22. https://doi.org/10.1017/S0958344020000130

New Media Consortium. (2008). *The horizon report*. Austin, TX: NMC. Retrieved from www.nmc.org/pdf/2008-Horizon-Report.pdf

Norris, J. M., & Ortega, L. (2000). Effectiveness of L2 instruction: A research synthesis and quantitative meta-analysis. *Language Learning*, 50(3), 417–528. https://doi.org/10.1111/0023-8333.00136

Ochsner, K. N., & Gross, J. J. (2008). Cognitive emotion regulation: Insights from social cognitive and affective neuroscience. *Current Directions in Psychological Science*, 17(2), 153–158. https://doi.org/10.1111/j.1467-8721.2008.00566.x

O'Dowd, R. (Ed.). (2007). *Online intercultural exchange: An introduction for foreign language teachers* (Vol. 15). London: Multilingual Matters. https://doi.org/10.21832/9781847690104

O'Dowd, R. (2011). Intercultural communicative competence through telecollaboration. *The Routledge handbook of language and intercultural communication* (pp. 342–358). London: Routledge.

O'Dowd, R. (2013). Telecollaborative networks in university higher education: Overcoming barriers to integration, *Internet and Higher Education*, 18, 47–53. https://doi.org/10.1016/j.iheduc.2013.02.001

O'Dowd, R. (2015). The competences of the telecollaborative teacher. *The Language Learning Journal*, 43(2), 194–207. https://doi.org/10.1080/09571736.2013.853374

O'Dowd, R. (2018). From telecollaboration to virtual exchange: State-of-the-art and the role of UNI collaboration in moving forward. *Journal of Virtual Exchange*, 1, 1–23. https://doi.org/10.14705/rpnet.2018.jve.1

O'Dowd, R., & Ritter, M. (2006). Understanding and working with "failed communication" in telecollaborative exchanges. *CALICO*, 61(2), 623–642.

O'Dowd, R., & Waire, P. (2009). Critical issues in telecollaborative task design. *Computer Assisted Language Learning*, 22(2), 173–188. https://doi.org/10.1080/09588220902778369

Omale, N., Hung, W. C., Luetkehans, L., & Cooke-Plagwitz, J. (2009). Learning in 3-D multiuser virtual environments: Exploring the use of unique 3-D attributes for online problem-based learning. *British Journal of Educational Technology*, 40(3), 480–495. https://doi.org/10.1111/j.1467-8535.2009.00941.x

Ortega, M. C., & Falconer, L. (2015). Learning spaces in virtual worlds: Bringing our distance students home. *Journal of Applied Research in Higher Education*, 7(1), 83–98. https://doi.org/10.1108/JARHE-02-2014-0026

Panichi, L., & Deutschmann, M. (2012). Language learning in virtual worlds: Research issues and methods. In M. Dooly & R. O'Dowd (Eds.), *Researching online foreign language interaction and exchange: Theories, methods and challenges* (pp. 205–232). Bern: Peter Lang.

Papadakis, S. (2016). Creativity and innovation in European education: Ten years eTwinning. Past, present and the future. *International Journal of Technology Enhanced Learning*, 8(3–4), 279–296. https://doi.org/10.1504/IJTEL.2016.082315

Pei-Ling Tan, J., Choo, S. S., Kang, T., Arief, D., & Liem, G. (2017). Educating for twenty-first century competencies and future-ready learners: Research perspectives from Singapore. *Asia Pacific Journal of Education*, 37(4), 425–436. https://doi.org/10.1080/02188791.2017.1405475

Phuong, D. T. D., & Shimakawa, H. (2015). Analyzing learning behavior of student persona toward non-negative matrix factorization. *International Journal of Information and Education Technology*, 5(11), 826. https://doi.org/10.7763/IJIET.2015.V5.620

Pink, D. H. (2005). *A whole new mind: Moving from the information age to the conceptual age*. New York: Riverhead Books.

Polka, W. (2001). Facilitating the transition from teacher centered to student centered instruction at the university level via constructivist principles and customized learning plans. *Educational Planning*, 13(3), 55–61.

Prasolova-Førland, E. (2008). Analyzing place metaphors in 3D educational collaborative virtual environments. *Computers in Human Behavior*, 24(2), 185–204. https://doi.org/10.1016/j.chb.2007.01.009

Ravitz, J., Hixson, N., English, M., & Mergendoller, J. (2012). Using project based learning to teach 21st century skills: Findings from a statewide initiative. In *American Educational Research Association Conference, Vancouver, Canada*, 16, 1–9.

Reinders, H. (Ed.). (2012). *Digital games in language learning and teaching*. London: Palgrave Macmillan. https://doi.org/10.1057/9781137005267

Reinhardt, J., & Sykes, J. M. (2012). Conceptualizing digital game-mediated L2 learning and pedagogy: Game-enhanced and game-based research and practice. In *Digital games in language learning and teaching* (pp. 32–49). London: Palgrave. https://doi.org/10.1057/9781137005267_3

Rieber, L. P. (2005). Multimedia learning in games, simulations, and microworlds. In R. E. Mayer, *The Cambridge handbook of multimedia learning* (pp. 549–567). Cambridge: Cambridge University Press. https://doi.org/10.1017/CBO9780511816819.034

Riley, S. K. L. (2008). Teaching in virtual worlds: Opportunities and challenges. *Setting Knowledge Free: The Journal of Issues in Informing Science and Information Technology*, 5(5), 127–135. https://doi.org/10.28945/1000

Ruzic, F. (1999). The future of learning in virtual reality environments. In M. Selinger & J. Pearson (Eds.), *Telematics in education: Trends and issues* (pp. 188–189). Oxford: Pergamon Press. https://doi.org/10.1016/B978-008042788-1/50014-4

Sadler, R., & Dooly, M. (2016). Twelve years of telecollaboration: What we have learnt. *ELT Journal*, 70(4), 401–413. https://doi.org/10.1093/elt/ccw041

Savery, J. R. (2015). Overview of problem-based learning: Definitions and distinctions. *Essential readings in problem-based learning: Exploring and extending the legacy of Howard S. Barrows*, 9, 5–15. https://doi.org/10.2307/j.ctt6wq6fh.6

Savery, J. R., & Duffy, T. M. (1995). Problem based learning: An instructional model and its constructivist framework. *Educational Technology*, 35(5), 31–38.

Savin-Baden, M. (2000). *Problem-based learning in higher education: Untold stories*. London: McGraw-Hill Education.

Schmidt, M., Laffey, J. M., Schmidt, C. T., Wang, X., & Stichter, J. (2012). Developing methods for understanding social behavior in a 3D virtual learning environment. *Computers in Human Behavior*, 28(2), 405–413. https://doi.org/10.1016/j.chb.2011.10.011

Seo, K. K. J. (2012). Inspiring equal contribution and opportunity in a 3d multi-user virtual environment: Bringing together men gamers and women non-gamers in Second Life®. *Computers & Education*, 58(1), 21–29. https://doi.org/10.1016/j.compedu.2011.07.007

Shah, C., & Kitzie, V. (2012). Social Q&A and virtual reference – Comparing apples and oranges with the help of experts and users. *Journal of the American Society for Information Science and Technology*, 63(10), 2020–2036. https://doi.org/10.1002/asi.22699

Siemens, G. (2005). Connectivism: A learning theory for the digital age. *International Journal of Instructional Technology and Distance Learning*, 2(1), 3–10.

Solomon, G. (2003). Project-based learning: A primer. *Technology and Learning*, 23(6), 20–23.

Stickler, U., & Hampel, R. (2015). Transforming teaching: New skills for online language learning spaces. In R. Hampel & U. Stickler (Eds.), *Developing online language teaching: Research-based pedagogies and reflective practices* (pp. 63–77). Basingstoke: Palgrave Macmillan. https://doi.org/10.1057/9781137412263_5

Stripling, B., Lovett, N., & Macko, F. C. (2009). Overview of project-based learning. *A guide to project-based learning in middle schools: Inspiring students to engage in deep and active learning*. New York: NYC Department of Education.

Tan, J. P.-L., Choo, S. S., Kang, T., & Liem, G. A. D. (2017). Educating for twenty-first century competencies and future-ready learners: research perspectives from Singapore. *Asia Pacific Journal of Education*, 37(4), 425–436. https://doi.org/10.1080/02188791.2017.1405475

Thomas, D., & Brown, J. S. (2011). *A new culture of learning: Cultivating the imagination for a world of constant change*, 219, Lexington, KY: CreateSpace.

Thomas, J. W. (2000). *A review of research on project-based learning*. California: Autodesk Foundation.

Thomas, M., Cinganotto, L., Philp, H., et. al. (2018). Digital game-based learning in 3D immersive environments: The GUINEVERE Project. *Innovation in Language Learning 2018* (pp. 1–5). Florence: Filodiritto Editore.

Thomas, M., & Reinders, H. (Eds.). (2010). *Task-based language learning and teaching with technology*. London: A&C Black.

Thomas, M., & Schneider, C. (2018). Language teaching in 3D virtual worlds with Machinima: Reflecting on an online Machinima teacher training course. *International Journal of Computer-Assisted Language Learning and Teaching (IJCALLT)*, 8(2), 20–38. https://doi.org/10.4018/IJCALLT.2018040102

Thorne, S. L. (2010). The 'intercultural turn' and language learning in the crucible of new media. *Telecollaboration*, 2, 139–164.

Thorne, S. L., Black, R. W., & Sykes, J. M. (2009). Second language use, socialization, and learning in internet interest communities and online gaming. *The Modern Language Journal*, 93, 802–821. https://doi.org/10.1111/j.1540-4781.2009.00974.x

Thorne, S. L., Cornillie, F., & Piet, D. (2012). ReCALL special issue: Digital games for language learning: Challenges and opportunities. *ReCALL Journal*, 24(3), 243–256. https://doi.org/10.1017/S0958344012000134

Tolosa, C., Ordóñez, C. L., & Alfonso, T. (2015). Online peer feedback between Colombian and New Zealand FL beginners: A comparison and lessons learned. *Profile Issues in Teachers Professional Development*, 17(1), 73–86. https://doi.org/10.15446/profile.v17n1.41858

Torp, L., & Sage, S. (2002). *Problems as possibilities: Problem-based learning for K–12 education*, 2nd edition. Alexandria, VA: ASCD.

Verdugo, D. R., & Belmonte, I. A. (2007). Primary teachers' insights on the use of the internet in their English as a foreign language lessons: A research case study. *Porta Linguarum*, 8, 63–83.

Virvou, M., & Katsionis, G. (2008). On the usability and likeability of virtual reality games for education: The case of VR-ENGAGE. *Computers & Education*, 50(1), 154–178. https://doi.org/10.1016/j.compedu.2006.04.004

Wang, J., Zou, B., Wang, D., & Xing, M. (2013). Students' perception of a wiki platform and the impact of wiki engagement on intercultural communication. *System*, 41(2), 245–256. https://doi.org/10.1016/j.system.2013.04.004

Wann, J., & Mon-Williams, M. (1996). What does virtual reality NEED?: Human factors issues in the design of three-dimensional computer environments. *International Journal of Human-Computer Studies*, 44(6), 829–847. https://doi.org/10.1006/ijhc.1996.0035

Warburton, S. (2009). Second Life in higher education: Assessing the potential for and the barriers to deploying virtual worlds in learning and teaching. *British Journal of Educational Technology*, 40(3), 414–426. https://doi.org/10.1111/j.1467-8535.2009.00952.x

Ware, P. (2005). Missed communication in online communication: Tensions in fostering successful online interactions. *Language Learning & Technology*, 9(2), 64–89. Retrieved from http://llt.msu.edu/vol9num2/default.html

Ware, P., & Kessler, G. (2016). Telecollaboration in the secondary language classroom: Case study of adolescent interaction and pedagogical integration. *Computer Assisted Language Learning*, 29(3), 427–450. https://doi.org/10.1080/09588221.2014.961481

Wiecha, J., Heyden, R., Sternthal, E., & Merialdi, M. (2010). Learning in a virtual world: Experience with using Second Life for medical education. *Journal of Medical Internet Research*, 12(1). https://doi.org/10.2196/jmir.1337

Zuiker, S. J. (2012). Educational virtual environments as a lens for understanding both precise repeatability and specific variation in learning ecologies. *British Journal of Educational Technology*, 43(6), 981–992. https://doi.org/10.1111/j.1467-8535.2011.01266.x

About the Authors

Silvia Benini works as research assistant in the School of Languages, Literatures and Cultures at the University College Cork. Areas of research interest include CALL, Games-Based Learning, Intercultural Communication, Language Policy and Planning. She has published on ICT and Language Learning. Her latest co-authored publication is "Extending digital literacies: Proposing an agentive literacy to tackle the problems of distractive technologies in language learning" (2020). She is a committee member of IRAAL (Irish Association for Applied Linguistics) and a member of CALS (Centre for Applied Language Studies).

Michael Thomas is Professor of Education and Chair of the Centre for Educational Research (CERES) at Liverpool John Moores University in the UK. He is the author or editor of over thirty books and peer-reviewed special editions and founding editor of four book series, including Advances in Digital Language Learning and Teaching (Bloomsbury), Digital Education and Learning (Palgrave), and Global Policy and Critical Futures in Education (Palgrave Macmillan). Among his other books on CALL are *Project-Based Language Learning with Technology* (Routledge 2017) and *Language Teaching with Video-Based Technologies* (Routledge 2020).

3 Business English Telecollaboration in Project-Based Learning: Indonesian and Saudi Arabian Contexts

Imelda V. Bangun and Adel Alfaifi

1 Introduction

Acknowledging the inherent value of computer-assisted language learning (CALL) (Chapelle, 2007) as applied to project-based learning (PBL) (e.g., Alsamani & Daif-Allah, 2016; Tseng & Yeh, 2017; Wahyudin, 2016), in this chaper we juxtapose the language teaching practices of a Southeast Asian country (i.e., Indonesia) and a Middle Eastern one (i.e., Saudi Arabia). Notably, we investigate how social entrepreneurship in an English for Business curriculum using telecollaboration (Dooly, 2017) can be used to accommodate metacognitive diversity across cultures (Proust & Fortier, 2018; Ünal & Papafragou, 2018). While both countries are generally collectivist societies, the degree of metacognitive skills (Chun, 2011; Mayer, 2005) may vary due to the pervasive pedagogical foundations implemented in each (Bangun et al., 2019). Therefore, we review and synthesize literature that focuses on technology-mediated PBL approaches (Debski & Gruba, 1999; Jeon-Ellis, Debski, & Wigglesworth, 2005; Sadler & Dooly, 2016) to guide the language teaching approaches for a collectivist society with diverse metacognitive skills to promote English as a Foreign Language (EFL) learners' linguistic proficiency and critical awareness (Freire, 1985).

PBL refers to a pedagogical approach where a curriculum is presented through projects (Bell, 2010) with the following principles: student-centered teaching, learner autonomy, collaborative learning, and learning through task completion (Hedge, 2000). Özdamli (2011: 3811) posited that,

> Project-based learning provides opportunities for students to pursue their interests and questions, make decisions about how they will find answers, and solve problems. In the classroom, project-based learning provides many unique opportunities for

> teachers to build a relationship with students. Shar[ing] student work ... includes documen[ting] ... the learning process and the student's final projects with other teachers, parents, mentors, and the business community who all have a stake in the students' education.

Comprehensive studies on PBL have been conducted in the English for Specific Purposes (ESP) and English as a Foreign Language (EFL) contexts in the last decades (Affandi & Sukyadi, 2016; Alsamani & Daif-Allah, 2016; Dooly & Masats, 2010; Foss, McDonald, & Rooks, 2008; Khanh, 2015; Meksophawannagul, 2015). The vast majority of these studies claimed that PBL effectively fosters collaborative work and improves digital literacy and linguistics skills. However, many of these studies did not directly focus on Business English in the EFL context, particularly in promoting social entrepreneurship. Accordingly, this systematic review aims to explore literature focusing on the trends (e.g., theoretical frameworks, PBL processes, telecollaboration PBL tools, and findings) of employing PBL within electronically-mediated environments in Business English.

With technology-mediated PBL approaches, EFL learners are encouraged to collaborate and cooperate with each other, incrementally improve their final project, presentation, and performance, be agents of change, and increase their intercultural communication (Dooly & Masats, 2010). Regarding telecollaboration, the learners could utilize CALL tools as follows: Google Docs to design a business plan and create an advertisement, Google Spreadsheets to plan a budget, and Google Slides to present a business executive summary. In this way, language learners can simulate real-world tasks and independent learning, collaborate across cultures using technology, and increase their metacognitive skills (Bangun et al., 2019).

2 Background and Description of the Research

A cross-curricular approach to teaching is characterized by knowledge, skills, and understanding from various subject areas (Barnes, 2015). According to Barnes (2015), the purpose of cross-curricular teaching and learning is to (1) motivate and encourage learners to have real-world experience; (2) explicitly draw on similarities in terms of subject content, pedagogical devices, and learning processes; (3) provide an interactive learning experience; (4) develop meaningful collaboration aligning with the curriculum; (5) contribute towards a more effective range of teaching and learning opportunities; (6) promote cognitive, personal, and social development;

(7) allow teachers the opportunity to evaluate and reflect on their pedagogical foundations and be more innovative in implementing the curriculum; and (8) foster meaningful collaborations among learners and educators.

Similar to the purpose and benefits of the cross-curricular approach, PBL is reported to be beneficial to the improvement of language skills such as writing (Calogerakou & Vlachos, 2011), increase students' motivation (Hsieh, 2014), cultural awareness (Eppelsheimer, 2012), intercultural competence (Steenhuis, Roland, & Kulik, 2018), and collaborative group work skills (Miller, Hafner & Fun, 2012), and enhance students' autonomy while sharing various roles in PBL (Gülbahar & Tinmaz, 2006; Lam & Lawrence, 2002). PBL, furthermore, promotes students' collaborative approach to learning (Stoller, 2006). Students involved in PBL are actively engaged in the learning process. The combination of both projects and pedagogy suggests that they can enhance language proficiency, such as speaking skills and vocabulary recognition (Rojas & Varon, 2019). Previous research in PBL in the L2 context has identified similar findings, as it claims that PBL provides the opportunity for L2 learners to explore comprehensible input and practice comprehensible output (Eyring, 1989). Tseng & Yeh (2019) conducted a study to determine the effects of PBL in developing EFL teachers' competencies in CALL. The authors recruited twelve prospective EFL teachers majoring in a foreign language program at the University of Science and Technology in Taiwan. The authors collected data using a pre- and post-technological pedagogical content knowledge (TPACK) survey to explore EFL teachers' development of CALL competencies. In addition, qualitative data including group discussion, class observation, lesson plans, and reflective essays were collected to complement survey results. The findings indicated that using PBL helped achieve a high level of CALL competencies and that PBL can be used to develop CALL competencies among EFL pre-service and in-service teachers.

Several research studies have discussed different learning approaches that concentrate on learner agency in constructing knowledge, such as problem-based learning, authentic learning, action learning, the case method, and inquiry-based learning (Steenhuis et al., 2018). These approaches are not necessarily synonymous with PBL. However, they share similar attributes in terms of meaning negations, problem-solving, learning by doing, inquiry, and research within projects (Beckett & Millers, 2006). In PBL, educators have a significant role in providing students with several topics to choose from, share technological tools, train students on how to use them, explain target performance, and end with formative assessment. Conversely, in second language classrooms, L2 learners should share responsibility for collecting, understanding, and reporting authentic information to succeed in implementing PBL (Beckett & Slater, 2019). In terms of PBL in business English, learners working collaboratively can produce a business product to promote social entrepreneurship by conducting fundraising events with a focus on specific problem-based and environmental issues. An issue worthy of further investigation in this context stems from the social setting and cultural aspects of PBL, while taking into account students' experiences because a particular topic can drive learning directions and shape the learning context (Barge, 2010).

A collaborative PBL approach in a business English context (see Table 3.1) aligns with constructivist theory which explains that educational experiences involve learners in the acquisition and co-construction of knowledge by interaction with others rather than learning individually (Lave & Wenger, 1991; Vygotsky, 1978; Wenger, McDermott, & Snyder, 2002). Collaboration in PBL also enhances teachers' potential ability to employ CALL instruction (Chapelle & Sauro, 2017) and scaffold learning activities, which may, in turn, help learners expand their current cultural and linguistic knowledge of business content. Moreover, the learners can improve their comprehension of specific topics by conducting a collaborative investigation into authentic problems (Blumenfeld et al., 1991) and projects (Nicol & MacLeod, 2005).

Various frameworks have been adopted in conducting PBL in business contexts based on three levels of competencies, such as communicative competence, technological competence, and business presentations in PBL (Dooly & Masats, 2010). To achieve communicative competence in PBL, students must understand instructions, recognize relevant information, utilize visual presentations or narrative methods, and create texts pertinent to the language content (Dooly & Masats, 2010). In terms of technological competence, students should show skills in designing scripts, using video and audio, exploring video editing software, and selecting and modifying video clips (Dooly & Masats, 2010; Wahyudin, 2016). Business presentations in PBL should demonstrate students' ability to understand the content, communicate effectively, apply critical thinking skills, and manage PBL questions and answers (Penrod, Tucker, & Hartman, 2015). To be effective in an L2 context, PBL should have clear goals defined by teachers and learners, an equal size and role in groups, products that can be shown to the audience, and the involvement of modalities such as textual and visual forms of representation (Kolber, 2012).

Table 3.1. The PBL Process in Business English

PBL Process in Business	Student Cooperation	Technology and Target Language Skills	Teachers' Support
Framing a business idea	Identifying a business idea based on specific problem and students' experience	Social media such as Twitter, Instagram Internet, Google Docs Language skills: reading and speaking	Helping students to identify a driving question, clarifying PBL expectations, and modeling when needed
Creating a product and needs analysis	Brainstorming, evaluating an existing idea, creating a needs analysis survey, interviewing an expert	Google survey, Skype Adobe Photoshop Language skills: writing and speaking	Facilitating a group discussion and enhancing metacognitive skills
Evaluation	Testing products, generating feedback, revising, communicating with a potential audience	Social media, Web-based, YouTube, Zoom Language skills: speaking and listening.	Providing feedback, encouraging revising, and providing suggestions

2.1 Metacognition across Cultures

Flavell (1979) defined metacognitive knowledge as "the knowledge concerning one's own cognitive processes and products, or anything related to them" and metacognitive skills as "the active monitoring and consequent regulation and orchestration of these processes" (p. 232). Several studies (e.g., Malcolm, 2009; McGrath, Berggren, & Mezek, 2016; Nergis, 2013) have investigated whether metacognitive growth is fostered in electronically-mediated environments by awareness-raising activities for metacognitive knowledge acquisition. Flavell's study showed that there was an interdependence between the degree to which these environments help language learners be more aware of their metacognitive skills, on the one side, and their abilities to demonstrate control and flexibility in the use of those skills (e.g., self-management, autonomy), on the other.

In teaching metacognitive awareness to L2 learners, educators must be aware of the learners' metacognitive diversity, which pertains to metacognition to represent learning practices and standards across cultures (Proust & Fortier, 2018). People from various socioeconomic and cultural groups have different ways of organizing their thoughts (Neisser, 1982). Proust & Fortier (2018) perceive that many eastern cultures adopt a teacher-centered teaching philosophy with less emphasis on critical thinking skills; however, western cultures are more familiar with student-centered teaching philosophies that emphasize critical thinking skills. Research also showed that linguistic and cultural differences, such as being raised in societies which are relatively more collectivist or individualistic, or being educated in a school system where being able to excel in evaluation is more valued than being able to think critically, may influence cognitive and metacognitive processes (Proust & Fortier, 2018; Ünal & Papafragou, 2018).

This discussion is further supported by a framework relating to metacognition (meta-level) and cognition (object-level) that gives attention to the monitoring and controlling process (Nelson & Narrens, 1990). For instance, monitoring may serve to compare and choose between two standards, and tracking may serve the purpose of deciding if the selected measure is still better than the other action (Dunlosky & Metcalfe, 2009). Thus, self-efficacy, which pertains to people's beliefs about the ability to complete a task, plays a pertinent role in increasing the learners' metacognitive profile (Bandura, 1977, 1997). The metacognitive perspective concurs with the cognitive perspective regarding the reading process, in that reading is an active process where readers construct meaning using linguistic information from the external printed text and their background knowledge (Askildson 2011; Carrell & Grabe 2002). These perspectives explain and frame the importance of teaching L2 learners the metacognitive strategies and awareness of the strategies being used when reading texts by activating background knowledge, identifying and planning reading tasks, and monitoring their reading (Boulware-Gooden et al., 2007). Additionally, these perspectives focus on noticing, working memory, or activating prior knowledge as a bridge to learning the new experience through the use of technology such as online or multimedia reading scaffolds (Liaw & English, 2017).

The findings of multiple studies also suggested that student factors, such as cultural and educational backgrounds, may influence the use of metacognitive strategies. Individual differences, including learning preferences (Plass et al., 1998), may also play an important role in metacognitive strategy choice. The findings of these studies further pointed to the valuable role metacognitive skills can play in L2 acquisition. Anderson (2005) strongly asserted that one of the most important skills teachers can develop in the classroom is helping their learners control their cognitive and metacognitive skills. Given the claim that CALL tools can play a valuable role in developing and supporting students' metacognitive strategies, metacognition across cultures may have a positive impact, and educational technology may play essential functions in helping L2 learners regulate their language acquisition and thus become more independent and motivated learners.

2.2 PBL and Telecollaboration

Telecollaboration in education uses computer and digital communication tools to promote learning through social interaction and collaboration to encourage independent learning (Dooly, 2017). With collaboration, L2 learners may engage in critical thinking and discussions and achieve a deeper understanding and longer retention of learned material (Scardamalia & Bereiter, 2006). A successful collaboration involves active contribution by the learners with an aim to find a solution to a problem (Rogoff, 1990). Collaborative learning is the key to knowledge transformation and construction (Tannenbaum & Tahar, 2008; Vygotsky, 1978). Through collaborative learning, students become aware of a higher learning process (Hertz-Lazarowitz & Bar-Natan, 2002) by providing feedback as they participate in online small group discussions (Janssen et al., 2007).

Lenkaitis, Calom, & Escobar (2019) conducted a study to investigate the interaction and communication between students from a Mexican university and American universities. Through the telecollaborative exchange, the authors aimed to explore how L2 learners of Spanish and English developed their intercultural communicative competence (ICC). Utilizing Zoom as a videoconferencing tool, the authors analyzed over six hours of video sessions of two participants based on the 15-category ICC framework. The findings indicated that communicative skills were the highest category coded following cultural self-awareness. Overall, the results showed that telecollaboration via synchronous computer-mediated communication (SCMC) is an effective tool that facilitates a collaborative approach in developing ICC. Therefore, the telecollaboration approach in L2 learning improves students' understanding of the target language and culture.

In this 21st century, technology has transformed interaction among English language learners in the classroom (Woodrich & Fan, 2017). Many researchers have noted that the affordances of various technological tools facilitate learners' collaborative work on PBL (see Table 3.2), and their ability to comment on each other's work, review revision history, perform voice typing, and insert images and tables (i.e., Google Docs features). Specifically, Kessler, Bikowski, & Boggs (2012) concluded that highly proficient non-native English speakers appreciated various aspects of Google Apps-supported collaborative writing activity and valued each member's role in the group. Suwantarathip & Wichadee (2014) reported how students in a Thai university who commented and critiqued each other's work via one of the Google Apps, Google Docs, gained a greater understanding of the writing process in general and performed better than those students who were placed in a face-to-face class setting. Bikowski & Vithanage (2016) found that collaborative writers using Google Docs outperformed individual writers. More importantly, both teachers and students reported positive perceptions of adopting Google Docs to support collaborative writing. Thus, it is of importance to implement both face-to-face and virtual collaboration.

Table 3.2. Findings on Telecollaboration and PBL

Telecollaboration and PBL	Participants	Technology	Outcomes
Marchewka & Raina (2019)	Students from the School of Management, India, Cracow University of Economics, Poland, and Erasmus students	Virtual exchange on Padlet.com	Improved students' understanding of cross-cultural communication
Lenkaitis, Calo, & Escobar (2019)	L2 learners of Spanish at a public university in the USA, L2 learners of English at a private university in Mexico	Zoom	Enhanced students' intercultural communication competence
Leh (2014)	Native English speakers with L2 speakers in the USA	Google Docs	Increased cultural knowledge and enhanced students' confidence
Bueno-Alastuey & Kleban (2016)	Canadian L2 learners of German and German L2 learners of English	Learning Management System (LMS) decussation, email, and messaging in Facebook	Understood learner communication, especially in an international context; enhanced language awareness among L2 teachers
Lee & Song (2019)	Different conditions: (1) American students in the study-abroad program, (2) Korean L2 learners of English, American L2 learners of Korean, (3) Korean L2 learners of English, American L2 learners of Chinese	KakaoTalk, a videoconference tool	Improved students' cognitive, engagement, confidence, and behavioral aspects of ICC

2.3 Theories, Approaches, and Model Guided PBL Studies

Several studies on PBL in Business English, telecollaboration, and cross-curricular contexts are discussed and summarized (see Table 3.3) in this section.

2.3.1 Sociocultural theory

This section presents a practice-theory-practice approach guided by sociocultural theory (Poehner & Lantolf, 2014; Vygotsky; 1978) on how CALL (Chapelle, 1998) and PBL may guide the cross-curriculum development of social entrepreneurship projects in an English for business course among two different cultures. Moreover, research on collaborative learning fits well with the core of Vygotsky's sociocultural theory, as Poehner & Lantolf (2014: 8) suggest, "Human consciousness arises through dialectical unity of our biologically endowed brain and 'auxiliary stimuli' appropriated during participation in social practices." Sociocultural theory, particularly the zone of proximal development (ZPD), maintains that social interaction has a pertinent role in allowing each individual to experience meaningful learning and development (Yang, Yeh, & Wong, 2010). Vygotsky (1978: 86) defines ZPD as:

> The distance between the actual development level as determined by independent problem-solving and the level of potential development determined through problem-solving under guidance or in collaboration with more capable peers.

2.3.2 Constructivist theory

The constructivist framework points to the benefit of collaborative learning that encourages learners to use prior knowledge and experiences to construct new knowledge (Piaget & Inhelder, 2000). Merriam, Caffarella, & Baumgartner (2007) noted that adult learners accumulated a growing reservoir of experience rich in resources for learning. Lightbown & Spada (2013) added that adult English learners typically possessed cognitive maturity and metalinguistic awareness to enable them to solve problems while engaging in discussions about language. However, they suggested that the use of these cognitive skills could interfere with second language acquisition. Specifically, adult English learners tend to produce sentences based on internal cognitive processes and prior knowledge that interacts with the language they hear around them.

Constructivist theory advocates students' collaboration in constructing new knowledge and solving a real-life problem that aligns with PBL (Tseng & Yeh, 2019). Krajcik & Blumenfeld (2006) identified three critical elements in PBL which were (1) creating a driving question, (2) developing artifices, and (3) developing a collaborative approach. In the first phase, along with teachers' scaffolding, L2 learners should create a driving question that is measurable, relevant to their real-life situations, and feasible in terms of students' ability. In the case of teacher training in PBL, creating effective driving questions should come from the teacher's engagement in class observation to determine a problem related to real-life teaching practices (Bell & Mladenovic, 2015). In the second phase, they develop artifacts involved in learners' collaborative efforts to produce solutions and answer driving questions. They collaborate to develop artifacts by designing the plan, collecting information, evaluating the information, and creating a product (Blumenfeld et al., 1991). These activities enhance learners' critical thinking and literacy skills (Garrison, 2007; Howard, 2002).

Whereas the significance of PBL has been well-documented in the research literature, few have investigated the limitations of PBL in terms of assessment. A study conducted by Gibbs (1999) noted the importance of assessment influencing the learning process and suggested that when employed correctly, assessment may enhance learning outcomes. However, PBL curriculum objectives are naturally complex, so it is pertinent to align the learning objectives with the assessment method to assess the students' knowledge and skills (Christensen, Henriksen, & Kolmos, 2006). Kolmos & Holgaard (2007) conducted an empirical investigation addressing the alignment between assessment and PBL at Aalborg University in Denmark. Their study investigated the overall experiences and the skills that are assessed among university students and found that individual examinations are appropriate to test disciplinary knowledge. Thus, they proposed several phases in the assessment system to be included in the PBL approach as follows: (1) ungraded oral presentations of the project, (2) ungraded short discussions, and (3) graded individual examinations.

2.3.3 CALL in PBL

CALL enhances the effectiveness of PBL and fosters its implementation (Condliffe et al., 2017) in facilitating communication and interaction between learners (Debski & Gruba, 1999). Different terms are used with respect to the integration of technology in PBL such as project-based CALL (Debski & Gruba, 1999), project-oriented computer-assisted language learning (PrOCALL) (Jeon-Ellis et al., 2005), and technology-enhanced project-based language learning (TEPBLL) (Sadler & Dooly, 2016). Perhaps the most challenging aspect of language learning in the EFL context is the lack of opportunity to practice English outside the classroom. However, technology increases the possibility of interaction and production using the target language.

In general, CALL in collaborative PBL creates an informal learning environment where EFL learners can communicate intensively, share information, and read from a variety of online resources. More importantly, learners in the CALL environment can produce the target language without hesitating to make mistakes. Although language learning is an accumulative process in PBL, interaction should be focused on the comprehension and production of the target language. Learning English as a Foreign Language in countries like Saudi Arabia and Indonesia can be difficult due to the lack of opportunities to interact and communicate in English outside the language classroom. However, social media platforms such as Twitter, Facebook, Snapchat, and Instagram open the possibility for EFL learners to use them and enhance their language skills. For instance, utilizing information and communication technology such as Twitter can overcome the challenge of exposing learners to the target language in foreign language contexts by enabling students to communicate with native language speakers (Kim, 2011; Sun, 2010).

2.3.4 Authentic project-based learning

Fostering authentic project-based learning (APBL) in higher education can be challenging for instructors (Lewis et al., 2019). It is pertinent to understand the challenges instructors face in implementing APBL in a manner that makes it a practical and innovative pedagogical approach (Frank & Barzilai, 2004; Prince & Felder, 2006). Lewis et al. (2019) argue that innovations in the existing APBL classroom can be adapted and integrated using CALL tools. APBL instructors in higher education are often required to implement a demanding state-of-the-art pedagogical approach and have significant autonomy to decide what innovations to adopt (Prince & Felder, 2006). In APBL, where technology innovations are involved, particularly the business English courses, students should work in a group with real users and clients to create a solution (e.g., idea, service, product) to a real-world problem with opportunities for implementing the solution. Effective APBL mirrors professional practice by having students work in teams using professional practices to solve real-life issues (Dym et al., 2005; Shaffer & Resnick, 1999). Such practices include giving students experience with teamwork and providing solutions to complex problems. While APBL provides tremendous learning experiences for students, the additional complexity caused by real-world problems (Parker et al., 2011, 2013) could create additional challenges for instructors; however, technology is well-placed to address these challenges.

This study further focuses on the adoption of innovations within APBL by instructors in higher education, who typically have significant pedagogical autonomy (Matusovich et al., 2014). While APBL is an effective approach to link students to the language used in real-life situations, the design and adaption of this approach is not an easy task. To manage difficulties and establish the foundation to integrate technology in APBL, Lewis et al. (2019) investigated the most common challenges in conducting APBL by interviewing 47 university instructors. The findings indicated four interrelated difficulties that included balancing students' needs, increasing curriculum flexibility while maintaining the standard of quality, providing scaffolding to the team, and accommodating students and other stakeholders. They suggested that in creating adaptable educational technology, innovators should incorporate instructors' needs, different stakeholders' needs, and state-of-the-art knowledge on learning (Easterday, Rees Lewis, & Gerber, 2016, 2018).

2.3.5 Collaborative Course Development model

The Collaborative Course Development (CCD) model argues that the classroom's power should shift to students by which they are allowed to be involved in the initial design of the course and class structure (Aiken et al., 2016). They elaborate that one innovative approach in the CCD model is to create an environment in which students move toward commitment rather than enrollment, facilitating active engagement instead of holding students to traditionally passive compliance. The expectation is that this investment and ownership in the course will lead to a more engaged student, which will lead in turn to a variety of positive outcomes. This work aims to explain how CCD practices can be implemented in a wide range of business courses. For example, first, in syllabus building, students are given a syllabus template that only includes instructor information and major headings (i.e., Course Objectives, Professor Responsibilities, Student Responsibilities, Assignments, Exams, etc.). After a specific time and clarification, students individually spend 10 to 15 minutes thinking about what they want in the template, and then they can collaborate to organize their template. They must reach a consensus on the course structure, goals, exams, and grading preferences. Next, the instructor leads students through a class-wide discussion. Here, groups are asked to present the pros and cons of their class plans.

Several other practices are flextures, elective choice assignments, creative theory building, competitive experimentation, and collaborative assignments. In "flextures" or flexible lectures, the educators in the CCD module might regularly provide five or six topics/issues/activities for the students to select from. Elective choice assignments, essentially, allow students to choose the tasks repeatedly. Creativity and collaboration enable students to name their new theory, investigate secondary research, and perhaps even design some research to test their hypothesis. In competitive experimentation, students learn to discuss and critique various aspects of research design. In collaborative assessment, students submit exam questions and design an upcoming exam either on paper or online.

Table 3.3. Theoretical Framework, Approaches and Model Utilized in PBL Studies

PBL Theories/ Approaches/ Model	Learning Process	Business English Context	Cross-curricular Context	Telecollaboration Context
Sociocultural Theory	Learners build their knowledge through mediation	Fundraising projects offer the opportunity to learn from each other	Possibility of interaction between two classes or two countries	Collaborations using CALL tools promote cultural awareness
Constructivist Theory	Building own knowledge through own learning experience	Business project completion offers knowledge construction	Cross-curriculum between two different subjects to produce a product	Hybrid collaborations provide more opportunity to construct knowledge
Authentic Project Based Learning (APBL)	Authentic learning experience using technology	An authentic project such us baking and selling cookies for a charity	Culinary students and EFL students in higher education combine curriculum	Culinary students and EFL students in higher education collaborate to produce videos on healthy eating habits
Collaborative Course Development (CCD)	A student-centered approach where learners are involved in classroom activities such as syllabus design, elective assignments, etc.	Students can create a new theory related to business English and test it	To test the new theory, cross-curricular interaction may happen between environmental engineering students and EFL students	Students can collaborate to write exams either on paper or online
Metacognitive within PBL	Learners must think about their thinking while working on their projects	As students plan their budget and advertisement, they should utilize the skills they have while receiving scaffolding from the teacher	Brainstorming between classes about metacognitive strategies	Students can collaborate to list and present various metacognitive strategies they can use in completing their projects

2.4 Project-Based Learning and Related Constructs

In the past, teaching cultural aspects of L2 such as habits and customs of a country received little attention in the research literature (Thanasoulas, 2001). Focusing on language teaching but ignoring cultural competence will affect students' abilities to communicate appropriately in authentic situations related to the cultural conventions (Seidl, 1998). As an alternative method to traditional practices in L2 teaching, the constructive approach provides the opportunity to construct knowledge about L2 language and culture. However, a constructive approach in PBL may lead students to make assumptions about some cultures, unrealize individual variations, and collect information from unreliable resources (Guest, 2002). To provide authentic communication in L2, the communicative approach fosters language learning in creating activities that involve both linguistic and cultural information (Canale & Swain, 1980; Liaw, 2006). Therefore, the communicative approach promotes awareness of language and cultures during the interaction between two languages (Lenkaitis et al., 2019). The idea of interaction and globalization in today's world raises the need for language learners to communicate effectively with others from various cultural backgrounds and countries, which are essential skills in the 21st century (Bennett & Bennett, 2004).

2.4.1 Project-based learning in Indonesia

Pembelajaran berbasis proyek (project-based learning in Bahasa Indonesia) has become the central approach to teaching English as a Foreign Language in the past decades in Indonesia (Mali, 2016; Wahyudin, 2016). Researchers agreed that PBL increases student engagement and autonomy (e.g., Brown, 2007; Richards, 2015; Tamin & Grant, 2013). A study on the effectiveness of PBL in teaching creative writing to improve English writing skills in the EFL context was conducted in Indonesia (Mali, 2016). In Mali's study, his students were assigned to write a poem in a particular style such as metaphor, acrostic, narrative, or haiku. Throughout the semester, the students were assigned to post their poems on a blog and comment on each other's blogs as part of their final project. The students were also asked to collaborate, during which they were monitored and scaffolded by the teacher via an online platform, Edmodo. The findings of his study showed that the students were actively involved, and the educators were compelled to be more creative and innovative with their instruction.

A study by Wahyudin (2016) focused on the PBL approach to promote learning English for business purposes (EFB) in the Indonesian context. The context of his study was higher education in Bandar Lampung,

Indonesia. His research aimed to examine the effect of PBL in promoting foreign language oral performance in EFB. In this part of Indonesia, stakeholders expressed their demand for having a local workforce who are competent in English in the business area to communicate with national customers. Therefore, the EFB program was designed for students majoring in computer engineering and informatic systems. A total of 60 participants were randomly selected for this study and were divided into experimental and control groups, with students in the experimental group learning through the PBL approach. A business presentation was utilized as a pre-test and post-test to evaluate students' speaking skills. For the evaluation of speaking performance, a scoring rubric was adapted that focused on various aspects of speaking, such as grammar, accent, vocabulary, comprehension, and fluency. This study's findings indicated that PBL contributed effectively to improving students' oral skills, including comprehension and fluency in the ESP context.

2.4.2 Project-based learning in Saudi Arabia

Telecollaboration in PBL opened the window for interaction between L2 learners from different countries. Alsamani & Daif-Allah (2016) conducted a study to investigate the impact of PBL in developing the English vocabulary of computer science majors at Qassim University in Saudi Arabia. The participants were divided into two groups, control and experimental. The control group received the content through traditional instruction, while the experimental group had PBL instruction. The quantitative data findings indicate that PBL was an effective approach in learning ESP, as well as enhancing students' learning autonomy by promoting self-directed learning. Consequently, the constructivist learning environment helped to shift the role of EFL teachers from controlling the whole to part of a task. Throughout they were able to cooperate with students in the learning process using authentic tasks.

Alsamani & Daif-Allah (2016) further explored how creating PBL involved several steps that included identifying the research question, creating products or solutions, conducting evaluations, and presenting projects. They argued that language teachers should encourage students to develop a business idea that stems from their experience and societal needs, and that PBL should be relevant to students' experience to enhance their motivation and sense of ownership. Technology tools in all phases helped improve progress, provide content resources, and facilitate collaborative efforts. One month of participation in PBL was provided for EFL learners from Saudi Arabia to travel to Indonesia. After reading about the English vocabulary used in business areas, students involved in the PBL approach became familiar with Indonesian culture. One group of students formulated a business idea that involved creating a travel agency focusing on Indonesia as the main travel destination. Here, students utilized several technology resources to collect information about famous Indonesian cities, weather, costs, culture, and food. Students had to design a business log and interview an Indonesian language teacher to collect information and present their ideas. By the end, students had created a video using a narrative style, designed a traveling logo and blog, and made a class presentation about their business idea.

3 Conclusion

The lack of teachers' and students' experience in utilizing technology in PBL may present challenges in EFL teaching. Unfamiliarity with the potential benefits of PBL within electronically-mediated environments in fostering social issues and metacognitive skills across cultures in business English may also lead to some resistance. Naturally, to implement these approaches, teachers can benefit from receiving training to improve their CALL competencies to help them integrate technology for teaching and learning (Goldsby & Fazal, 2000). Furthermore, teachers of business English who would like to promote telecollaboration in a cross-curricular setting of students from collectivist countries such as Indonesia and Saudi Arabia may also benefit from being aware of the pertinence of the PBL approach as applied to CALL (e.g., Alsamani & Daif-Allah, 2016; Mali, 2016; Wahyudin, 2016). As confirmed by Tseng & Yeh (2019), PBL helped achieve a high level of CALL competencies by implementing PBL among pre-service and in-service EFL teachers. The findings in various studies, furthermore, confirmed that the employment of PBL accompanied by technological tools increased students' understanding of cross-cultural communication, their confidence, language awareness, cognition, and engagement in the classroom. The technology used included Padlet, Zoom, and other videoconference tools, Google Docs, various Learning Management Systems, email, and social media.

Constructivist theory, authentic project-based learning, collaborative course development, metacognition within PBL, and sociocultural theory are some of the frameworks that guided the studies in project-based learning. Implementing the PBL approach as applied to CALL in business English in countries such as Indonesia and Saudi Arabia may be challenging since these countries are collectivist societies where citizens have a broad range of metacognitive skills. Additionally, the PBL approach is student-centered, whereas these countries are mostly familiar with the teacher-centered approach. However, when the teachers and the students are informed of PBL and trained well, PBL offers the opportunity for them to overcome several of these challenges. As posited by Alsamani & Daif-Allah (2016), whose study investigated the impact of PBL in developing English vocabulary for computer science majors at Qassim University in Saudi Arabia, PBL was an effective approach in learning ESP, as well as enhancing students' learning autonomy by promoting self-directed learning. Consequently, the constructivist learning environment helped to shift the role of EFL teachers from controlling the whole task to cooperating with students throughout the learning process involving authentic tasks.

A few recent studies on PBL and collaborative approaches utilized technological accessibility and affordance to deliver effective authentic learning. However, there are various aspects to consider when discussing the efficiency of this approach due to the type of technology, time spent in communication, PBL group sizes, internet access, and technological affordances that may affect overall students' performance. Although many of the quantitative studies show significant outcomes in students' language skills, this literature review recommends a mixed-methods approach to exploring students' interaction from a sociocultural perspective as mixed methods may provide a more complex understanding of the phenomenon (Creswell & Plano Clark, 2011; Johnson, Onwuegbuzie, & Turner, 2007; Johnson & Turner, 2003). Future research on the effectiveness of fostering social entrepreneurship in English for business in a curriculum that utilizes a telecollaborative approach in the EFL context should also be investigated and explored.

References

Affandi, A., & Sukyadi, D. (2016). Project-based learning and problem-based learning for EFL students' writing achievement at tertiary level. *Rangsit Journal of Educational Studies*, 3(1), 23–40.

Aiken, K. D., Heinze, T. C., Meuter, M. L., & Chapman, K. J. (2016). Innovation through collaborative course development: Theory and practice. *Marketing Education Review*, 26(1), 57–62. https://doi.org/10.1080/10528008.2015.1091679

Alsamani, A. S., & Daif-Allah, A. S. (2016). Introducing project-based instruction in the Saudi ESP classroom: A study in Qassim University. *English Language Teaching*, 9(1), 51–64. https://doi.org/10.5539/elt.v9n1p51

Anderson, N. (2005). L2 learning strategies. In E. Hinkel (Ed.), *Handbook of research in second language teaching and learning* (pp. 757–771). Mahwah, NJ: Lawrence Erlbaum Associates.

Askildson, L. R. (2011). A review of CALL and L2 reading: Glossing for comprehension and acquisition. *International Journal of Computer-Assisted Language Learning and Teaching (IJCALLT)*, 1(4), 49–58. https://doi.org/10.4018/ijcallt.2011100104

Bandura, A. (1977). Self-efficacy: Toward a unifying theory of behavioral change. *Psychological Review*, 84, 191–215. https://doi.org/10.1037/0033-295X.84.2.191

Bandura, A. (1997). *Self-efficacy: The exercise control*. New York: Freeman.

Bangun, I., Mannion, P., Li, Z., & Cheng, K. (2019). Integrating CALL to develop metacognitive and English proficiency skills in EAP classrooms. *The Florida Journal of Educational Research*, 5(72), 90–108.

Barge, S. (2010). *Principles of problem and project-based learning: The Aalborg PBL model*. Aalborg, Denmark: Aalborg University.

Barnes, J. (2015). An introduction to cross-curricular learning. In P. Driscoll, A. Lambirth, & J. Roden (Eds.), *The creative primary curriculum*, 2nd edition (pp. 260–283). Newbury Park, CA: Sage Publishing.

Beckett, G. H., & Millers, P. C. (2006). *Project-based second and foreign language education: Past, present and future*. Greenwich, CT: Information Age Publishing.

Beckett, G., & Slater, T. (Eds.). (2019). *Global perspectives on project-based language learning, teaching, and assessment: Key approaches, technology tools, and frameworks*. New York: Routledge. https://doi.org/10.4324/9780429435096

Bell, A., & Mladenovic, R. (2015). Situated learning, reflective practice and conceptual expansion: Effective peer observation for tutor development. *Teaching in Higher Education*, 20(1), 24–36. https://doi.org/10.1080/13562517.2014.945163

Bell, S. (2010). Project-based learning for the 21st century: Skills for the future. *The Clearing House*, 83, 39–43. https://doi.org/10.1080/00098650903505415

Bennett, J. M., & Bennett, M. J. (2004). Developing intercultural sensitivity: An integrative approach to global and domestic diversity. In: D. Landis, J. Bennett, & M. Bennett (Eds.), *Handbook of intercultural training* (pp. 147–165). Thousand Oaks, CA: Sage. https://doi.org/10.4135/9781452231129.n6

Bikowski, D., & Vithanage, R. I. (2016). Effects of web-based collaborative writing on individual L2 writing development. *Language Learning & Technology*, 20, 79–99.

Blumenfeld, P. C., Soloway, E., Marx, R. W., Krajcik, J. S., Guzdial, M., & Palincsar, A. (1991). Motivating project-based learning: Sustaining the doing, supporting the learning. *Educational Psychologist*, 26(3–4), 369–398. https://doi.org/10.1207/s15326985ep2603&4_8

Boulware-Gooden, R., Carreker, S., Thornhill, A., & Malatesha, J. (2007). Instruction of metacognitive strategies enhances reading comprehension and vocabulary achievement of third-grade students. *The Reading Teacher*, 61(1), 70–77. https://doi.org/10.1598/RT.61.1.7

Brown, H. D. (2007). *Principles of language learning and teaching*, 5th edition. New York: Pearson Education, Inc.

Bueno-Alastuey, M. C., & Kleban, M. (2016). Matching linguistic and pedagogical objectives in a telecollaboration project: A case study. *Computer Assisted Language Learning*, 29(1), 148–166. https://doi.org/10.1080/09588221.2014.904360

Calogerakou, C., & Vlachos, K. (2011). Films and blogs: An authentic approach to improve the writing skill – An intercultural project-based framework in the Senior High State School. *Research Papers in Language Teaching and Learning*, 2(1), 98–110.

Canale, M., & Swain, M. (1980). Theoretical bases of communicative approaches to second language teaching and testing. *Applied Linguistics*, 1(1), 1–47. https://doi.org/10.1093/applin/1.1.1

Carrell, P. L., & Grabe, W. (2002). Reading. In N. Schmitt (Ed.), *An introduction to applied linguistics* (pp. 233–250). London: Edward Arnold.

Chapelle, C. A. (1998). Multimedia CALL: Lessons to be learned from research on instructed SLA. *Language Learning & Technology*, 2(1), 21–39. Retrieved from http://llt.msu.edu/vol2num1/article1/

Chapelle, C. A. (2007). Technology and second language acquisition. *Annual Review of Applied Linguistics*, 27, 98–114. https://doi.org/10.1017/S0267190508070050

Chapelle, C. A., & Sauro, S. (2017). *The handbook of technology and second language teaching and learning*. Hoboken, NJ: John Wiley & Sons. https://doi.org/10.1002/9781118914069

Christensen, J., Henriksen, L. B., & Kolmos, A. (2006). *Engineering science, skills, and building*. Aalborg, Denmark: Aalborg University Press.

Chun, D. M. (2011). Computer-assisted language learning. In E. Hinkel (Ed.), *Handbook of research in second language teaching and learning* (pp. 663–680). New York: Routledge.

Condliffe, B., Quint, J., Visher, M. G., Bangser, M. R., Drohojowska, S., Saco, L., & Nelson, E. (2017). *Project-based learning: A literature review (working paper)*. New York: MDRC.

Creswell, J. W., & Plano Clark, V. L. (2011). *Designing and conducting mixed methods research*, 2nd edition. Thousand Oaks, CA: Sage.

Debski, R., & Gruba, P. (1999). A qualitative survey of tertiary instructor attitudes towards project-based CALL. *Computer Assisted Language Learning*, 12(3), 219–239. https://doi.org/10.1076/call.12.3.219.5715

Dooly, M. (2017). Telecollaboration. In C. Chapelle & S. Sauro (Ed.), *The handbook of technology and second language teaching and learning* (pp. 169–183). Hoboken, NJ: Wiley Blackwell. https://doi.org/10.1002/9781118914069.ch12

Dooly, M., & Masats, D. (2010). Closing the loop between theory and praxis: New models in EFL teaching. *ELT Journal*, 65(1), 42–51. https://doi.org/10.1093/elt/ccq017

Dunlosky, J., & Metcalfe, J. (2009). *Metacognition*. Thousand Oaks, CA: Sage Publications.

Dym, C. L., Agogino, A. M., Eris, O., Frey, D. D., & Leifer, L. J. (2005). Engineering design thinking, teaching, and learning. *Journal of Engineering Education*, 94(1), 103–120. https://doi.org/10.1002/j.2168-9830.2005.tb00832.x

Easterday, M. W., Rees Lewis, D. G., & Gerber, E. M. (2016). The logic of the theoretical and practical products of design research. *Australasian Journal of Educational Technology*, 32(4), 125–144. https://doi.org/10.14742/ajet.2464

Easterday, M. W., Rees Lewis, D. G., & Gerber, E. M. (2018). The logic of design research. *Learning: Research and Practice*, 4(2), 131–160. https://doi.org/10.1080/23735082.2017.1286367

Eppelsheimer, N. (2012). Food for thought: Exotisches und hausmannskost zum interkulturellen lernen. *Journal of the American Association of Teachers of German*, 45(1), 5–19. https://doi.org/10.1111/j.1756-1221.2012.00114.x

Eyring, J. L. (1989). *Teacher experience and student responses in ESL project work instruction: A case study*. Los Angeles, CA: University of Los Angeles.

Flavell, J. H. (1979). Metacognition and cognitive monitoring: A new area of cognitive-developmental inquiry. *American Psychologist*, 34(10), 906–911. https://doi.org/10.1037/0003-066X.34.10.906

Foss, P. N. C., McDonald, K., & Rooks, M. (2008). Project-based learning activities for short-term for intensive English program. *The Philippine ESL Journal*, 1, 57–76.

Frank, M., & Barzilai, A. (2004). Integrating alternative assessment in a project-based learning course for pre-service science and technology teachers. *Assessment & Evaluation in Higher Education*, 29(1), 41–61. https://doi.org/10.1080/0260293042000160401

Freire, P. (1985). *The politics of education: Culture, power, and liberation*. Granby, MA: Bergin & Garvey. https://doi.org/10.1007/978-1-349-17771-4

Garrison, D. R. (2007). Online community of inquiry review: Social, cognitive, and teaching presence issues. *Journal of Asynchronous Learning Networks*, 11(1), 61–72. https://doi.org/10.24059/olj.v11i1.1737

Gibbs, G. (1999). Using assessment strategically to change the way students learn. In S. Brown and A. Glasner (Eds.), *Assessment matters in higher education*. London: The Society for Research into Higher Education and Open University Press.

Goldsby, D. S., & Fazal, M. B. (2000). Technology's answer to portfolios for teachers. *Kappa Delta Pi Record*, 36(3), 121–123. https://doi.org/10.1080/00228958.2000.10532035

Guest, M. (2002). A critical "checkbook" for culture teaching and learning. *ELT Journal*, 56(2), 154–161. https://doi.org/10.1093/elt/56.2.154

Gülbahar, Y., & Tinmaz, H. (2006). Implementing project-based learning and e-portfolio assessment in an undergraduate course. *Journal of Research on Technology in Education*, 38(3), 309–327. https://doi.org/10.1080/15391523.2006.10782462

Hedge, T. (2000). *Teaching and learning in the language classroom*. Oxford: Oxford University Press.

Hertz-Lazarovitz, R. & Bar-Natan, I. (2002). Writing development of Arab and Jewish students using cooperative learning and computer-mediated communication. *Computers & Education*, 39(1), 19–39.

Howard, J. (2002). Technology-enhanced project-based learning in teacher education: Addressing the goals of the transfer. *Journal of Technology and Teacher Education*, 10(3), 343–364.

Hsieh, T. L. (2014). Motivation matters? The relationship among different types of learning motivation, engagement behaviors and learning outcomes of undergraduate students in Taiwan. *Higher Education*, 68(3), 417–433. https://doi.org/10.1007/s10734-014-9720-6

Janssen, J., Erkens, G., Kanselaar, G., & Jaspers, J. (2007). Visualization of participation: Does it contribute to successful computer-supported collaborative learning? *Computers and Education*, 49(4), 1037–1065.

Jeon-Ellis, G., Debski, R., & Wigglesworth, G. (2005). Oral interaction around computers in the project-oriented CALL classroom. *Language Learning & Technology*, 9(3), 121–145.

Johnson, R. B., Onwuegbuzie, A. J., & Turner, L. A. (2007). Toward a definition of mixed methods research. *Journal of Mixed Methods Research*, 1(2), 112–133. https://doi.org/10.1177/1558689806298224

Johnson, R. B., & Turner, L. A. (2003). Data collection strategies in mixed methods research. In A.Tashakkori & C. Teddlie (Eds.), *Handbook of mixed methods in social and behavioral research* (pp. 297–319). Thousand Oaks, CA: Sage.

Kessler, G., Bikowski, D., & Boggs, J. (2012). Collaborative writing among second language learners in academic web-based projects. *Language Learning & Technology*, 16(1), 91–109.

Khanh, N. V. (2015). Towards improving ESP teaching/learning in Vietnam's higher education institutions: Integrating Project-Based Learning in ESP courses. *International Journal of Languages, Literature, and Linguistics*, 227–232. https://doi.org/10.18178/IJLLL.2015.1.4.44

Kim, T. (2011). Korean elementary school students' English learning demotivation: A comparative survey study. *Asia Pacific Education Review*, 12(1), 1–11. https://doi.org/10.1007/s12564-010-9113-1

Kolber, M. (2012). Metodaprojektu – czytylko ornament dydaktyczny*? Języki Obce w Szkole*, 4, 3235.

Kolmos, A., & Holgaard, J. E. (2007). Alignment of PBL and assessment. *Journal of Engineering Education Washington*, 96(4), 19.

Krajcik, J. S., & Blumenfeld, P. C. (2006). Urban schools' teachers enacting project-based science. *Journal of Research in Science Teaching*, 43(7), 722–745. https://doi.org/10.1002/tea.20102

Lam, Y., & Lawrence, G. (2002). Teacher-student role redefinition during a computer-based second language project: Are computers catalysts for empowering change? *Computer Assisted Language Learning*, 15(3), 295–315. https://doi.org/10.1076/call.15.3.295.8185

Lave, J., & Wenger, E. (1991). *Situated learning: Legitimate peripheral participation*. Cambridge: Cambridge University Press. https://doi.org/10.1017/CBO9780511815355

Lee, J., & Song, J. (2019). Developing intercultural competence through study abroad, telecollaboration, and on-campus language study. *Language Learning & Technology*, 23(3), 178–198.

Leh, A. (2014). Using project-based learning and Google Docs to support diversity. In *Proceedings of the ICET '14: International conferences on educational technologies sustainability, technology and education*. San Bernardino, CA: California State University San Bernardino.

Lenkaitis, C. A., Calo, S., & Venegas Escobar, S. (2019). Exploring the intersection of language and culture via telecollaboration: Utilizing videoconferencing for intercultural competence development. *International Multilingual Research Journal*, 13(2), 102–115. https://doi.org/10.1080/19313152.2019.1570772

Lewis, D. G. R., Gerber, E. M., Carlson, S. E., & Easterday, M. W. (2019). Opportunities for educational innovations in authentic project-based learning: Understanding instructor perceived challenges to designing for adoption. *Educational Technology Research and Development*, 67, 953–982. https://doi.org/10.1007/s11423-019-09673-4

Liaw, M. (2006). E-learning and the development of intercultural competence. *Language Learning & Technology*, 10, 49–64.

Liaw, M., & English, K. (2017). Technologies for teaching and learning L2 reading. In C. Chapelle & S. Sauro (Eds.), *The handbook of technology and second language teaching and learning* (pp. 62–76). Hoboken, NJ: John Wiley & Sons, Inc. https://doi.org/10.1002/9781118914069.ch5

Lightbown, P. M., & Spada, N. (2013). *How languages are learned*. Oxford: Oxford University Press.

Malcolm, D. (2009). Reading strategy awareness of Arabic-speaking medical students studying in English. *System*, 37, 640–651. https://doi.org/10.1016/j.system.2009.09.008

Mali, Y. C. G. (2016). Project-based learning in Indonesian EFL classrooms: From theory to practice. *IJEE (Indonesian Journal of English Education)*, 3(1), 89–105. https://doi.org/10.15408/ijee.v3i1.2651

Marchewka, M., & Raina, R. (2019). "FORE-UEK Telecollaboration 2017" – Virtual exchange in business studies. In A. Turula, M. Kurek & T. Lewis (Eds.), *Telecollaboration and virtual exchange across disciplines: In service of social inclusion and global citizenship* (pp. 49–55). Research-publishing.net. Retrieved from https://doi.org/10.14705/rpnet.2019.35.939

Matusovich, H. M., Paretti, M. C., McNair, L. D., & Hixson, C. (2014). Faculty motivation: A gateway to transforming engineering education. *Journal of Engineering Education*, 103(2), 302–330. https://doi.org/10.1002/jee.20044

Mayer, R. E. (2005). Cognitive theory of multimedia learning. In R. E. Mayer, *The Cambridge handbook of multimedia learning* (pp. 31–48). Cambridge: Cambridge University Press. https://doi.org/10.1017/CBO9780511816819.004

McGrath, L., Berggren, J., & Mezek, S. (2016). Reading EAP: Investigating high proficiency L2 university students' strategy use through reading blogs. *Journal of English for Academic Purposes*, 22, 152–164. https://doi.org/10.1016/j.jeap.2016.03.003

Meksophawannagul, M. (2015). Teacher and learner views on effective English teaching in the Thai context: The case of engineering students. *English Language Teaching*, 8(11), 99–166. https://doi.org/10.5539/elt.v8n11p99

Merriam, S. B., Caffarella, R. S., & Baumgartner, L. M. (2007). *Learning in adulthood: A comprehensive guide*. San Francisco, CA: John Wiley & Sons, Inc.

Miller, L., Hafner, C. A., & Fun, C. N. K. (2012). Project-based learning in a technologically enhanced learning environment for second language learners: Students' perceptions. *E-Learning and Digital Media*, 9(2), 183–195. https://doi.org/10.2304/elea.2012.9.2.183

Neisser, U. (1982). *Memory observed: Remembering in natural contexts*. San Francisco, CA: W. H. Freeman.

Nelson, T. O., & Narens, L. (1990). Metamemory: A theoretical framework and new findings. In G. H. Bower (Ed.), *The psychology of learning and motivation* (pp. 125–141). New York: Academic Press. https://doi.org/10.1016/S0079-7421(08)60053-5

Nergis, A. (2013). Exploring the factors that affect reading comprehension of EAP learners. *Journal of English for Academic Purposes*, 12(1), 1–9. https://doi.org/10.1016/j.jeap.2012.09.001

Nicol, D. J., & MacLeod, I. A. (2005). Using a shared workspace and wireless laptops to improve collaborative project learning in an engineering design class. *Computers & Education*, 44(4), 459–475. https://doi.org/10.1016/j.compedu.2004.04.008

Özdamlı, F. (2011). The experiences of teacher candidates in developing instructional multimedia materials in project-based learning. *Procedia Social and Behavioral Sciences*, 15, 3810–3820. https://doi.org/10.1016/j.sbspro.2011.04.378

Parker, W. C., Lo, J., Yeo, A. J., Valencia, S. W., Nguyen, D., Abbott, R. D., Nolen, S. B., Bransford, J. D., and Vye, N. J. (2013). Beyond breadth-speed-test: Toward deeper knowing and engagement in an advanced placement course. *American Educational Research Journal*, 50(6), 1424–1459.

Parker, W. C., Mosborg, S., Bransford, J., Vye, N., Wilkerson, J., and Abbott, R. (2011). Rethinking advanced high school coursework: Tackling the depth/breadth tension in the AP US government and politics course. *Journal of Curriculum Studies*, 43(4), 533–559.

Penrod, C., Tucker, M., & Hartman, K. (2015). Assessing business presentation skills: Assuring learning through assessment, analysis, and curriculum improvement. *Journal of Behavioral Studies in Business*, 8, 1–6.

Piaget, J., & Inhelder, B. (2000). *The psychology of the child*. New York: Basic Books.

Plass, J. L., Chun, D. M., Mayer, R. E., & Leutner, D. (1998). Supporting visual and verbal learning preferences in a second-language multimedia learning environment. *Journal of Educational Psychology*, 90(1), 25–36. https://doi.org/10.1037/0022-0663.90.1.25

Poehner, M. E., & Lantolf, J. P. (2014). *Sociocultural theory and the pedagogical imperative in L2 education: Vygotskian praxis and the research/practice divide*. New York: Routledge.

Prince, M. J., & Felder, R. M. (2006). Inductive teaching and learning methods: Definitions, comparisons, and research bases. *Journal of Engineering Education*, 95(2), 123–138. https://doi.org/10.1002/j.2168-9830.2006.tb00884.x

Proust, J., & Fortier, M. (2018). *Metacognitive diversity: An interdisciplinary approach*. Oxford: Oxford University Press. https://doi.org/10.1093/oso/9780198789710.001.0001

Richards, J. C. (2015). *Key issues in language teaching*. Cambridge: Cambridge University Press.

Rogoff, B. (1990). *Apprenticeship in thinking: Cognitive development in social context*. Oxford: Oxford University Press.

Rojas, L. R., & Varon, J. R. (2019). Teaching English through task and project-based learning to Embera Chamí students. *Colombian Applied Linguistics Journal*, 21(1), 80–92. https://doi.org/10.14483/22487085.13109

Sadler, R., & Dooly, M. (2016). Twelve years of telecollaboration: What we have learnt. *ELT Journal*, 70(4), 401–413.

Scardamalia, M., & Bereiter, C. (2006). Knowledge building: Theory, pedagogy, and technology. In K. Sawyer (Ed.), *Cambridge handbook of the learning sciences* (pp. 97–118). New York: Cambridge University Press.

Seidl, M. (1998). Language and culture: Towards a transcultural competence in language learning. *Forum for Modern Language Studies*, 34(2) 101–113. https://doi.org/10.1093/fmls/XXXIV.2.101

Shaffer, D. W., & Resnick, M. (1999). "Thick" authenticity: New media and authentic learning. *Journal of Interactive Learning Research*, 10(2), 195–215.

Steenhuis, H.-J., Roland, L., & Kulik, B. (2018). *Project-based learning: How to approach, report, present, and learn from course-long projects*. New York: Business Expert Press.

Stoller, F. (2006). Establishing a theoretical foundation for project-based learning in second and foreign language contexts. In G. H. Beckett & P. C. Miller (Eds.), *Project-based second and foreign language education: Past, present, and future* (pp. 19–40). Greenwich, CT: Information Age.

Sun, Y. (2010). Developing reflective cyber communities in the blogosphere: A case study in Taiwan higher education. *Teaching in Higher Education*, 15(4), 369–381. https://doi.org/10.1080/13562510903556075

Suwantarathip, O., & Wichadee, S. (2014). The effects of collaborative writing activity using Google Docs on students' writing abilities. *The Turkish Online Journal of Educational Technology*, 13(2), 148–156.

Tamin, S. R., & Grant, M. M. (2013). Definitions and uses: Case study of teachers implementing project-based learning. *Interdisciplinary Journal of Problem-Based Learning*, 7(2), 71–101. https://doi.org/10.7771/1541-5015.1323

Tannenbaum, M., & Tahar, L. (2008). Willingness to communicate in the language of the other: Jewish and Arab students in Israel. *Learning and Instruction*, 18, 283–294.

Thanasoulas, D. (2001). The importance of teaching culture in the foreign language classroom. *Radical Pedagogy*, 3(3), 1–25.

Tseng, S., & Yeh, H. (2019). Fostering EFL teachers' CALL competencies through project-based learning. *Journal of Educational Technology & Society*, 22(1), 94–105.

Ünal, E., & Papafragou, A. (2018). The relation between language and mental state reasoning. In J. Proust & M. Fortier (Eds.), *Metacognitive diversity: An interdisciplinary approach*. Oxford: Oxford University Press. https://doi.org/10.1093/oso/9780198789710.003.0008

Vygotsky, L. (1978). Interaction between learning and development. *Readings on the Development of Children*, 23(3), 34–41.

Wahyudin, A. Y. (2016). The effect of project-based learning on L2 spoken performance of undergraduate students in English for Business class. In *CONAPLIN 9, Proceedings of the Ninth International Conference on Applied Linguistics* (pp. 42–46). Beijing: Atlantis Press. https://doi.org/10.2991/conaplin-16.2017.9

Wenger, E., McDermott, R. A., & Snyder, W. (2002). *Cultivating communities of practice: A guide to managing knowledge*. Boston, MA: Harvard Business Press.
Woodrich, M., & Fan, Y. (2017). Google docs as a tool for collaborative writing in the middle school classroom. *Journal of Technology Information: Research*, 16, 391–410.
Yang, Y., Yeh, H.-C., & Wong, W. (2010). The influence of social interaction on meaning construction in a virtual community. *British Journal of Educational Technology*, 41(2), 287–306.

About the Authors

Imelda V. Bangun, PhD, has worked with adult immigrants, refugees, and international students for eight years as an educator and administrator. She is currently working as an ESOL literacy instructor at the Adult Education Center of Palm Beach County. Her research interests include CALL, e-learning, metacognition, L2 motivation, corpus, project-based learning, and multiliteracy.

Adel Alfaifi is a PhD candidate in Technology in Education and Second Language Acquisition at the University of South Florida with four years of teaching experience in Arabic as a Foreign Language. His research interests include authentic learning materials, foreign language assessment, project-based learning, and CALL.

PART II

Project-Based Language Learning in Pedagogical Contexts

4 Project-Based English Language Learning through Multimodal Videos: An Online Learning Case Study

Valentina Morgana

1 Introduction

The potential for new technologies to support and inform project-based language learning environments has been widely recognized by recent research (Dooly & Sadler, 2016; Pitura & Berlinska-Kopeć, 2018; Thomas, 2017). However, the ability of project-based learning (PBL) to connect students and teachers around the world, crossing physical and geographical barriers, suddenly became a reality in winter 2020 when schools moved online, and the COVID-19 emergency forced students and teachers to study from home. Even though in the field of learning English as Foreign Language (EFL) digital content has been developed for years, planning a technology-mediated project with adolescent learners appeared nonetheless quite challenging. Millennial learners are not only fervent users of digital media, but they are also digital content producers (Gee, 2015). As a result, they are expert in interacting with technologies, and contributing to and modifying online content, both synchronously and asynchronously. Therefore, their learning experience is significantly different from their peers of 10 years ago. Drawing on learners' needs and abilities to create personalized digital content and experiences, this chapter reports on a research study of a multimodal video project conducted during the COVID-19 emergency with 24 lower-secondary school students in Italy.

The situation required a move from the standard task-based approach to a more content-based approach, capable of motivating students during the emergency and providing them with an alternative social community. Nowadays, the idea of community permeates our daily lives and as such project-based learning fosters the creation of a community where both teachers and students are members (Beckett & Miller, 2006; Stoller, 2002). The final product was a short, multimodal video to be shared with classmates and provided opportunities for the students to engage in autonomous learning and demonstrate their independence. In this chapter I describe and evaluate the implementation of the multimodal video project, drawing attention to the supporting role of the technological tools and the virtual classroom community in the development of English skills. The following research questions guided the study: What are the effects of a digital video project on EFL learning processes? Does it help to reach specific linguistic goals?

2 Review of the Research

At the beginning of the 21st century, Warschauer (2000) was already proposing the idea that a school curriculum should make space for the use of purposeful digital technologies that would foster language learning. Many studies since then have investigated the use of such technologies for second language learning in various educational contexts (Chun, 2016; Thomas, Reinders, & Warschauer, 2012). Meanwhile, as technologies have become more portable, research has also focused on out-of-class learning, considering the opportunities offered to access authentic materials anytime, anywhere (Kukulska-Hulme, 2013; Lai & Zheng, 2018; Wrigglesworth, 2020). However, formal and informal practices have always been considered as separate, each with their own potential and capabilities. In this study, the online teaching situation imposed by the COVID-19 emergency offered a unique opportunity to blend formal and informal learning practices, but also required careful design in terms of a pedagogical framework and technological practices. In this respect, a form of student-centered pedagogy that offered opportunities for independent and self-regulated language learning was implemented (Miller, Hafner, & Fun, 2012). Project-based language learning seemed particularly suitable for such a situation as it fosters language learning by building up a series of activities and tasks all aimed towards the realization of a project perceived as meaningful and linked to students' needs (Beckett & Miller, 2006; Stoller, 2002).

2.1 The Features of Project Work in English Language Learning

Project-based language learning characteristics seem particularly suitable for the English language classroom, as confirmed by recent studies in various second and foreign language settings (Hafner & Miller, 2011; Thomas,

2017; Tsiplakides & Fragoulis, 2009). Project-based learning is a student-centered approach, based on the constructivist principles of social interaction, knowledge sharing, and active participation of the student in the learning process (Stoller, 2002). In project-based work, students deal with authentic questions and problems linked with real-world situations, and this process leads them to meaningful learning experiences (Kokotsaki, Menzies, & Wiggins, 2016). Students are engaged in communicative activities and focused on achieving their goal as a group. In this respect, PBL is interconnected with similar student-centered approaches like task-based language teaching (TBLT). Students are requested to collaborate to achieve a shared goal. However, the focus of TBLT is on individual tasks, often focused on only one language skill.

In contrast, a PBL approach involves using various skills to collaboratively solve a problem over a more extended period (Stoller, 2002). Thus, completing project-work requires a wide range of skills that are not only linguistic such as critical thinking skills, organization and project management skills, as well as intercultural skills. Additionally, in technology-mediated environments, project-based language learning helps learners develop digital literacy skills (Thomas, 2017). In the present study, for example, students need to collaborate online on a digital story project.

In PBL, the language used and context in which communication takes place are strongly interrelated; indeed, they should be inseparable, as in real life (Stoller, 2002). Language educators have been concerned that focusing on the content could put less emphasis on explicit language focus. In reality, the rationale behind project-based language learning is that students should be equipped with the language they need to successfully perform a sequence of tasks. Therefore, it allows for the explicit teaching of linguistic aspects (e.g., grammar, discourse markers). The use of English language teaching projects provides opportunities for learners to use and interact with authentic situations. Although research literature has generally reported positive attitudes, there is an issue related to some EFL learners' perceptions of the usefulness of PBL (Beckett & Slater, 2005). In particular, despite their final results, learners are not always convinced about the efficacy of PBL on their learning of English, mainly because they do not feel involved in the choice and design of project goals (Moulton & Holmes, 2000). To overcome this issue, Beckett & Slater (2005) proposed a Project Framework to inform students about 'the language, content and skills development which occurs through project work' (Beckett & Slater, 2005: 110). The teacher-researcher in this project followed a similar approach.

2.2 Digital Video and Stories in EFL

Of particular interest for this study is the area of PBL literature related to the use and production of multimodal digital videos as pedagogical tools to develop second language skills, as well as a wide range of other literacies. Research into these educational practices highlights the importance of bridging the gap between how students use digital videos outside the classroom and what students actually do with videos in the language classroom (Godwin-Jones, 2012). Multimodal digital videos are compositions that can include digital text, images, sound effects, and videos, and they have been recognized as particularly powerful for various types of learning (Hafner, 2014; Miller et al., 2012; Wagener, 2006). In the area of English language learning, research studies focusing on the creation of digital stories to improve communicative competence have been successfully implemented (Kim, 2014; Miller et al., 2012). In digital story projects, learners narrate, inform, or instruct on a particular topic, and present historical or scientific findings (Robin & McNeil, 2019) with the support of video, audio, and a soundtrack. Nowadays, students are exposed to various types of digital stories on social networks. As Hafner & Miller (2011) note, multimodal video projects allow them to create a personalized digital product that resembles the stories they watch and share in their daily lives. They are also a great opportunity to learn different skills, both linguistic (writing, speaking, presentation) and non-linguistic (digital, organizational, etc.) as they require the combination of various multimodal literacies. In their study on the use of a collaborative video project in an English for Science context, they drew upon lessons from learner autonomy in informal practices and brought them to formal settings. From an EFL perspective, the same could be done for linguistic objectives and language features, using learners' strategies to understand a popular YouTuber or Instagrammer's video, bringing them to the language class. Teachers could invite learners to analyze linguistic features, including vocabulary and collocations, but also pronunciation issues (Godwin-Jones, 2012).

3 Theoretical Background

Over the last twenty years, second language acquisition (SLA) theories have served as a theoretical framework for research in CALL (computer-assisted language learning) and technology-mediated environments (Morgana, 2020). The planning and design of the study was informed by key concepts of sociocultural theory as developed by Lantolf & Thorne (2007). In particular, this study focused on the concepts of mediation and personalization.

According to Vygotsky (1978), psychological or semiotic tools (e.g., language) mediate human activities, while physical tools or artifacts (e.g., digital tools) contribute to construct knowledge. Moreover, from a sociocultural perspective, through these tools second language learners have the chance to construct new meanings (personalization).

This study is grounded in the application of sociocultural theory (Lantolf, Thorne, & Poehner, 2014) in content- and project-based learning that sees the classroom as a social context that fosters language development. This type of instruction allows explicit focus on linguistic features to prepare students for the language demands of the project. In particular, the interaction among students, teachers, tasks, and technology mediates, scaffolds, and activates the conscious awareness of language features through, for example, noticing (Morgana, 2020). In a sociocultural classroom, where Vygotskian ideas are applied, the teacher encourages learners to engage in dialogue both with the teacher and with each other, and to think by asking questions of each other (Brooks & Brooks, 1999). Furthermore, activities and tasks themselves mediate action and interaction, and the way they are designed and presented could also influence how learners orient themselves (Lantolf & Appel, 1994).

4 Methodology

This study follows a mixed methods approach, triangulating qualitative data with quantitative results in order to shed light on the learning processes and linguistic outcomes of the project. Qualitative data included lesson recordings (N=8), observation notes, and the students' written comments (N=24). In order to identify similar patterns in the data, they were analyzed using a standard qualitative coding method. A qualitative interpretive approach (Richards, 2003) proved to be particularly relevant to describe digital environments and behaviors, as such realities are complex and dynamic (Hafner & Miller, 2011; Lier, 1998). Additionally, learners' assessment scores after the first task were compared with scores on the final project, in an attempt to compare linguistic objectives and outcomes, and answer the second research question.

The project started in March 2020 and was implemented over a period of five weeks. Due to the emergency lockdown imposed by the Italian Government, all lessons took place online using Google Meet, a videoconferencing application. For research purposes, a series of linguistic objectives was set at the beginning of the project and all lessons were video-recorded.

4.1 Research Context

The participants were 24 students attending the second year of a lower secondary school (7th grade) in Milan, Italy. All students were between 12 and 13 years old at the time of the study. The teacher-researcher had known the students for two years and was also familiar with the school environment, thus supporting the need for a rigorous design in interpretive qualitative research (Miles & Huberman, 1994). All lessons took place from home due to the full lockdown imposed by the government. The Italian Ministry of Education requires learners in the 7th grade to have three 1-hour English lessons per week, but due to the emergency, the timetable was adapted to two 1-hour slots per week. Students connected from home using the videoconference app Meet, part of the GSuite platform for education. Although the learners' digital literacy was not formally examined, all students were able to use the tools and technology required by the study as the teacher-researcher had used them for other language projects in the previous school year. Most learners used a laptop computer to follow the lessons and to perform the tasks; two students used a tablet; and one of them connected with his smartphone. This study looked in particular at the different uses of the technological tools and at the strategies employed by the teachers and the learners in response to such mediation in relation to the project tasks.

4.2 Pedagogical Framework

This project follows the multiple-step, project-based design framework proposed by Stoller (2002). The framework proposes ten easy steps to guide the implementation of the project: from the choice of a shared theme to the project evaluation. For the purposes and context of this study, the framework was adapted in order to include an inductive task at the beginning of the project and also to provide space for the digital tools involved. The inductive task was then used as a first assessment tool. In addition, an extra step on language focus was added, as requested by students. According to Stoller (2002), in order to be effective, a project should be linked to a real-world concern. In this particular case, learners were spending most of their time at home and since cooking in Italy represents the basics of family and traditions, it easily became part of their daily lives. The project was, in fact, designed to answer the need for exchanging recipe and video-related activities.

Stoller (2002) advises involving students in the design and planning of the initial steps of the language learning project. However, given the particular situation, all stages and decisions related to the project (e.g., topic, technological tools, linguistic objectives, and final product) were specified and organized by the teacher-researcher. In order to overcome any potential learner issues relating to the usefulness of a project-based approach to learning English (Beckett & Slater, 2005), the teacher-researcher gave a pre-project lesson to discuss and explain the linguistic goals of the project to the students. An outline of the five-week project, including expected learning outcomes, cross-cultural skills, and specific target tasks, is presented in Table 4.1.

Table 4.1. Project Outline

Target Task	Linguistic Objectives, Communicative Function, and/or Specific Vocabulary	Skills and Competences – Digital Literacies
Week 1: *"A favorite family dish"* – Written text + Individual oral presentation	Using food vocabulary (countable/uncountable nouns) Selecting, organizing and sequencing information	Use of search engine (Google) Creating and sharing a Google document Giving an online oral presentation
Week 2: *"Cook with Amber"* – Listen to and watch a teen chef's video recipe Compare and contrast	Listening for detailed information Language focus: cooking verbs	Analyzing the components of a digital video: light, audio/music, shot from above, etc.
Week 3: *"The menu"* – Read and watch food recipes for a complete menu Write and present a menu	Reading and listening comprehension Selecting and using key vocabulary	Use of Google doc, Google presentations, Jamboard, and/or Canva for the virtual menu
Week 4: *"My video recipe"* – Plan, rehearse, and record a video recipe based on the virtual menu Presentation checklist	Use of key presentation and food vocabulary (how to start, linking words, cooking verb collocations)	Shooting, recording, and sharing a digital video recipe using a smartphone or tablet Use of various technological tools and applications (e.g., Canva, Animoto, Movie maker, etc.)
Week 5: Project assessment and evaluation	Peer-to-peer comments on video recipe	

4.3 Project Design and Technological Tools

Based on the school curriculum, by the end of the school year learners had to reach a set of language objectives in English. The language objectives included: the use of countable and uncountable nouns, the use of cooking verb collocations, the use of selected discourse linkers and organizers, and correct pronunciation. For this reason, the first step of the project was to carefully select a series of linguistic goals that served as a guideline for the following steps. Additionally, it was expected that at this level learners should be able to talk about a personal experience (e.g., a favorite recipe) and give a short presentation about a familiar content they had previously selected.

The study used a wide range of free, multimodal internet resources that helped participants in the planning and completion of the digital video project. In particular, technological tools were used to: (a) do background research; (b) write and share texts; (c) watch authentic digital videos and use them as modelling samples; (d) create and edit a multimodal digital video; and (e) present final work to students and teacher. The multimodal videos produced by the students shared many characteristics with digital stories and were a blend of the students' linguistic competences, communication skills, and digital literacies.

Collaboration is a key aspect of PBL as it supports the development of critical and problem-solving skills (Thomas, 2017). However, due to the health emergency, only individual video projects were produced in this study. In order to overcome the issue, the whole class acted as a collaborative group, and any necessary support and scaffolding was always provided for linguistic as well as technical issues and concerns. In addition, the teacher provided students with a timeline to help them manage the project and follow the steps correctly.

4.4 Project Implementation

In week 1, students were introduced to the topic with an inductive content approach. They were asked to select and present one of their favorite family recipes. The task was specifically designed to elicit vocabulary related to food, guide learners towards the structure of the text, and assist them in transferring their L1 presentation skills into L2. Technology played a mediator role throughout the project. In week 1, learners developed the ability to search and select content (on Google), compose a written text synchronously using Google Documents, and use it as a guideline to orally present their family recipe to the class. The shared Google document also allowed teacher and peers to provide synchronous and personalized feedback to students.

Tasks were designed to gradually increase in complexity. In week 2, learners watched a digital video recipe performed on YouTube by an American teenage chef. The video served to provide learners with key vocabulary and language use. It was also used as a model for the digital video final project. Learners were able to play the recorded video as many times as they needed and perform the guided tasks at their own pace. The weekly tasks included both language focus activities to prepare learners for their own performance, and digital literacy activities such as the analysis of video performance. In particular, students were asked to identify and take notes of the features of popular video recipes (e.g., lights, music, length, colors used, camera effects, etc.).

Week 3 focused on the collaborative creation of a virtual menu using some of the technological tools learners would use to record their own digital videos. A series of standard sample menus were presented to students. During the synchronous lesson, learners discussed the pros and cons of each menu and then collaboratively constructed their class menu. Students worked on a shared Jamboard (a virtual board embedded in GSuite for Education) and the teacher acted as a facilitator. Three learners were then selected to transform the Jamboard into an official virtual menu using the Canvas application. In the discussion and planning stage of week 3, students learned to deal with a large group discussion online, taking turns and providing constructive feedback. The teacher also assisted them in reflecting on the roles in the team and identifying who did what. For example, students with strong language skills were responsible for selecting sources and content from the web, while others with strong presentation skills worked on the digital menu design.

Week 4 was devoted to the planning, rehearsal, and implementation of the final project. Each student worked on his/her task individually. Although they were not allowed to share their content or any part of their digital video with the class before the end of the project, they were encouraged to ask for support from the teacher and exchange opinions with peers in the group. The teacher also posted a step-by-step guide on how to create a successful video recipe on the virtual classroom for students to use as a reference. The guide was a co-constructed file based on the notes and assumptions made in the previous week by the group. Additionally, students could record part of their presentation and ask the teacher to provide them with individual feedback. At the end of week 4, the students' video recipes were published online on the class website where all participants could provide supportive and constructive feedback to their peers.

In week 5, the teacher individually assessed all the video recipes and provided each learner with a language mark (between 5 and 10). Projects were assessed according to four main criteria, based on curriculum requirements: the use of countable/uncountable nouns, selected linkers, range of vocabulary, and pronunciation. At the end of the project, students were asked to reflect on their experience and provide a short comment on what they thought they had learned in the previous five weeks, despite the distance learning modality. Most of them also provided the teacher with useful suggestions for future projects.

5 Analysis

The qualitative data of the study included classroom observation notes based on lesson recordings (*N*=8) and the students' final written comments on the project (*N*=24). Observation notes were taken during and right after each English lesson thanks to the support of video recordings (Kahn, 2012). The researcher also wrote detailed notes immediately after each live session, including selected verbatim records of the students' interactions (Vaca Torres & Gómez Rodríguez, 2017). Classroom observation notes included comments on the students' engagement, questions, issues raised, learning modality (e.g., turn taking, discussion management), motivation, and reflection on language learning episodes. Each dataset was analyzed using a qualitative content analysis of emergent themes approach (Elo & Kyngäs, 2008; Silverman, 2004). This entailed an open coding of the students' and teachers' interviews, lesson plans, and classroom observation notes. All the coding units selected were analyzed using the qualitative analysis software Nvivo (version 10.8). Classroom observation notes and the students' comments were coded and grouped into themes and categories.

In order to get a clear picture of the project outcomes, qualitative data were triangulated with data from the learners' initial and final assessments. The students' speaking scores from the pre-project task were compared to their scores at the end of the project task (video recipe) to check if linguistic objectives were achieved. The pre-project task took place at the beginning of the first week and it was performed live during the online weekly English class. Students were aware that the performance was being recorded for research purposes and that it was to be assessed based on the linguistic objectives of the project. The final project task was the multimodal digital video that each student recorded and uploaded to the class website at the end of the project. Students were allowed about five minutes to perform their task. The teacher-researcher provided students with an evaluation grid, which included the expected linguistic outcomes. In order to ensure reliability, all tasks and performances were assessed by the teacher-researcher and by a research assistant.

The scores for each linguistic objective (countable/uncountable nouns; selected linkers and organizers; vocabulary range; pronunciation) were entered into JASP 0.14.1 for statistical analysis.

6 Results

Results from the qualitative analysis helped to answer the first research question on what learning processes EFL learners activate during project-based work mediated by technology. Two main categories emerged most often from the data analysis: language awareness and independent learning. Results from each category are presented in the following sections, evidenced by extracts from live lesson recordings and the students' written comments. Following the ethical rules and regulations to conduct research with secondary school students, proper names have been removed and replaced with numbers (e.g., student 3).

6.1 Language Awareness

Extracts from the observation notes show that students frequently asked questions about the correct vocabulary to use before presenting or interacting with other students. Most of them took notes and cross-checked with the group if definitions or translations found on the internet were appropriate, as in the following extract from week 2 of the project:

> Student 5: But … teacher … do you prepare a ***pizza base***? Or a **pizza dough.** Google says **pizza dough.** I don't know how to say it …

Moreover, as a result of the authentic video comprehension activity from week 2, learners seemed particularly interested in the detection and understanding of specific language chunks (e.g., cooking method, home cooking, ready meal, set menu, etc.) and expressions related to eating and drinking. Questions on collocations frequently appeared in the data, either spontaneously or prompted by the teacher, and they often led to lively classroom discussions as in the example below:

> (Learners had just watched the video recipe of Amber's home-made chicken nuggets twice: the first as a group and the second individually, at their own pace)
> Teacher: *Have you noticed any particular verb coming before the name of the food mentioned?*

> Student 1: ***Cook*** *chicken nuggets*
> Student 2: *No, no ... it's* ***do*** *real chicken nuggets*
> Student 3: *I don't understand* **season the potatoes**. *Season is ... like summer* (laughing).

The reflection on language learning is also confirmed by the students' final comments. Most of them reported a perceived language improvement in their speaking and presentation skills, particularly in the area of pronunciation and vocabulary.

> Comment 1: *I think the best thing I learnt is pronunciation. The first time I was bad ... I recorded the video 10 times.*
> Comment 2: *I liked the video from YouTube. In the afternoon I read the subtitle with the speaker ... to have the American pronunciation, like Amber.*
> Comment 3: *My English is better now. I like using YouTube and also making my video. Sometimes Amber speaks too fast, but with sottotitoli [subtitles] it's ok.*

The video project allowed learners to focus attention on pronunciation subskills, such as intonation and connected speech, and also on the use of a wider range of vocabulary. Digital technologies gave the students the chance to plan and rehearse their oral presentation. Over the five weeks of the project, learners gradually became aware of their language competence and skills and this encouraged them to work on their perceived language weaknesses, as indicated by the students' comments and observation notes.

6.2 Learner's Autonomy

As noted above, the second main category emerging from the analysis was learner autonomy. The distance learning context where this study took place naturally allowed for autonomy and self-directed learning and the situation forced students to take more responsibility for their learning. Observation notes from lesson recordings showed how students felt engaged and responsible particularly during the research and investigation phases, when they were required to find content for their video and scan it for useful information:

> Student 22: *I am doing my research on the internet. It's [everything is] in English, but it's ok. I try to understand. I like watching videos on You Tube, can I watch more video recipes from Amber's channel? Faccio io! [I'll do it!]*
> (Partly translated from Italian)

Even though they sometimes had issues with the language level of the content, since they were working with authentic materials, they always recognized the language practice aspect and responded positively to the challenge. In addition, virtual classroom discussions often focused on what activities they could perform autonomously.

> Student 9: *The best thing is to make the video. Can I try? Copio e incollo le cose più utili. [I can cut and paste the most useful things.]*

Many of them were concerned about planning and working on a personalized video project that would allow them to express their preferences and show their language improvements.

> Student 1: *Can I use post-it so I can remember words? Or I write the steps of the recipe. In television they have it.*
> Student 15: *How many times can we record and provare il video [rehearse the video]?*

Generally, comments showed a positive attitude towards the tasks as students felt engaged in purposeful, meaningful activities, involving authentic language use (Stoller, 2002).

> Student's final comment: *I love making videos for TikTok, but this video was cool. Ci ho messo una vita! [It took me ages!], but I'm happy ... very happy.*
> *I cooked everything by myself.*
> Student 5: *So we learn how to make video bellissimi su Instagram [lovely videos on Instagram as well].*

6.3 Assessment of the Students' Tasks

In order to answer the second research question and see if linguistic goals set at the beginning of the project were reached, scores from the two assessment tasks were compared. Table 4.2 shows the comparison between the pre- and the post-project assessments based on the four different language objectives. Scores for each objective ranged from 5 to 10. Generally, the data demonstrated that learners significantly improved their marks over the five-week project and were able to meet the project's linguistic requirements.

The Shapiro-Wilk test showed that the data were normally distributed, so a statistical analysis of means was conducted to measure pre- and post-project differences in relation to language objectives. The PRE scores are based on recorded performances during live classes in week 1, and the

POST scores are based on the students' multimodal video recipe. Scores on countable and uncountable nouns (Mean 7.042 > 8.25) and use of selected linkers (Mean 6.708 > 7.833) show a quite significant difference in means. Results show that student competence was good at the start in terms of the first two linguistic objectives and they seemed to have reached their goal. The most significant difference between the two groups was revealed by the scores on vocabulary, including the use of collocations, and on pronunciation (Table 4.2). By comparing the scores from the first task on presenting a family recipe and from the final video project, it became evident that the group significantly enhanced their competences in terms of content and communication skills. Learners constantly increased the lexis related to cooking in general and were able to retain quite a large range of vocabulary throughout the project. It is interesting to note that one of the teacher's concerns about using exclusively authentic digital material to scaffold and prepare students for the project was that learners would get confused and not be able to retain key cooking vocabulary. Results demonstrated the opposite.

Table 4.2. Descriptive Statistics of Students' Scores in Communication and Vocabulary

	PRE Communication (Fluency + Pronunciation)	POST Communication (Fluency + Pronunciation)	PRE Vocabulary (Collocations + Range)	POST Vocabulary (Collocations + Range)
Valid	24	24	24	24
Mean	6.417	7.875	6.875	8.292
Standard Deviation	0.881	0.947	0.900	0.908

7 Discussion

Investigating the use of digital video in the English language learning curriculum has been quite a popular area of recent research into PBL (Assaf, 2018; Dooly & Sadler, 2016; Hafner & Miller, 2011). However, the implementation of video projects to improve second language skills and digital literacies in an online learning environment with secondary learners has not been investigated.

This study was guided by two main research questions: What are the effects of a digital video project on EFL learning processes? Does it help to reach specific linguistic goals? Although multiple variables could have influenced the learning process over the five weeks (e.g., time spent online, on digital videos, or on YouTube), there were two main areas that benefited significantly from the digital video project work. First, the analysis and creation of a digital video fostered spontaneous reflection on various aspects of language learning. Second, the implementation of a digital video project encouraged learner autonomy, not only in terms of learning "independently," but also in terms of learning "collaboratively" with teachers and peers.

Students were actively engaged in finding the correct term or noticing the suitable combination of words. In their comments, they emphasized the importance of mastering the right vocabulary to perform the various tasks, but also to comprehend the authentic videos and texts used in the project, thereby confirming the results in Vaca Torres & Gómez Rodríguez (2017).

An assumption often made about project-based instruction is that it is strongly content-oriented, and as a result language focus is often overlooked. In fact, a project-based approach focuses on content, but it also allows explicit language focus activities (Stoller, 2002). The students' comments and interactions from this study suggest that they found the language focus experience an important step to support them in the subsequent oral task performance. They were strongly motivated to reflect on language aspects, and this can be attributed to the fact that their final digital video was intended for a real audience (the class website). Other studies confirm the importance of providing meaningful digital video experiences for learners (Thorne & Reinhart, 2008; Winke, Gass, & Sydorenko, 2010; Hafner & Miller, 2011; Nikitina, 2011).

In the context of this project, learner autonomy and independence are intended outcomes as learning collaboratively supported by the project group (teachers and peers) is an important integral element of the approach. Observation notes and the students' comments provided an insight into the strategies implemented to successfully perform tasks, but also to overcome some issues. Learners were gratified to be able to control their learning, and often mentioned this during lessons and in their comments. The term "independent" was, in fact, the most frequent word in the data. They felt independent in selecting their sources and materials; they appreciated the independence in practicing and rehearsing their oral performance; and they independently supported their peers when in need or elicited questions during online classes. As in Hafner & Miller (2011) and in Kim (2014), learners took independent action towards their learning and towards the learning of the community to which they belong. The digital video project also provided opportunities for self-assessment. Learners' comments on linguistic objectives during online lessons were often critical and reflective, and this attitude apparently guided them to gain better linguistic outcomes, as confirmed by assessment results.

Behind the design of this project was the idea that technology mediates our learning and that the online class is a socially constructed environment in which students contribute to each other's advancement in learning. The online digital tools used, particularly Google Meet, effectively mediated online communicative practices, as it helped, for example, to manage turn-taking during interactions and provided learners with a virtual space to meet (Lenkaitis, 2020).

In the present study, students produced videos that were similar to the most popular YouTube videos of a teenage chef. The language they used was obviously simpler, but they followed the same format, thus showing that they invested time and effort in the project, and they found it fun. Based on this premise, this study argues that a technology-mediated project-based curriculum should take into account what is relevant for language learners in a broader sense, not only in terms of technological tools or language requirements, but also in terms of real-life pedagogical resources.

8 Conclusion

The unprecedented situation of COVID-19 has forced language educators to become flexible and innovative. This chapter has presented a case study implemented with lower secondary school students in an online distance learning modality in Italy. The study was designed in order to create new opportunities for language learning and keep young students engaged in their own learning and within the school community.

Although the findings of this study are limited, they show how the implementation of project-based practices to learn English in online distance modality can contribute to the development of autonomous learning and foster language awareness. As seen above, students perceived the digital video project as responding to their needs and actively participated in the design and realization of their own digital product. Moreover, despite the isolated condition they were experiencing, the language project contributed to making them feel part of a community. The changes that education has experienced in the last year are opening new opportunities for language learning and teaching. This research study shows that tasks and projects provide one potential way of blending formal and informal learning with online with face-to-face learning. The findings presented in this chapter aim to contribute to understanding the new dynamics that are produced as a result.

Although a series of lessons can be drawn from this study, it also has several limitations that it is essential to acknowledge. The sample of students and teachers was relatively small in size, and the context where the project took place was also unusual. It is not possible, therefore, to generalize the research findings.

Nevertheless, the insights provided by the study clearly indicate that there are some directions that future research in this area can take. Considering the relevance of PBL in EFL contexts, it will be worthwhile to examine the relationship between long-term project work and students' English language competence in secondary schools and to explore what specific linguistic skills may benefit from a PBL approach.

References

Assaf, D. (2018). Motivating language learners during times of crisis through project-based learning: Filming activities at the Arab International University (AIU). *Theory and Practice in Language Studies*, 8(12), 1649. https://doi.org/10.17507/tpls.0812.10

Beckett, G. H., & Miller, P. C. (Eds.). (2006). *Project-based second and foreign language education: Past, present, and future*. North Carolina: IAP.

Beckett, G. H., & Slater, T. (2005). The project framework: A tool for language, content, and skills integration. *ELT Journal*, 59(2), 108–116. https://doi.org/10.1093/eltj/cci024

Brooks, J. J. G., & Brooks, M. G. (1999). *In search of understanding: The case for constructivist classrooms*. Alexandria, VA: Association for Supervision and Curriculum Development.

Chun, D. M. (2016). The role of technology in SLA research. *Language Learning and Technology*, 20(2), 98–115.

Dooly, M., & Sadler, R. (2016). Becoming little scientists: Technologically-enhanced project-based language learning. *Language Learning and Technology*, 20(1), 54–78.

Elo, S., & Kyngäs, H. (2008). The qualitative content analysis process. *Journal of Advanced Nursing*, 62(1), 107–115. https://doi.org/10.1111/j.1365-2648.2007.04569.x

Gee, J. (2015). *Social linguistics and literacies*. New York: Routledge. https://doi.org/10.4324/9781315722511

Godwin-Jones, R. (2012). Emerging technologies digital video revisited: Storytelling, conferencing, remixing. *Language, Learning and Technology*, 16(1), 1–9.

Hafner, C. A. (2014). Embedding digital literacies in English language teaching: Students' digital video projects as multimodal ensembles. *TESOL Quarterly*, 48(4), 655–685. https://doi.org/10.1002/tesq.138

Hafner, C. A., & Miller, L. (2011). Fostering learner autonomy in English for science: A collaborative digital video project in a technological learning environment. *Language Learning and Technology*, 15(3), 68–86.

Kahn, G. (2012). Open-ended tasks and the qualitative investigation of second language classroom discourse. *Journal of Ethnographic & Qualitative Research*, 6, 90–107.

Kim, S. (2014). Developing autonomous learning for oral proficiency using digital storytelling. *Language Learning and Technology*, 18(2), 20–35.

Kokotsaki, D., Menzies, V., & Wiggins, A. (2016). Project-based learning: A review of the literature. *Improving Schools*, 19(3), 267–277. https://doi.org/10.1177/1365480216659733

Kukulska-Hulme, A. (2013). *Re-skilling language learners for a mobile world.* Monterey, CA: The International Research Foundation for English Language Education. Retrieved from http://www.tirfonline.org/english-in-the-workforce/mobile-assisted-language-learning/

Lai, C., & Zheng, D. (2018). Self-directed use of mobile devices for language learning beyond the classroom. *ReCALL*, 30(3), 299–318. https://doi.org/10.1017/S0958344017000258

Lantolf, J. P., & Appel, G. (1994). *Vygotskian approaches to second language research.* Norwood, NJ: Ablex Publishing Corporation.

Lantolf, J. P., & Thorne, S. (2007). Sociocultural theory and second language learning. In B. van Patten & J. Williams (Eds.), *Theories in second language acquisition* (pp. 201–224). New York: Routledge.

Lantolf, J. P., Thorne, S. L., & Poehner, M. E. (2014). Sociocultural theory and second language development. In B. van Patten & J. Williams (Eds.), *Theories in second language acquisition: An introduction* (pp. 207–226). New York: Routledge.

Lenkaitis, C. A. (2020). Technology as a mediating tool: Videoconferencing, L2 learning, and learner autonomy. *Computer Assisted Language Learning*, 33(5–6), 483–509. https://doi.org/10.1080/09588221.2019.1572018

Lier, L. Van. (1998). All hooked up: An ecological look at computers in the classroom. *Studia Anglica Posnaniensia: International Review of English Studies*, 281–302.

Miles, M. B., & Huberman, A. (1994). *An expanded sourcebook: Qualitative data analysis* (2nd Edition). London: Sage.

Miller, L., Hafner, C. A., & Fun, C. N. K. (2012). Project-based learning in a technologically enhanced learning environment for second language learners: Students' perceptions. *E-Learning and Digital Media*, 9(2), 183–195. https://doi.org/10.2304/elea.2012.9.2.183

Morgana, V. (2020). *Fostering English speaking and writing subskills for the Cambridge B2 First through technology-mediated tasks* [Manuscript submitted for publication].

Moulton, M. R., & Holmes, V. L. (2000). An ESL capstone course: Integrating research tools, techniques, and technology. *TESOL Journal*, 9(2), 23–28.

Nikitina, L. (2011). Creating an authentic learning environment in the foreign language classroom. *International Journal of Instruction*, 4(1), 33–45.

Pitura, J., & Berlinska-Kopeć, M. (2018). Learning English while exploring the national cultural heritage: Technology-assisted project-based language learning in an upper-secondary school. *Teaching English with Technology*, 18(1), 37–52.

Richards, K. (2003). *Qualitative inquiry in TESOL*. London: Palgrave Macmillan. https://doi.org/10.1057/9780230505056

Robin, B. R., & McNeil, S. G. (2019). Digital storytelling. In R. Hobbs & P. Mihailidis (Eds.), *The international encyclopedia of media literacy* (pp. 1–8). New York: Wiley. https://doi.org/10.1002/9781118978238.ieml0056

Silverman, D. (Ed.) (2004). *Qualitative research: Issues of theory, method and practice*. London: Sage. https://doi.org/10.1073/pnas.0703993104

Stoller, F. (2002). Project work: A means to promote language content. In W. Richards & J. Renandya (Eds.), *Methodology in language teaching: An anthology of current practice* (pp. 107–119). Cambridge: Cambridge University Press. https://doi.org/10.1093/elt/58.1.80

Thomas, M. (2017). *Project-based language learning with technology: Learner collaboration in an EFL classroom in Japan*. London & New York: Routledge. https://doi.org/10.4324/9781315225418

Thomas, M., Reinders, H., & Warschauer, M. (Eds.) (2012). *Contemporary computer-assisted language learning*. London: Bloomsbury Academic.

Thorne, S., & Reinhart, J. (2008). "Bridging activities," new media literacies, and advanced foreign language proficiency. *CALICO Journal*, 25(3), 558–572. https://doi.org/10.1558/cj.v25i3.558-572

Tsiplakides, I., & Fragoulis, I. (2009). Project-based learning in the teaching of English as a foreign language in Greek primary schools: from theory to practice. *English Language Teaching*, 2(3), 113–119. https://doi.org/10.5539/elt.v2n3p113

Vaca Torres, A. M., & Gómez Rodríguez, L. F. (2017). Increasing EFL learners' oral production at a public school through project-based learning. *PROFILE Issues in Teachers' Professional Development*, 19(2), 57–71. https://doi.org/10.15446/profile.v19n2.59889

Vygotsky, L. S. (1978). *Mind in society: The development of higher psychological processes*. Cambridge: Cambridge University Press.

Wagener, D. (2006). Promoting independent learning skills using video on digital language laboratories. *Computer Assisted Language Learning*, 19(4–5), 279–286. https://doi.org/10.1080/09588220601043180

Warschauer, M. (2000). The changing global economy and the future of English teaching. *TESOL Quarterly*, 34(3), 511–535. https://doi.org/10.2307/3587741

Winke, P., Gass, S., & Sydorenko, T. (2010). The effects of captioning videos used for foreign language listening activities. *Language Learning & Technology*, 14(1), 66–87.

Wrigglesworth, J. (2020). Using smartphones to extend interaction beyond the EFL classroom. *Computer Assisted Language Learning*, 33(4), 413–434. https://doi.org/10.1080/09588221.2019.1569067

About the Author

Valentina Morgana is Adjunct Professor of English Linguistics in the Faculty of Language Sciences and Foreign Literature at the Università Cattolica del Sacro Cuore in Milan, Italy. She holds a Doctorate in Education from the Department of Languages of the Open University, UK. Her research interests include Applied Linguistics (MALL and TBLT) and Corpus Linguistics. Her recent publications focus on mobile English language learning and technology-mediated task-based language teaching.

5 Project-Based Learning in Online Synchronous Writing Classrooms: Enhancing EFL Learners' Awareness of the Ethics of Writing

Fatemeh Nami

1 Introduction

Teaching writing has always been one of the most challenging tasks for language teachers particularly in foreign language learning contexts. The time-consuming nature of writing, widely available online writing samples and resources, and limited writing proficiency and knowledge about ethics of writing have promoted a copy/paste habit in many students. Additionally, the conventional deductive teaching styles that are reliant on knowledge transfer through direct instruction usually fail to effectively improve students' second/foreign language skills (see Essien, 2018). These challenges are usually intensified in online synchronous classrooms in which students do not have the opportunity to physically meet peers or the teacher.

New technological advances and the emergence of online writing tools and technologies have opened up new horizons for language teachers in order to overcome the aforementioned problems. Additionally, previous research highlights the potential of problem-driven writing projects for enhancing learner engagement in and knowledge of technical skills in writing (e.g., Hoopingarner, 2009; Kessler, Bikowski, & Boggs, 2012). In an attempt to contribute to this research base, the present chapter reports a study on a group of Masters' level students who attended an online synchronous writing course in a state university of technology in Tehran. To promote their understanding of ethics in writing and referencing, students were engaged in three rounds of writing and sharing review projects throughout a 13-session course. The project sharing was followed by online classroom discussions. The overall purpose was to provide students with an opportunity to view and reflect on their own and their peers' work to gain a better grasp of the focus of the task. Students' pre- and post-treatment writings were analyzed and compared with the pre- and post-treatment writings of a control group who received conventional treatment in an online synchronous course. The overall purpose was to explore how project-based learning (PBL) strategy shaped students' knowledge of correct referencing, paraphrasing, and the essence of avoiding plagiarism in writing. The findings offer useful insights for teachers and educators on the potential of technology-enhanced PBL for language classrooms.

2 Literature Review

2.1 Project-Based Learning: Theoretical Groundings and Empirical Research

Research on second and foreign language learning has widely advocated the potential of learner interaction and group work for student learning. Inspired by Vygotsky's (1978) notion of social constructivism, it is suggested that knowledge is socially constructed through personal experience and social interaction with the other members of a community or an environment. Also referred to as collective scaffolding (Donato, 1994), problem-solving through interactive tasks plays a determining role in enhancing learners' control over their learning.

To effectively promote knowledge construction, such interaction should occur between explicit and tacit knowledge (DeFillippi, 2001), or the known (i.e., theory) and the knower (i.e., practice and inquiry) (Heo, Lim, & Kim, 2010; also Amineh & Asl, 2015). This way, interaction, be it social or with the coursework, can "develop their [students'] cognitive skills and fosters their full potential" (Nami & Marandi, 2014: 484). For this to happen, students should be given an opportunity to take responsibility for their own learning (Praba', Artini, & Ramendra, 2018) by actively partaking in problem-oriented learning projects, namely through "learning by doing" (Barron et al., 1998). In effect, students can construct their knowledge of different concepts through building on their prior course of knowledge.

Of different teaching/learning models proposed so far, PBL is believed to better satisfy the abovementioned needs, building on the tenets of social constructivism and action learning (see Heo et al., 2010). It stands for a dynamic student-centered learning approach that practically integrates collaborative/individual hands-on project work in a meaningful learning context (DeFillippi, 2001) to solve authentic curriculum-based problems (also Blumenfeld et al., 1991). As Putri, Artini, & Nitiasih (2017: 1148) put it, in the "PBL classroom, students plan, implement, reflect, and evaluate their own learning by working on authentic tasks, such as solving a problem or [on a] task which is constructed based on real-world issues." To help students develop a deep understanding of the instructional content, the teacher should engage students in authentic problem-solving tasks. Engagement in curriculum-related projects to produce meaningful outputs as an illustration of learning can also develop learner autonomy (Grant, 2002).

Effective integration of PBL into the language classroom, according to Stoller (2006), requires:

- a shift in the teacher's role from the sage-on-the-stage to a facilitator and in students' roles from passive recipients of the information to the center of the classroom;
- an attention to different language skills;
- an opportunity for students to partially own the project and develop an understanding of its goal and focus;
- a project scheduled for a (usually extended) time period;
- student engagement in the process of data collection and analysis to solve the problem in the learning scenario;
- an opportunity for student collaboration and individual activity;
- presentation of final project output; and
- learner engagement in reflection on the process and the product of learning.

Simpson (2011), similarly, defines PBL as a student-centered learning approach which (a) engages students in a process of information collection and presentation, (b) gradually develops over varying time scales, (c) stems from a real-life challenging problem, (d) draws upon the potential of teacher and peer feedback, (e) involves the use of different language skills and production of meaningful artifacts, and (f) considers the essence of assessing both the process and product of learning.

In other words, PBL involves students in a process of collective or individual inquiry to find a solution for an authentic problem or question posed under the supervision of an instructor (Bell, 2010). As posited in constructionism, learning is expected to be more effective when students produce a meaningful output, share it with peers, and experience reflecting on their artifacts (see Grant, 2002). Artifacts "are representations of the students' problem solutions that reflect emergent states of knowledge" (Blumenfeld et al., 1991: 372). The project outputs are concrete and, hence, can be reflected upon and shared with others. Artifact sharing is one of the main indications of student learning and knowledge construction which distinguishes PBL from the conventional inquiry-oriented teaching/learning procedures (see Sadeghi, Biniaz, & Soleimani, 2016).

It is worth mentioning that despite its productive nature, PBL may be accompanied by some challenges. The first and foremost relates to the lack of a clear understanding, on the part of educators and instructors, about what comprises a "project." For some educators and teachers, any kind of coursework or assignments are considered as projects. To be effective, however, project-work must move beyond the conventional realization of assignments to embrace *meaningful inquiry*. Furthermore, as Grant (2002) puts it, this learning strategy might not be apt for every individual learner, considering the differences in learning styles and preferences. This problem coupled with the time-consuming nature of the strategy can negatively affect the quality of PBL in different contexts, particularly if the teachers do not have relevant coping experience.

A careful review of research on PBL in second and foreign language learning contexts brings a plethora of empirical studies to the forefront. These studies mainly highlight a positive connection between PBL and language skills development. Additionally, PBL is suggested to be effective for promoting critical thinking and learner engagement, compassion, and resilience (see Essien, 2018). Sadeghi, Biniaz, & Soleimani (2016), for instance, applied PBL strategy to develop 36 English as a Foreign Language (EFL) students' knowledge of writing comparison and contrast paragraphs. The results of *t*-test analysis revealed that the students who were engaged in PBL outperformed those who received the conventional treatment. Putri et al. (2017), in another study, examined the potential of PBL for improving English language learners' writing and speaking skills. In addition to developing learners' writing and speaking proficiency, the experience positively enhanced their confidence in collaborative and self-directed learning.

Drawing on interview, observation, and students' writings, Praba' et al. (2018) found project-based learning effective for promoting learners' communication, critical thinking, creativity, and English language writing proficiency. Essien (2018), similarly, reported a positive relation between PBL and learners' English language proficiency and perception towards this experience.

2.2 PBL in Online Real-Time (Synchronous) Language Learning Classrooms

As discussed above, PBL draws on the potential of project work and interaction to promote student-centered learning. Scaffolding, interaction, and project work require a rich social learning context to be effectively experienced (see Twu, 2009). The "public and participatory and inquiry-oriented nature of Web 2.0 technologies" (Nami, 2019: 484) – ranging from WebQuests to virtual learning environments and learning management systems (LMSs) – makes them apt for satisfying this need. Despite the abundance of research on the potential of PBL for second/foreign language learning, empirical data on how PBL might contribute to technology-enhanced or computer-assisted language learning (CALL) remains scant. Even fewer are the studies that explore PBL in online and virtual learning environments and its potential for enhancing learners' productive skills (e.g., writing).

Parallel with the advances in information and communication technologies (ICTs) and the proliferation of online management and learning environments, "the delivery of learning programs has gradually shifted from local desktop to online-based applications" (Cavus & Ala'a, 2009: 19). Today, many courses and programs are offered in online synchronous mode through LMSs of different universities across the globe. According to Nami (2019: 170), "learning management systems are considered as ubiquitous learning environments as the services and content offered in these systems are accessible through different compatible devices." Since LMSs are relatively new to the language teaching profession, studies that focus on the productivity of online real-time classrooms for developing learners' language proficiency are still emerging. Given the potential of online platforms for facilitating learner interaction, access to resources, and feedback generation and reception, such learning environments appear to be apt for operationalizing project-based learning strategy.

2.3 Project-Based Writing Development in Online Language Classrooms

Technology has proved to be useful for writing practice and development (Kessler et al., 2012). In line with the emergence of new educational technologies, consensus has grown on their potential for encouraging students not only "to engage in the writing process and display their finished products" (Hoopingarner, 2009: 228) but also to learn about the dynamics of writing and form. Studies on technology-enhanced PBL for writing development are growing. Kessler et al. (2012), for instance, investigated how collaborative writing projects created with a web-based word-processing tool contribute to students' writing development. They observed an overall improvement in students' attention to meaning and more accurate grammatical structures after getting engaged in the projects.

When it comes to the integration of PBL in online language learning contexts, research remains limited. The contribution of PBL to learners' knowledge of the ethics of writing in an online synchronous writing course has not been previously explored. Parallel with the growing popularity of online real-time classrooms in higher education contexts for second and foreign language learning/instruction, investigating how different learning strategies (including PBL) may shape learners' language knowledge in these contexts is imperative.

Throughout a decade of teaching academic writing to graduate students, I have observed that while students' overall knowledge of thesis-writing generally improves after the course completion, their attention to the ethics of writing and their experience in writing and paraphrasing seriously lags behind. In practice, students' written texts usually contain instances of self/plagiarism, patchwriting, inadequate or missing references, and limited or no use of paraphrasing.

As noted by Li & Casanave (2012), the most effective precaution against plagiarism and patchwriting is the development of learners' referencing and paraphrasing skills. In the absence of these skills, students draw on patchwriting and self/plagiarism as a coping strategy. Howard (1993: 233) defines patchwriting as a process of "copying from a source text and then deleting some words, altering grammatical structures, or plugging in one-for-one synonym substitutes." Although it is not considered as deceptive as plagiarism, patchwriting should be avoided as it signals writers' limited writing and language proficiency.

Hence, the problems commonly observed in students' texts can be attributed to restricted practice opportunities and deductive teaching strategies that cannot effectively prepare students for academic writing. This problem is intensified in the context of online writing classrooms with limited classroom time and lack of face-to-face physical access to peers and the instructor. Project-based learning can engage learners in a process of collective/individual reflection on and exploration of written samples to offer a practical solution for writing problems. This way, students are anticipated to experience meaningful learning.

The study reported in this chapter aimed to explore the effectiveness of PBL for students' writing knowledge and skill development. The following research question was addressed: Did the students who were engaged in PBL in an online real-time writing classroom demonstrate a better understanding of the ethics of writing compared to those in a control group?

3 Background and Description of the Research

A quasi-experimental research design was applied to explore the possible impact of PBL on students' knowledge of and attention to the ethics of academic writing. Since the performance of the control and experimental groups was compared using pre- and post-treatment analyses, the study can be considered quasi-experimental.

3.1 Participants and Research Context

A convenience sample comprising two groups of Teaching English as a Foreign Language (TEFL) major Masters' level (MA) students who registered for a two-credit online academic writing course in a state university of technology in Tehran, Iran, in the Fall semester of 2018, participated in the study. The first group was engaged in PBL and included 10 students (eight females and two males). The control group comprised 10 students (six females and four males) and received the conventional classroom treatment. Pseudonyms will be used throughout to refer to the participants. All of the courses in this MA program are offered online through the learning management system of the university. The academic writing courses comprised 13 once-a-week two-hour sessions which were delivered via the Adobe Connect environment. These courses aim at preparing students to write different sections – abstract, introduction, literature review, methodology, results, discussion, and conclusion – of a thesis (see Figure 5.1). Specifically, the focus is on the introduction and practice of the required moves, proper word choice, technical structure, and adherence to the codes of ethics and referencing (according to the American Psychological Association: APA manual) in writing. A summary of the conventional and project-oriented online courses' syllabi can be found in the Appendix.

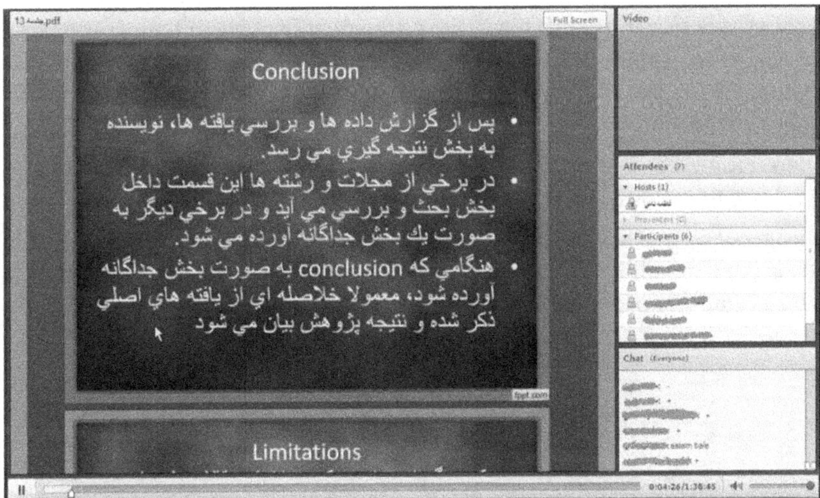

Figure 5.1. Screenshot of the Online Academic Writing Course's Synchronous Session

The classroom discussions and exchanges were mainly audio- and text-based using microphones and text-chat box. Live video streaming was avoided to safeguard against possible connection problems especially for the students with slower internet connections. The sessions were recorded and available for download in FLV and MP4 formats after each session.

3.2 The Conventional Online Real-Time Academic Writing Course

The conventional academic writing course comprised 13 two-hour online real-time sessions. The first two sessions were dedicated to the introduction of plagiarism and patchwriting, APA referencing, paraphrasing techniques, and plagiarism detection and proofreading software as the best strategies to avoid self/plagiarism and patchwriting. The instructor noted that although "the Internet made textual borrowing strategies easier, it has also made detection of copied material easier" (Li & Casanave, 2012: 167). A screencast was played showing students how to use online detection software such as Grammarly and Plagscan for plagiarism checks.

From week 3 onwards, one section of a thesis (i.e., the abstract, introduction, literature review, methodology, results and discussion, or conclusion) was introduced and worked on for two to three sessions. During each classroom meeting, students' watched animated PowerPoint presentations accompanied by the instructor's notes and highlights on the structure, word choice, moves, and punctuation patterns commonly used in different sections of a thesis. The instructor also uploaded well- and ill-structured written samples, highlighting the plagiarized and/or patchwritten texts or proper uses of paraphrasing and referencing techniques in them. Following the online real-time sessions, each student was asked to write a sample section (with a specified word limit) and email it to the instructor within one week. The writings were read and commented on the by instructor and were then returned to the students. The main course reading included Swales & Feak (2004). By the end of the course, each individual had written a 150–300 word abstract, a 400–500 word introduction, a 600–800 word literature review, a 700–800 word methodology section, a 700–900 word results and discussion section, and a 400–500 word conclusion, along with a reference list according to the APA manual of style.

3.3 The Project-Oriented Online Real-Time Academic Writing Course and PBL Tasks

The content and delivery of the instructional material were exactly the same for the experimental group. However, rather than having the teacher highlight the plagiarized/patchwritten parts and/or proper use(s) of paragraphing and referencing techniques, the samples were emailed to each individual after particular sessions. The students were asked to use these samples as the main sources in their PBL tasks.

The PBL tasks were scheduled for weeks 5 (review report on thesis introduction), 8 (review report on thesis literature review), and 11 (review report on thesis results and discussion). After introducing the essence and structure of the *Introduction* section and the use of references, in-text citations, paragraphing, and the essential moves (used in introductions) during sessions 3 and 4, the students received a Word file containing two anonymized Introduction sections. One featured an ill-structured text with plagiarism, patchwriting, and referencing problems. These texts were selected from the instructor's digital library of students' writings collected throughout years of instruction. The second sample contained a well-written text taken from an article published in a peer-reviewed journal. The students were recommended to use plagiarism detection software to examine the texts. The samples were copied in a Word file (using the same font type and size) to avoid providing any hint on the quality of the texts.

Inspired by Putri et al. (2017), PBL implementation steps were followed. The overall purpose of the writing projects was introduced to the learners and an agreement was reached on the way to carry out and present their projects. Considering the focus of the project, which was to enhance students' knowledge of the ethics of writing and paraphrasing, it was decided to have the projects presented in written format. Students were asked to find and highlight in/appropriate referencing, APA style in-text citation, and paraphrasing along with the presence and/or absence of plagiarism or patchwriting in texts. They were also required to offer suggestions for improvement. Written reports were to be submitted within one week.

The sessions following the collection of students' reports were dedicated to the collective review of the sample texts. The instructor uploaded a PDF file containing the texts with some sentences highlighted in yellow. She then invited the students to comment on the highlighted parts, drawing on what they had learned from the review process. These collective post-task discussions aimed at engaging students in a process of reflection on and analysis of their PBL product (see Stoller, 2006).

At the end of these sessions, the instructor revealed which text was well-written and which one was poorly structured. Additionally, the student reports that correctly addressed the problems or identified the proper use of the aforementioned qualities were shared with the class to provide other students with better insights. This way, it was hoped that the required conditions for effective PBL, as discussed by Stoller (2006), were addressed in the study. For the second PBL task, the *Literature Review* section of two sample papers with the qualities discussed above was selected and shared with participants. The focus of the third task was on the *Results and Discussion* section.

3.4 Data Sources and Analysis

The data sources used in this study included control and experimental groups' pre- and post-treatment writings. Prior to the beginning of the course, the participants were asked to write an introduction (within a word limit of 800–1,000 words), accompanied by a reference list, on the topic they were going to work on for their thesis project. After the course completion, a new introduction essay with the same word limit was written by the participants. Pre- and post-PBL writings were compared. A comparison was also made between the essays written by the participants in the control and experimental groups to spot possible differences.

The pre- and post-PBL writings were reviewed for instances of (1) plagiarism, (2) patchwriting, (3) paraphrased text, (4) correct in-text citation, (5) end-of-the-text reference list, and (6) correct in-text references. Post-PBL writings were expected to be original, featuring instances of proper paraphrasing, in-text references/citations, and an end-of-the-text reference list in alignment with APA style.

4 Research Findings and Discussion

The presence of plagiarism, patchwriting, paraphrased text, in-text direct citation, APA style reference list, and in-text referencing in pre- and post-treatment writings of the experimental and control groups is indicated in Tables 5.1 and 5.2, respectively. As shown in the tables, an overall improvement was observed in the final writings across the two groups. While there were several instances of plagiarized texts in both groups' pre-treatment writings, a careful analysis of their post-treatment writings using Grammarly software revealed the originality of 100% of the writings in the experimental group and 80% of the texts written by control group students.

A similar progress pattern was observed in correctly referenced and paraphrased texts across the two groups (see Tables 5.1 and 5.2). Hence, conventional and PBL treatments proved effective for enhancing students' consciousness about and knowledge of the ethics of writing and plagiarism/patchwriting avoidance strategies.

Table 5.1. Attention to Ethics of Writing in Experimental Group Students' Pre- and Post-PBL Writings

Participants	Pre-PBL Writing						Post-PBL Writing					
	Plagiarism	Patchwriting	Paraphrasing	In-text Direct Citation	End of the Text Referencing	In-Text Referencing	Plagiarism	Patchwriting	Paraphrasing	In-text Direct Citation	End of the Text Referencing	In-Text Referencing
Kaveh	—	✓	—	—	—	✓	—	—	✓	—	✓	✓
Maryam	—	✓	—	—	—	✓	—	—	✓	✓	✓	✓
Shirin	✓	—	—	—	—	—	—	✓	—	—	✓	✓
Neda	✓	—	—	—	—	—	—	—	✓	✓	✓	—
Soraya	✓	—	—	—	—	—	—	—	✓	✓	✓	—
Pegah	✓	—	—	—	—	—	—	—	✓	—	✓	✓
Golshan	✓	—	—	—	—	—	—	—	✓	—	✓	—
Arezoo	✓	—	—	—	—	—	—	—	✓	—	✓	✓
Ladan	✓	—	—	—	—	—	—	—	✓	✓	✓	✓
Pedram	✓	—	—	—	—	—	—	✓	—	✓	✓	✓

Table 5.2. Attention to Ethics of Writing in Control Group Students' Pre- and Post-PBL Writings

Participants	Pre-Treatment Writing						Post -Treatment Writing					
	Plagiarism	Patchwriting	Paraphrasing	In-text Direct Citation	End of the Text Referencing	In-Text Referencing	Plagiarism	Patchwriting	Paraphrasing	In-text Direct Citation	End of the Text Referencing	In-Text Referencing
Mobin	✓	—	—	—	—	—	✓	—	—	—	—	✓
Bahareh	—	✓	—	—	—	—	—	✓	—	✓	—	✓
Ehsan	—	✓	—	—	—	✓	—	—	✓	—	—	✓
Elmira	—	—	✓	—	—	—	—	✓	—	✓	✓	✓
Bita	—	✓	—	—	—	✓	—	—	✓	✓	✓	✓
Sanaz	✓	—	—	✓	—	—	—	✓	—	✓	—	✓
Hussein	✓	—	—	—	—	—	—	✓	—	✓	✓	—
Mahsa	✓	—	—	—	—	✓	—	—	✓	✓	—	✓
Mehran	✓	—	—	—	—	—	—	✓	—	✓	✓	—
Shadi	—	—	✓	—	—	—	✓	—	—	—	✓	✓

In order to gain more insights into the possible differences, the frequency and percentage of non-plagiarized and non-patchwritten texts and the presence of correctly paraphrased texts, in-text direct citation, in-text references, and end-of-the-text reference list were calculated in post-PBL writings (see Table 5.3 and Figure 5.2). As illustrated in Figure 5.2, although there was a decrease in the number of plagiarized texts in control group writings, 50% still included instances of patchwriting. Consistent with Li & Casanave (2012), it is suggested that, in the absence of the required skill for paraphrasing borrowed texts, these students have drawn on patchwriting as a copy strategy. The large number of direct in-text citations (i.e., 70% of the texts) and the limited number of correctly paraphrased text chunks (i.e., 30% of the texts) confirm this justification. Although in-text direct citations are useful techniques for highlighting the content when its significance might be lost in the process of paraphrasing, the overuse of direct citation might indicate the author's limited knowledge and skill of paraphrasing.

Table 5.3. The Frequency and Percentage of the Factors Identified in Control and Experimental Groups' Post-Treatment Writings

Groups	Post-PBL Writing											
	Absence of Plagiarism		Absence of Patchwriting		Correct Paraphrasing		In-text Direct Citation According to APA		End of the Text Referencing According to APA		In-Text Referencing According to APA	
	Freq.	%	Freq.	%	Freq.	%	Freq.	%	Freq.	%	Freq.	%
Experimental	10	100	8	80	8	80	5	50	10	100	7	70
Control	8	80	5	50	3	30	7	70	5	50	8	80

Participants in the experimental group, on the contrary, demonstrated a better grasp of the code of ethics in academic writing and plagiarism/patchwriting avoidance strategies. Eighty percent of post-treatment writings in this group did not contain any patchwriting and at the same time featured correct use of the paraphrasing technique. In other words, students in the experimental group made a more balanced use of different technical writing strategies to ensure the originality of their text.

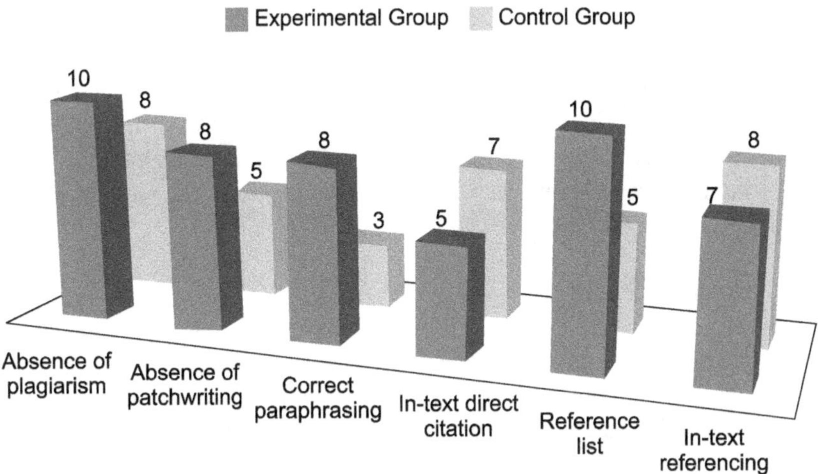

Figure 5.2. The Frequency of Indicators of Ethical Writing in Control and Experimental Groups

This can be attributed to the potential of the PBL experience for understanding the course content (Essien, 2018). Not adhering to the code of ethics in writing can stem from students' unawareness of such rules or their limited writing proficiency. Meaningful review of well-written and ill-structured texts and sharing and discussing the findings during classroom meetings might have helped learners address the aforementioned real-life problems in their own writing. Additionally, integrating language skills (i.e., reading and writing) and reporting the project outcomes in written mode might have placed the students in a situation which required real-life language use and thus improved their production skills (see Fried-Booth, 1997).

Consistent with the available literature on PBL in second and foreign language learning contexts, it is suggested that having students' PBL reports (or artifacts) uploaded, reflected upon, and discussed during the classroom meetings might have helped students develop better control over and understanding of the instructional content and course-related problems compared to having the points presented by the instructor. In line with Kessler et al. (2012), it can be claimed that collective review, reflection, and discussion or scaffolding enable students "to pool their linguistic knowledge and analyze their language production" (p. 103). This reflects what Praba' et al. (2018) consider as the potential of PBL for providing students with an opportunity to take responsibility for their own learning process – learning by doing (see Barron et al., 1998).

Furthermore, having their written reports shared and praised during classroom meetings might have better encouraged students in the experimental group to address effective referencing strategies when borrowing texts to avoid plagiarism and patchwriting (see Nami, 2019). As Liaw (2008) argues, environmental satisfaction in the context of e-learning positively contributes to learner engagement in the process of learning.

5 Conclusion

The study reported in this chapter presented an attempt to explore the potential of PBL in online real-time writing courses for enhancing students' awareness of the ethics of writing and developing their plagiarism and patchwriting avoidance skills. The findings indicated an overall improvement in the quality of post-treatment writing for both groups. However, project-based writing tasks which focused on the review of well- and ill-structured sample texts, written report production, and classroom reflection and sharing of the outputs proved more effective than mere deductive instruction followed by learner writing practice. More specifically, it was observed that students in the experimental group demonstrated a better command in expressing their views in writing through the appropriate use of referencing and paraphrasing strategies. Control group participants, while similarly attentive to the essence of avoiding plagiarism, were less successful in transferring their ideas through the balanced use of paraphrased and cited texts as their post-treatment writings still contained patchwritten chunks. It can be concluded that engaging students in real-life problem-oriented writing projects can be more productive than direct instruction and conventional writing practice. This way, students find the opportunity to not only understand the concepts introduced throughout the course, but also reflect on and apply them in order to successfully accomplish the projects and solve the problem.

Considering the abovementioned points, a number of pedagogical implications can be drawn from the study. First, the findings highlight the essence of redefining writing instruction/practice in online language classrooms by drawing on the potential of PBL and the incentives of the digital real-time learning environments for developing different language skills, namely writing. In the same vein, it requires the development of relevant instructional materials and language learning projects/scenarios that address the peculiarities of the technology-enhanced learning platforms as well as the learning needs of the students. Furthermore, PBL in CALL cannot be fully professional without adequately prepared language teachers. This necessitates the design of relevant professional development and preparation plans that aim at promoting language teachers' understanding of PBL in technology-enhanced learning platforms and their ability to develop appropriate integration scenarios for such contexts.

This study entailed a number of limitations that should be acknowledged. In addition to the sampling procedure and a small scale, the study was limited to a 13-week (3-month) period. For language skills to be better developed and their knowledge internalized, longer exposure and practice time is recommended. Hence, future research is advised to explore the way online project-based writing practice in longitudinal studies shapes students' knowledge of the codes of ethics and related writing skills. Furthermore, this study relied on students' writings as the main source of data. Different results might have been achieved if data were collected from more diverse sources.

In order to gain a more comprehensive insight into the productivity of any approach for students, it is essential to explore its effectiveness from their perspective. This study, however, did not explore participants' perceptions of project-based online writing practice. Future studies should gain additional insights from students and instructors using self-report data. The study was carried out in an online real-time learning platform. Future research could also explore whether the modality of the learning platform – namely online, blended, or face-to-face classes – contributes to or impedes effective project-based writing practice. Project-based language learning can be realized individually and collectively. The PBL projects explained and focused on in this study were individually carried out by the participants. How collective PBL contributes to students' knowledge construction and language development, specifically in online learning platforms, can be focused on in future studies. The possible impact of individual differences and learning styles on student project-based language learning can be another research strand.

As online learning platforms continue to grow in popularity across various disciplines, identifying the best learning/teaching practices for such platforms is increasingly important. Given the context of the present study, problem-oriented writing projects can be considered as viable learning activities to promote students' knowledge of second and/or foreign language. While the integration of project-based language learning scenarios in technology-enhanced learning platforms might not necessarily ensure the effectiveness of language learning practice, it can provide opportunities for better learner engagement with and reflection on the writing tasks that may result in deeper understanding.

Appendix

A summary of the conventional and project-oriented online courses' syllabi

Syllabus for Advanced Writing Course
Fall 2018

SPECIAL NOTE: If you need to contact me, please apply the term "advanced writing" in the subject line of the email. Thank you.

Course Description:
As a writing course for MA students, *Advanced Writing* aims at fulfilling the general requirements in upper-level advanced writing, i.e., improving students' skills in writing a thesis and other academic texts. Accordingly, the techniques applicable to different types of advanced writing will be covered. Through reviewing sample texts and writing practice, students are expected to learn how to improve their skills in academic writing.

Advanced Writing tends to be an interactive and workshop-oriented course. Thereby, classroom sessions will be divided between professional instruction and discussions focusing on students' writings. That's why consistent attendance is one of the requirements of this course.

Course Requirements:
Participation: Active participation is required for this course. Students are expected to have carefully read the assigned readings prior to scheduled class discussion to prep for in-class review and critique. The quality of the contributions demonstrated in all tasks and discussions determines the participation grade.

Weekly assignments: Students are required to (1) perform small writing tasks to draft different parts of a research article or thesis and (2) analyze the codes of ethics, rhetorical and linguistic features, usage, grammar, spelling conventions, and mechanics of different texts.

Regular attendance: The course sessions require mandatory attendance. Students are permitted two absences during the semester. Five percentage points will be deducted from the final score of those who miss more than two sessions. Missing four or more classes will automatically result in student's failing the course. Please log into the class on time. Tardiness, twice throughout the course, is counted as one absence.

Weekly Schedule (for the conventional online writing course)

Sessions	Session Foci	Weekly Tasks
1	Introduction to • the course syllabus and its specifications, and • self/plagiarism and patchwriting, in-text citation, paraphrasing, and online plagiarism detection and proofreading technologies	
2	• proposal outline, article types, • APA style of writing, documentation, and citation (integrating basic paraphrases, quotes, and summarized ideas, and avoiding plagiarism), and • length and structure	
3	• the essential moves in the *Introduction* and *Lit Review Sections*, and • strategies for avoiding biased language	
4	• continued discussion on the *Introduction* and *Lit Review Sections*, and • review of the well- and ill-structured sample writings	Write mini *Introduction* and *Lit Review Sections* (400–500 words for the introduction and 600–800 words for the lit review) on a selected topic and carefully address the moves and referencing requirements of a scholarly written text. Email your text in the Word File prior to the beginning of the next session.
5	• the structure of and moves in the *Methodology Section*, and • precision in writing	
6	• continued discussion on the *Methodology Section*, and • review of the well- and ill-structured sample writings	Write a mini *Methodology Section* (700–800 words) and carefully address the moves and referencing requirements of a scholarly written text. Email your text in the Word File prior to the beginning of the next session.
7	• the structure of and the essential moves in the *Results and Discussion Section*, and • the use of tables, figures, illustrations, and artworks	

8	• continued discussion on the *Results and Discussion Section*, and • review of the well- and ill-structured sample writings	Write a mini *Results and Discussion Section* (700–900 words) and carefully address the moves and referencing requirements of a scholarly written text. Email your text in the Word File prior to the beginning of the next session.
9	• continued discussion on the *Results and Discussion Section*, and • review of the well- and ill-structured sample writings	
10	• the structure of and the essential moves in the *Conclusion Section*	
11	• continued discussion on the *Conclusion Section*, and • review of the well- and ill-structured sample writings	Write a mini *Conclusion Section* (400–500 words) and carefully address the moves and referencing requirements of a scholarly written text. Email your text in the Word File prior to the beginning of the next session.
12	• the structure and types of Abstracts in Applied Linguistics	Write a mini *Abstract* (400–500 words) and carefully address the structure and type requirements of a scholarly written abstract. Email your text in the Word File prior to the beginning of the next session.
13	• the structure of titles and subtitles in scholarly written texts, and • concluding remarks	

Weekly Schedule (for the project-oriented online writing course)

Sessions	Session Foci	Weekly Tasks
1	Introduction to • the syllabus, course specifications, and the expected outcomes, and • self/plagiarism and patch-writing, in-text citation, paraphrasing, and online plagiarism detection and proofreading technologies	

2	• proposal outline, article types, • APA style of writing, documentation, and citation (integrating basic paraphrases, quotes, and summarized ideas, and avoiding plagiarism), and • length and structure	
3	• the essential moves in the *Introduction* and *Lit Review Sections*, and • strategies for avoiding biased language	Write mini *Introduction* and *Lit Review Sections* (400–500 words for the introduction and 600–800 words for the lit review) on a selected topic and carefully address the moves and referencing requirements of a scholarly written text. Email your text in the Word File prior to the beginning of the next session.
4	• continued discussion on the *Introduction* and *Lit Review Sections*	Review the two sample writings shared by the instructor in terms of authors' attention to the codes of ethics in writing (i.e., plagiarism avoidance, direct citation, paraphrasing and referencing, etc.). Share your review in the form a Word File with the instructor prior to the beginning of the next session.
5	**(In-Class Workshop)** collective class review of the two sample writings	
6	• the structure of and moves in the *Methodology Section* and • precision in writing	Write a mini *Methodology Section* (700–800 words) and carefully address the moves and referencing requirements of a scholarly written text. Email your text in the Word File prior to the beginning of the next session.
7	• continued discussion on the *Methodology Section*	Review the two sample writings shared by the instructor in terms of authors' attention to the codes of ethics in writing (i.e., plagiarism avoidance, direct citation, paraphrasing and referencing, etc.). Share your review in the form a Word File with the instructor prior to the beginning of the next session.

8	**(In-Class Workshop)** collective class review of the two sample writings	
9	• the structure of and the essential moves in the *Results and Discussion Section*, and • using tables, figures, illustrations, and artworks	Write a mini *Results and Discussion Section* (700–900 words) and carefully address the moves and referencing requirements of a scholarly written text. Email your text in the Word File prior to the beginning of the next session.
10	• continued discussion on the *Results and Discussion Section*	Review the two sample writings shared by the instructor in terms of authors' attention to the codes of ethics in writing (i.e., plagiarism avoidance, direct citation, paraphrasing and referencing, etc.). Share your review in the form a Word File with the instructor prior to the beginning of the next session.
11	**(In-Class Workshop)** collective class review of the two sample writings	
12	• the structure of and the essential moves in the *Conclusion Section*, and • the structure and types of Abstracts in Applied Linguistics	Write a mini *Conclusion Section* (400–500 words) and carefully address the moves and referencing requirements of a scholarly written text. Email your text in the Word File prior to the beginning of the next session.
13	• the structure of titles and subtitles in scholarly written texts and • concluding remarks	Write a mini *Abstract* (400–500 words) and carefully address the structure and type requirements of a scholarly written abstract. Email your text in the Word File prior to the beginning of the next session.

References

Amineh, R. J., & Asl, H. D. (2015). Review of constructivism and social constructivism. *Journal of Social Sciences, Literature and Languages*, 1(1), 9–16.

Barron, B. J., Schwartz, D. L., Vye, N. J., Moore, A., Petrosino, A., Zech, L., & Bransford, J. D. (1998). Doing with understanding: Lessons from research on problem-and project-based learning. *Journal of the Learning Sciences*, 7(3–4), 271–311. https://doi.org/10.1080/10508406.1998.9672056

Bell, S. (2010). Project-based learning for the 21st century: Skills for the future. *Clearing House: A Journal of Educational Strategies*, 83(2), 39–43. https://doi.org/10.1080/00098650903505415

Blumenfeld, P. C., Soloway, E., Marx, R. W., Krajcik, J. S., Guzdial, M., & Palincsar, A. (1991). Motivating project-based learning: Sustaining the doing, supporting the learning. *Educational Psychologist*, 26(3–4), 369–398. https://doi.org/10.1207/s15326985ep2603&4_8

Cavus, N., & Ala'a, M. M. (2009). Computer aided evaluation of learning management systems. *Procedia: Social and Behavioral Sciences*, 1(1), 426–430. https://doi.org/10.1016/j.sbspro.2009.01.076

DeFillippi, R. J. (2001). Introduction: Project-based learning, reflective practices and learning. *Management Learning*, 32(1), 5–10. https://doi.org/10.1177/1350507601321001

Donato, R. (1994). Collective scaffolding in second language learning. In J. P. Lantolf & G. Appel (Eds.), *Vygotskian approaches to second language research* (pp. 33–56). Norwood, NJ: Ablex.

Essien, A. M. (2018). The effects of project-based learning on students' English language ability. In *The 2018 International Academic Research Conference, Vienna*, 438–443.

Fried-Booth, D. L. (1997). *Project work*, 8th edition. Oxford: Oxford University Press.

Grant, M. M. (2002). Getting a grip on project-based learning: Theory, cases and recommendations. *Meridian: A Middle School Computer Technologies Journal*, 5(1), 83.

Heo, H., Lim, K. Y., & Kim, Y. (2010). Exploratory study on the patterns of online interaction and knowledge co-construction in project-based learning. *Computers & Education*, 55(3), 1383–1392. https://doi.org/10.1016/j.compedu.2010.06.012

Hoopingarner, D. (2009). Best practices in technology and language teaching. *Language and Linguistics Compass*, 3(1), 222–235. https://doi.org/10.1111/j.1749-818X.2008.00123.x

Howard, R. M. (1993). A plagiarism pentimento. *Journal of Teaching Writing*, 11(3), 233–245.

Kessler, G., Bikowski, D., & Boggs, J. (2012). Collaborative writing among second language learners in academic web-based projects. *Language Learning & Technology*, 16(1), 91–109.

Li, Y., & Casanave, C. P. (2012). Two first-year students' strategies for writing from sources: Patchwriting or plagiarism? *Journal of Second Language Writing*, 21(2), 165–180. https://doi.org/10.1016/j.jslw.2012.03.002

Liaw, S. S. (2008). Investigating students' perceived satisfaction, behavioral intention, and effectiveness of e-learning: A case study of the Blackboard system. *Computers & Education*, 51(2), 864–873. https://doi.org/10.1016/j.compedu.2007.09.005

Nami, F. (2019). Exploring the effectiveness of online synchronous learning management systems: The case of a Masters' level academic writing course.

In M. Kruk (Ed.), *Assessing the effectiveness of virtual technologies in foreign and second language instruction* (pp. 168–190). Hershey: IGI Global. https://doi.org/10.4018/978-1-5225-7286-2.ch007

Nami, F., & Marandi, S. S. (2014). Wikis as discussion forums: exploring students' contribution and their attention to form. *Computer Assisted Language Learning*, 27(6), 483–508. https://doi.org/10.1080/09588221.2013.770036

Praba, L. T., Artini, L. P., & Ramendra, D. P. (2018). Project-based learning and writing skill in EFL: are they related? In *SHS Web of Conferences* (Vol. 42, p. 00059). EDP Sciences. https://doi.org/10.1051/shsconf/20184200059

Putri, N. L. P. N. S., Artini, L. P., & Nitiasih, P. K. (2017). Project-based learning activities and EFL students' productive skills in English. *Journal of Language Teaching and Research*, 8(6), 1147–1155. https://doi.org/10.17507/jltr.0806.16

Sadeghi, H., Biniaz, M., & Soleimani, H. (2016). The impact of project-based language learning on Iranian EFL learners comparison/contrast paragraph writing skills. *International Journal of Asian Social Science*, 6(9), 510–524. https://doi.org/10.18488/journal.1/2016.6.9/1.9.510.524

Simpson, J. (2011). Integrating project-based learning in an English language tourism classroom in a Thai university. Unpublished doctoral dissertation, Australian Catholic University.

Stoller, F. (2006). Establishing a theoretical foundation for project-based learning in second and foreign language contexts. In G. H. Beckett, & P. C. Miller (Eds.), *Project-based second and foreign language education: Past, present, and future* (pp. 19–40). Greenwich, CT: Information Age.

Swales, J. M., & Feak, C. B. (2004). *Academic writing for graduate students: Essential tasks and skills* (Vol. 1). Ann Arbor, MI: University of Michigan Press.

Twu, H. L. (2009). Effective wiki strategies to support high-context culture learners. *Tech Trends*, 53, 16–21. https://doi.org/10.1007/s11528-009-0318-2

Vygotsky, L. S. (1978). *Mind in society: The development of higher psychological processes*. London: Routledge.

About the Author

Fatemeh Nami is an assistant professor in the Department of Foreign Languages at Amirkabir University of Technology in Iran. She holds a PhD in Teaching English Language with a focus on computer-assisted language learning (CALL). Her research interests include: e-learning, interactive digital content authoring, problem and project-based learning, CALL teacher education, digital storytelling, and mobile-assisted language learning (MALL), on which she has published several articles in scholarly journals, book chapters, and an edited volume.

6 Incorporating Digital Projects into an Advanced Japanese Course: Effectiveness and Implementation

Kai Xie

1 Introduction

Project-based learning (PBL) has been used in the field of second language acquisition for about two decades (Hedge, 1993). Since it aligns well with the student-centered learning approach currently advocated in second language education, PBL has received support from many educators and researchers. Numerous scholars consider this method effective in language learning (e.g., Beckett & Slater, 2018; Fried-Booth, 2002; Haines, 1989; Lam & Lawrence, 2002; Lee, Li, & Lee, 1999; Legutke & Thomas, 1991; Papandreou, 1994; Stoller, 2012; Thomas, 2017). An increasing number of empirical research studies on project-based language learning (PBLL) have also emerged (e.g., Beckett & Miller, 2006; Beckett & Slater, 2005; Carpenter & Matsugu, 2019; Dressler et al., 2019; Eyring, 1989; Fang & Warschauer, 2004; Kobayashi, 2004; Mohan & Beckett, 2003).

However, most of these studies focus on English as a Second Language (ESL), and few works have examined the Less Commonly Taught Languages (LCTLs). Moreover, much room remains for empirical research on project-based approaches that involve technology (Beckett, Slate, & Mohan, 2019; Dooly & Sadler, 2016). Rapid technological development has led to a great potential for using technology in second language teaching and learning. Moreover, the new generation of learners is accustomed to absorbing knowledge via digital tools. Although technology cannot and likely will not be able to replace teachers or traditional classroom learning, used properly, this tool can supplement language learning in many ways (Blake, 2016; Blyth, 2018; Egbert, Hanson-Smith, & Chao, 2007; Felix, 2008; Godwin-Jones, 2014; Hong et al., 2016; Kessler, 2018; Reinders & White, 2016). On the other hand, scholars have pointed out general limitations of technology and PBL for language learning (Beckett, 1999; Eyring, 1989; Ford & Kluge, 2015; Foster, 2009; Terrazas-Arellanes, Knox, & Walden, 2015). Therefore, more empirical research is needed to evaluate the effectiveness of technology-enhanced project-based language learning (TEPBLL). Dooly & Sadler (2016: 54) specifically stressed the need for more varied research into TEPBLL with the observation that "studies into TEPBLL should not only focus on validating the approach via individual results of products stemming from its application, but extensive investigation of processes should be carried out."

This chapter describes the use of digital video projects in an advanced Japanese language course at Kenyon College, a private liberal arts college located in a rural area in the Midwest of the United States. The course was redesigned to be content-based, both to attract students and to accommodate learners with diverse levels, incorporating PBL and seeking to integrate language and content learning. According to Beckett & Slater (2018: 1), PBL allows students to focus on "the development of language, content, and skills in an integrated and meaningful way." This chapter examines whether the digital video projects were effective in students' learning of language, content, and skills. Included is a discussion of how to implement digital projects more effectively, along with consideration of the assessment process, which several scholars have indicated to require more attention in the literature (Chen & Hirch, 2019; Condlife, 2016; Gleason & Link, 2019; Kuo et al., 2019).

2 Review of Previous Studies

This section reviews previous studies related to my research questions and that guided my course design. It will first discuss research on PBLL and then review the studies on computer-assisted language learning (CALL), especially TEPBLL. Finally, the section surveys studies on the assessment of PBLL.

Research has demonstrated the effectiveness of PBL in integrating the four language skills, integrating language and content learning, developing problem-solving and decision-making skills, cultivating students' interests, increasing student autonomy and flexibility among instructor and student roles, and promoting cooperation (Beckett, 2002; Beckett & Miller, 2006; Beckett & Slater, 2018; Fried-Booth, 2002; Haines, 1989; Henry, 1994; Hsieh, 2012; Jordan, 1997; Lam & Lawrence, 2002; Van Lier, 1996). The benefits of PBL for content-based language teaching also include authenticity and real-life application (Foss et al., 2007) and improved writing skills

(Calogerakou & Vlachos, 2011). On the other hand, researchers have also pointed out the limitations of PBL in language learning. For example, ESL students sometimes cannot understand how PBL helps them learn form (Beckett, 1999; Eyring, 1989). Ford & Kluge (2015) considered students' use of their first languages a major limitation, while Foster (2009) thought that measuring the outcomes of learning approaches such as PBLL was difficult. This chapter focuses on two projects using CALL technologies, examining whether the above-mentioned benefits and limitations apply to them.

Egbert et al. (2007: 3) claimed that "educators do not need a discrete theory of CALL to understand the role of technology in the classroom; a clear theory of SLA and its implications for the learning environment serves this goal." In this study, I mainly apply theories of SLA to evaluate the effectiveness of the use of CALL technologies in language acquisition. According to Spolsky's (1989) theory of conditions for language acquisition, knowledge and skills in the future are a result of knowledge in the present. This is connected to abilities, motivation, and opportunity. Abilities include physiological, biological, intellectual, and cognitive skills. Opportunity refers to the learning environment or time multiplied by exposure to the language. This study will discuss how technology influences motivation and opportunity, especially the learning environment. Thus, the text will analyze whether the digital projects under discussion provided conditions for the optimal language learning environments listed in Egbert et al. (2007: 5; see Table 6.1).

Table 6.1. Conditions for Optimal Language Learning Environments

1.	Learners have opportunities to interact and negotiate meaning.
2.	Learners interact in the target language with an authentic audience.
3.	Learners are involved in authentic tasks.
4.	Learners are exposed to and encouraged to produce varied and creative language.
5.	Learners have enough time and feedback.
6.	Learners are guided to attend mindfully to the learning process.
7.	Learners work in an atmosphere with an ideal stress/anxiety level.
8.	Learner autonomy is supported.

Note. Adapted from Egbert et al. (2007).

Numerous scholars have discussed the effectiveness of using technology in language learning, including Beckett & Slater (2018), Chapelle & Jamieson (2008), Golonka et al. (2014), Salpeter (2005), and Zhao & Beckett (2014). Kessler (2018) stressed that technologies facilitate learner-centered instruction and collaborative learning, especially when supporting project-based experiences. Cope & Kalantzis (2013: 188) claimed that technology-mediated PBLL allows "alternative starting points for learning (what the learner perceives to be worth learning, what engages the particularities of their identity)" and "alternative pathways and comparable destination points in learning." At the same time, this approach can help students develop the necessary knowledge and skills "to be active and informed citizens and workers in a changing world – a world of diversity and one in which our means of communication and access to information change rapidly" (Cope & Kalantzis, 2013: 191). In particular, video-making projects have also proved effective in many ways. For example, such projects have both provided a stimulus for speaking (Pearson, 1990) and improved students' confidence in speaking a foreign language (Charge & Giblin, 1988; Marsh, 1989). This type of project has also led to higher motivation and collaboration (Coleman, 1992; Hsieh, 2012) and helped students acquire and improve skills in and beyond language learning (Gardner, 1995). However, not all students could discern how the use of technology is helpful in language learning (Terrazas-Arellanes et al., 2015). Vinogradova (2011) stressed the importance of having explicit and systematic instruction and scaffolding to make video projects more effective. This chapter builds on these existing studies, focusing on Less Commonly Taught Languages instead of ESL.

On the topic of assessing PBLL, scholars have previously agreed that traditional methods are not sufficient (Van den Bergh et al., 2006). Since the learning process in PBLL is complex and influences many aspects of development, various types of assessment are necessary. Researchers have proposed and used self-assessment and peer assessment, performance-based assessment, portfolio assessment, guidelines for formative language, and content analysis (Beckett & Slater, 2005; Lee & Lim, 2002; Slater, Beckett, & Aufderhaar, 2006; Van den Bergh et al., 2006). However, Beckett & Slater (2018: 5) thought that existing assessment instruments "do not address how learning takes place through PBLL or technology-integrated PBLL." This study uses diverse assessment methods and examines whether these methods are effective and sufficient.

3 Methodology

3.1 Participants

The study was conducted in JAPN 322, an advanced Japanese language course at Kenyon College in the United States. Kenyon College is a small liberal arts college with about 1,700 students. The Japanese program is small, comprising one to three Japanese majors and two to five Japanese minors per year. First- and second-year Japanese language courses typically have 12 to 16 students and five to 15 students, respectively, and they use *Genki* as the textbook. Once students finish the second-year course, they can take any advanced courses (all numbered at the 300-level, including the course under discussion). Since very few students meet the requirements for taking advanced courses, only one advanced course is offered each semester. A significant challenge of this curriculum is the difficulty in teaching the advanced courses due to a large variance in the enrolled students' language background and ability. Among the 10 students who took JAPN 322 during the time of this study, two were seniors returning from a year of study abroad in Japan (one was advanced-mid in reading and advanced-low in writing, listening, and speaking according to the American Council on the Teaching of Foreign Languages [ACTFL] standards; the other was intermediate-high in all skills), two were half-Japanese who were advanced-low to -mid in listening and speaking before coming to Kenyon but needed improvement in reading and writing, especially kanji (their reading and writing were roughly intermediate-low to -mid), and two were juniors who had completed the first- and second-year courses at Kenyon and planned to study abroad in Japan in the coming spring (one participated in the intensive summer language program at Middlebury College immediately before taking this course). The remaining four were sophomores, two of whom were placed in the second-year course upon arriving at Kenyon during their freshman year. The other two took the first-year course at Kenyon during their freshman year and completed a second-year course elsewhere during the summer. In general, Kenyon students are academically competitive, and this class was no exception. Among the 10 students, three received a grade of A+, four received A, two received A–, and one received B+ for the course.

3.2 Course Design

JAPN 322 consisted of three 50-minute classes per week for 14 weeks, taught in Japanese. In the past, advanced language courses taught at Kenyon had used *Tobira* as the textbook and focused on language proficiency. Usually, only students who had completed the second-year course at Kenyon enrolled, and those with higher language proficiency did not feel the need to enroll in such a course. For example, in Fall 2017, the advanced course had only four students, including two who had completed first- and second-year courses at Kenyon, a freshman who was placed into the advanced course, and a senior who was placed into the second-year level during her study abroad in Japan and thus needed this advanced course to fulfill the requirements for a Japanese minor. In Spring 2018, the advanced course was cancelled due to insufficient enrollment (students usually study abroad in Japan during the spring semester).

JAPN 322 was redesigned into a content-based course, attracting students from various backgrounds as detailed in the previous section. The course covered four topics, including manga and anime, old tales, mass media, and marriage and family. Students read and watched a wide range of authentic materials in Japanese, including manga, anime, fictional works, essays, newspapers, blogs, and TV dramas. In class, we discussed these materials in Japanese while students practiced vocabulary, kanji, and grammar not covered in first- and second-year courses. Table 6.2 lists the course goals and objectives.

Table 6.2. Course Goals and Objectives

1.	Deepening understanding of Japanese culture and society.
2.	Expanding speaking, listening, reading, and writing skills in Japanese language.
3.	Solidifying the vocabulary, kanji, and grammar foundation built in previous Japanese courses.
4.	Acquiring new grammar patterns, vocabulary, kanji, and idioms.
5.	Becoming familiar with different writing and speech types and styles.
6.	Developing skills of skimming, summarizing, critical thinking, and problem-solving.
7.	Improving skills of discussion, presentation, and research in Japanese language.

Compared to the advanced courses in the past, which mainly emphasized points 2 to 5, this course placed much more emphasis on 1, 6, and 7.

3.3 Digital Projects

The course combined traditional classroom teaching with project-based learning outside the classroom. Vocabulary, kanji, and grammar quizzes ensured that students studied the linguistic form regularly. However, the primary assignments were projects rather than tests. In the past, the major projects for advanced Japanese language courses consisted of three oral presentations and one research paper in Japanese. This time, students were asked to complete two digital projects, to be shown to the wider Kenyon community. One oral presentation and one skit were also assigned for comparison purposes. Students' grades were calculated according to Table 6.3.

Table 6.3. Assessment

Categories	Percentage
Attendance and participation	10%
Homework	10%
Writing assignments	12%
Grammar quizzes	12%
Kanji quizzes	10%
Vocabulary quizzes	8%
Skits	3%
Presentation	4%
Voice-dubbing project	10%
Final project	20%
Japanese table	1%
Total	100%

For the midterm, students formed a group of three to four members and completed a voice-dubbing project. Each group was given an episode of a Japanese animation TV series (7 to 10 minutes). Students watched the original version in Japanese and studied its plot. Then they carried out voice-dubbing using appropriate Japanese language and added English subtitles.

The final project was a video introduction to a topic related to Japanese culture. Each student chose their own topic, found and read resources in both English and Japanese, and finally made a 6- to 10-minute video about the topic. They added voice in Japanese and subtitles in English. The midterm project served as a warm-up for the final project. On the one hand, students became familiar with the process of adding voice and subtitles with no need to worry about images. On the other hand, working in groups allowed students to learn from each other and better prepare themselves for the final project, which was accomplished individually.

Both projects were scaffolded. Students first chose an episode/topic for their project and then participated in an interactive workshop conducted by a technical expert at Kenyon to learn the necessary technological skills. After they finished each project, we watched their completed works together and undertook peer review in class. Students worked on the projects for the whole semester (14 weeks of instruction plus an exam week). Table 6.4 presents a detailed timeline.

At the time, Kenyon had a Digital Storytelling Initiative funded by the Andrew W. Mellon Foundation. The initiative supported summer workshops for faculty to learn how to incorporate digital storytelling projects into their courses and provided funding to support teaching projects. I participated in the summer workshop before this course, and I also received a grant from this initiative to cover software purchases ($210 in total) as well as the books and DVDs ($600 in total) that students needed to complete their projects. The initiative also allowed for a technician from our Center for Innovative Pedagogy to assist our projects along the way, including offering workshops for students and providing consultation and help on technical issues for both students and instructors.

Table 6.4. Timeline of the Digital Projects

Week	Assignments
1	I uploaded several episodes of anime on Moodle. Students signed up for the episode they wanted to work on.
2	Workshop (50 minutes) with technical expert (learned how to use WeVideo, a cloud-based video editing software).
3–4	Students watched anime and studied plot together with their group members, then submitted first draft of script in both Japanese and English.
5	Students revised the script based on my feedback and submitted the final version of the script.
6–7	Students carried out voice-dubbing and added English subtitles. In week 7, there was another interactive workshop with the technical expert, which helped students finalize their voice-dubbing project and discussed how to make a good digital story. Students submitted their voice-dubbing project by the last class of week 7. They watched the completed works together and did peer review in class.
8	Students submitted a proposal for the final project, including a one-paragraph description in Japanese and a bibliography.
9–10	Students worked on written script and submitted the first draft.
11	Students revised the script based on my feedback and submitted the final draft of script.
12–14	Students created videos. In the last class of week 14, students watched completed videos together and did peer review in class.
15	Students revised their project based on peer review and submitted their final project.

3.4 Digital Project Topics

For the voice-dubbing project, students formed three groups and completed one episode each for *Doraemon*, *Chibimarukochan*, and *Ranma 1/2*. The topics for the final project included: supernatural cat in Japanese culture, cuteness in Japan, Tokyo street style, Japanese fashion, the Japanese education system, Karuta (a Japanese card game), noh (a form of Japanese performing art), seclusion policy in early modern Japan, Japanese humor seen in the manga series *Tensai Bakabon*, and Geisha.

3.5 Data Collection

Because students completed both digital and non-digital projects, I was able to compare their performance. The skit and oral presentation assignments served as helpful reference points for the voice-dubbing project and the final project, respectively. Additionally, students filled out an anonymous evaluation for each digital project and the course as a whole. Lastly, students completed peer-review forms.

4 Findings and Discussion

Beckett & Slater (2018: 1) suggested that PBLL could promote the development of "language, content, and skills in an integrated and meaningful way." This section will first examine the effectiveness of the digital projects in developing language, content, and skills. Then it will address the limitations of the projects. Finally, it will discuss how to effectively implement and assess the projects.

4.1 Effectiveness

As noted in Beckett et al. (2019), not much experimental research has investigated how PBL promotes the development of language form and function, especially in technology-mediated PBLL contexts. To determine whether the two digital projects were effective in developing language skills, I compared the voice-dubbing project with the skit and the final project with the oral presentation. Neither the voice-dubbing project nor the skit required creativity, as students were asked to reenact scenes from anime and dialogues from books, respectively. Their performances were less influenced by their level of language proficiency than how hard they worked. All the students did an excellent job in both assignments: Their speeches were fluent, and their acting was good. However, in general, their utterances were closer to those of native speakers in the voice-dubbing project than in the skit. One reason is that for the voice-dubbing project, they had a model speech to emulate. In the peer-review class session, several students also mentioned that originally their speed of speech was slower than that in the anime, making it impossible to match their voice with the images. They had to practice many times until they were able to reach the same speed as the original. The student with the lowest proficiency level could not reach the same speed, even after practice; instead, he had to adjust the speed of the video to match his voice. A downside of the voice-dubbing project was that the students had to imitate the childish way of speaking found in anime, meaning they generally could not use their original voices. Also, as the class had only two male students, several female students had to dub the male voices. A different selection of anime series (e.g., anime with more mature characters and female characters) might work better. The other major difference between the two assignments was that listening skills were practiced in the voice-dubbing project but not in the skit. In the peer-review class session, students mentioned that they had to watch the anime repeatedly to be able to transcribe the dialogues. In the skit assignment, students needed to read the dialogues. In general, the students found reading easier than listening. According to the evaluations for the digital projects, the students spent an average of 7 to 10 hours on the voice-dubbing project, presumably significantly more than the time they had spent on the skit.

When comparing the final digital project with the oral presentation, the differences in students' performance were more noticeable. For both projects, students were graded on content, comprehension, productivity, accuracy, and effort. While the final project was also graded on other categories in addition to these five, in this section I only focus on the aspects related to language skills. (See assessment section for more details on assessment methods.) In both cases, students needed to use enough complicated grammatical structures to obtain a high grade for "productivity." They were also graded on whether they were able to use the grammar structures correctly. Students submitted a first draft for their script and had a chance to revise their script based on my feedback. These efforts aimed at making sure that students consciously practiced target grammar and had more accurate productions.

In general, the students did better in the categories of comprehension, accuracy, and effort in the digital project than the oral presentation. It is also worth noting that the variance in students' performances was lower in the digital project than the oral presentation. For the digital project, the highest grade for the five categories was 100%, while the lowest was 84%.

However, for the oral presentation, the highest grade was 97.5%. The student who received the lowest score for the oral presentation, 70%, was not well prepared and was too nervous, causing him to forget part of what he planned to say. The digital project was less focused on memorization and provided a low-stress learning environment for those who were not confident in their language abilities. In the peer-review class session, students also mentioned that for the digital project, they practiced reading the script many times. The recording part of the process enabled them to listen to their utterance, recognize what they needed to improve, and re-record as many times as they wanted. This approach provided an incentive to keep practicing until they reached near perfection. Students often underestimate the time and energy required for an oral presentation assignment, and they seldom have a chance to evaluate their performance themselves. The self-evaluation embedded in the digital project motivated students to make their best effort to produce a work that they were satisfied with. Compared to the oral presentation, however, this project contributed less to developing the students' public speaking skills.

In spite of the fact that the students spent much more time on the two digital projects, none of them complained about the workload, and all students liked the course in general. Among the nine students who completed the course evaluation, all thought that the workload for the course was reasonable. The evaluation showed that 88.89% strongly agreed that "the instructor made the course material interesting," while the remaining 11.11% chose "agree" for this category. Moreover, 77.77% strongly agreed that "the instructor was effective in teaching this course." The remaining 22.22% chose "agree" for this category.

In addition, most students enjoyed the digital projects. All 10 students completed the evaluation for the two digital projects. For the voice-dubbing project, 80% agreed that this exercise was useful and meaningful. Comments included "I really enjoyed the project" and "It is interesting to do voice dubbing." Regarding the two students who did not completely agree, one thought that it might be more useful to dub an English show into Japanese. The other enjoyed the subtitle component but thought that "it took a lot of time just to figure out the logistics of doing a dub and that felt like a waste of time at periods."

All but one student enjoyed the final project. Positive feedback included the responses that it was interesting and they were proud of what they had accomplished. The student who did not like the project commented,

> I think making the Dub video and final project video was difficult because I had never used technology like that before. I felt like we

had to spend more time figuring out how to make a video rather than gathering research materials on the topic.

All the other students seemed comfortable with using technology as it was applied in this class. According to the technician who conducted workshops and helped with the video-making throughout the process, the students seemed able to master the use of WeVideo quickly, and only one student sought help outside the classroom.

According to Spolsky (1989), motivation and opportunity (especially the learning environment) are two of the most important factors in language acquisition. As discussed, the digital projects significantly increased students' motivation and interest. This result accords with previous studies on the benefits of PBL and use of technology and video projects (e.g., Coleman, 1992; Hsieh, 2012). The students were willing to spend much more time on these projects, and investing more time and energy naturally led to better language production. In fact, the required minimum length for the final video project was 5 minutes, but most students made an 8- to 10-minute video. In contrast, when assigned a research paper or oral presentation, students rarely do significantly more work than the requirement. Language learning has no shortcuts; the only way to improve is to practice. In this sense, boosting learners' motivation and interest to encourage them to spend more time on practicing is essential in language education, and the digital projects were highly effective in this regard.

Evidence also showed that these two digital projects were better at creating optimal language learning environments than the oral presentation and skit in the following two categories proposed in Egbert et al. (2007: 5): "6. Learners are guided to attend mindfully to the learning process" and "7. Learners work in an atmosphere with an ideal stress/anxiety level" (see Table 6.1 for a full list). As discussed earlier, anxiety negatively affected students' performance in the oral presentation, especially when they were not confident in their language ability or not fully prepared. Making digital projects was much less stressful because students had plenty of time to ensure correctness and could revise their finished product as many times as they wanted. Self-evaluation and self-correction also made students more mindful of the learning process, allowing them to make improvements more consciously.

In addition to helping improve students' language ability, the digital projects also contributed to the development of content and skills not directly related to language acquisition. In the case of the final project, students could choose a topic that interested them. Moreover, they found related sources and conducted research before finally creating a work based on their research. Through this process, the students acquired deep knowledge about a topic related to Japanese culture and cultivated skills related to creativity, communication, research, problem-solving, and critical thinking. Compared to a research paper or oral presentation, the digital project required the students to add visuals and sound, encouraging them to further research the topic and convey information in a more engaging way. Moreover, because the students were making their videos for the wider Kenyon community, they learned how to tell a story to a general audience effectively. As an added bonus, the voice-dubbing project required the students to work in groups, which cultivated their communicative and collaborative skills. Lastly, these projects improved the students' technology literacy, especially their video-making and editing skills. As Egbert et al. (2007: 4) noted, "Along with traditional text literacy and numeracy, visual, information, technological, and media literacies are crucial to help learners succeed outside of classrooms." The skills that the participants gained by completing these projects went beyond language acquisition, and they will remain beneficial to these students in the long run.

4.2 Limitations

Despite their benefits, these digital projects also presented limitations. First, they could not completely replace the oral presentations or skits, which were better at meeting the first two conditions for optimal language learning environments proposed by Egbert et al. (2007: 5): "1. Learners have opportunities to interact and negotiate meaning" and "2. Learners interact in the target language with an authentic audience." Therefore, combining digital projects with oral presentations as assignments in the same course would offer an ideal solution. Such projects would allow students more opportunities to practice in a low-stress environment and thereby become better prepared to interact with an authentic audience.

Moreover, in order to help students acquire knowledge and learn to use the technologies necessary for completing the projects, two workshops conducted in English were held during class time. This preparation reduced the time that students were exposed to Japanese language in class and confirmed the limitation of using the first language that Ford & Kluge (2015) addressed. Furthermore, as Terrazas-Arellanes et al. (2015) indicated, not all students saw the usefulness of technology. Although the students generally spent much more time on the digital projects, they did not use all of that time for language learning. This outcome was especially the case for those who were less competent in technology: They needed to spend more time on understanding the technological issues and consequently might have felt frustrated and confused about how this requirement was connected to the course's objectives. As mentioned, one student in particular did not like the projects. She talked to me about her frustrations and gave a score of 4 out of 10 for her technological skills in the peer-review form. In the course evaluation, one student wrote that not making the final project digital would be better. While the student's frustrations in this case were understandable, I think that students who are less skilled in technology need this kind of training most. In other words, educators will sometimes find it necessary to challenge students and push them to expand their comfort zones. Technology literacy, though not directly related to language learning, constitutes an important part of college education in this new age. Our department recently adopted a new policy incorporating a digital portfolio into the senior capstone experience for all majors to showcase what students have accomplished during their studies. Thus, digital projects could prepare them for the senior capstone.

The potential frustration is not limited to digital projects. As Beckett (1999) and Eyring (1989) pointed out, ESL students sometimes cannot perceive how PBL helps them to focus on the learning of linguistic form. Beckett & Slater (2005) suggested that it is crucial to help students see the value of PBL. In my case, the students might have appreciated the digital projects better if I had explained the benefits more explicitly. At the beginning of the semester, talking about how these projects integrate language learning with developing other vital skills for students' general education would be worthwhile. Adding skills such as collaboration and technology literacy to the course objectives in the syllabus may also help. I allocated one class to peer review for each project, where we watched the projects together and discussed how they could be improved. Giving the students more time to reflect on the process and discuss what they had learned might have provided a better understanding of the value of the projects. When the student who had trouble in technology consulted me, I primarily focused on helping her solve the technological problems. I could have communicated better with her about the importance of learning the technology.

4.3 Implementation

As discussed earlier, proper implementation may overcome several of the limitations related to the use of digital projects. The effectiveness of digital projects also depends on how they are implemented. In order to make digital projects more effective in language learning, educators need to consciously design projects that meet the following conditions for optimal language learning environments outlined in Egbert et al. (2007: 5): "3. Learners are involved in authentic tasks," "5. Learners have enough time and feedback," and "8. Learner autonomy is supported." The digital projects under discussion made the case that students would present their videos to the wider Kenyon community. As Stoller (2012) suggested, this type of project can provoke authentic and purposeful language practice. In addition, students had autonomy throughout the process of deciding on a topic, finding useful materials, making videos, and grading and giving feedback to others' works. The real-life application, autonomy, and flexibility motivated the students to create a video that they had much control of and appealed to a wide audience.

Various scholars consider scaffolding an essential component to support student learning in PBL (Darling-Hammond et al., 2008; Putambekar & Hubscher, 2005; Vinogradova, 2011). This approach, used in the two digital projects, played an important role in helping students succeed. Each project was divided into several steps, and the voice-dubbing project prepared students for the final project. Scaffolding helped the students stay on track, allotting enough time for each step. In such a process, teachers could also provide timely feedback to help students improve. In the evaluation for the digital projects, one student commented that "the benchmarks for turning in transcription/translation were really helpful and helped us to stay on track." One student suggested applying scaffolding even more, writing that "it would be easier for us to work on the final project if we have deadlines set for several drafts of the video (not only for drafts of the script)."

Although one student complained about spending much time trying to understand the logistics of technologies, none of the other students was overwhelmed by the technology. One reason for this is that the projects required students to use only one software application (WeVideo), which was user-friendly and not too difficult to learn. Technical workshops also helped most of the students stay on the same page in terms of the technology required for the projects. When incorporating digital projects, keeping the technological aspect simple, without using too many new tools all at once, and providing technical support when necessary are important. If similar projects are implemented across the courses in the same program or department, then students only need to learn the technology tools once. As a result, they may become more comfortable using these tools going forward. In fact, several students have voluntarily chosen to make videos as their final project for my other courses – not limited to language courses. Using simple technology tools also makes implementing digital projects easier for instructors. I was lucky to have a college initiative to support my projects, but even without the outside support, learning and teaching the use of one software application would have been feasible.

4.4 Assessment

Since PBLL involves many aspects of development, traditional methods of assessment are not always sufficient (Slater et al., 2006; Van den Bergh et al., 2006). Based on suggestions from previous studies (Beckett & Slater, 2005; Lee & Lim, 2002; Van den Bergh et al., 2006), I adopted various types of assessment instruments, including self-assessment, peer assessment, and instructor assessment, evaluating many aspects of learning, as the following discussion details.

For the voice-dubbing project, in addition to grading all the completed projects (including their own) on a scale of 1 to 10, students also evaluated the members in the same group (including themselves) in the categories of "understanding and transcribing the video," "voice-dubbing," "technology skills," "collaboration skills," and "overall performance," using a scale of 1 to 10 for each category. I graded their projects related to the categories of "transcription," "English translation," "speaking clearly and fluently," "acting (voice only)," and "effort" on a scale of 1 to 10 for each category. The final grade for the project consisted of the peer-review grade on the project (20%), the peer-review grade on the group members (30%), and grades that I gave (50%).

The grade for the final project was calculated based on the proposal (10%), script (20% for the first draft and 30% for the final draft), and final product (20% student + 20% instructor). I graded the script on the categories of "content," "comprehension," "productivity," "accuracy," and "effort" on a scale of 1 to 5. Both peer students and I graded the final product in the categories of "speaking (whether the utterance is fluent and easy to understand)," "visual aspect (whether he/she used informative, appropriate, and effective images)," and "effectiveness of storytelling (whether the video effectively conveyed information on this topic)."

This complex and comprehensive grading system allowed me to emphasize assessing students' language skills while at the same time attempting to cover all the other skills associated with the projects. Self-assessment and peer assessment gave students some autonomy and provided me with information that I would not have had otherwise (e.g., collaboration between students, each student's contribution to the whole project). One problem with the peer assessment was that since we had a small Japanese program, students in the advanced language courses knew each other well, making it difficult for them to be objective when evaluating each other. In general, the grades they gave to their peers were on the high side. (In contrast, in a literature course I taught where most students did not know each other, the grades they gave to their peers were more objective.) On the other hand, Kenyon students generally tend to be humble. For most students, the lowest grade they received was from themselves, and some good students gave themselves low grades in certain categories (especially technological skills), even if they did a good job. This outcome emphasizes the need for instructors to adjust assessment methods based on the circumstances of each course. The next time I teach this course, I will ask students to evaluate themselves only on "effort" and "overall performance" rather than specific skills, and I will make the percentage for self-assessment and peer evaluation lower.

Compared to traditional language tests, the assessment system used in the digital projects was more appropriate for evaluating students with diverse language backgrounds and abilities. Instead of assessing for learning the same knowledge and skills, the digital projects – especially the final project – allowed the students to learn what they were genuinely interested in according to their own language level and at their own pace. As long as they used more than five grammar structures learned in the course and more than 10 grammar structures learned from the second-year course, they were able to achieve full points for the "productivity" category. All the other grading criteria were not related to a fixed scope of knowledge or skills, giving students the freedom to learn vocabulary related to their area of interest and practice grammar and four language skills corresponding to their levels. The students' final projects varied significantly in terms of their levels of language proficiency, but most were able to achieve a grade in the A range. This kind of assessment system can adapt to an individual student's level and fits well in content-based courses where students' levels vary.

5 Conclusion

My findings arising from this research study support Beckett & Slater's (2018: 1) claim that PBL allows students to focus "on the development of language, content, and skills in an integrated and meaningful way." The two digital projects, comprising a voice-dubbing project and a video-making project, were effective not only in developing language skills but also in deepening understanding of Japanese culture and cultivating skills related to creativity, communication, collaboration, research, problem-solving, and critical thinking. In addition, working on the projects improved visual, information, technological, and media literacies that have become increasingly important. The most significant benefits of the digital projects included increasing motivation and interest and creating an optimal learning environment. Furthermore, the authenticity, autonomy, and flexibility made students more motivated to engage with both content and language. Most of the students spent more time practicing the language without feeling overwhelmed or bored, and they were proud of their achievements. Additionally, students were able to learn in a low-stress environment at their own pace. This kind of open-ended project is also ideal for courses where students have diverse language backgrounds and abilities.

The use of technology led to higher levels of student motivation, but learning (often resorting to their first language) and applying technology tools was time-consuming, which might in turn cause frustration and confusion. Thus, using simple tools (ideally one at a time) and being prepared to provide technical support when necessary are critical parts of the process. An explicit explanation at the beginning of the semester and a group reflection when each project is finished may help students better understand the benefits of technology-enhanced PBLL and the importance of acquiring skills not related to language acquisition. Additionally, when I incorporate digital projects in the future, I will offer the option of doing the final project individually or in pairs. This approach will allow students who are not confident in their technology skills to pair with another student who can provide support.

When implementing such projects, scaffolding is also essential, as it helps students stay on track and receive timely support when necessary. An appropriate assessment system is vital as well, since traditional methods do not reflect the complex and integrated learning objectives of digital projects. I used a comprehensive system that integrated self-assessment, peer assessment, and instructor assessment, evaluating several kinds of skills associated with the projects while allocating a higher percentage of the score to language skills. Instructors must adjust the percentage of each category and each assessment method based on the specific circumstances. Although digital projects are ideal for assessing students at different levels, I think that combining them with traditional assessment methods such as homework and quizzes would help to ensure that students spend enough time to study the form regularly. In addition, providing students the opportunity to present in front of and interact with an authentic audience is necessary, since students cannot practice public speaking and interaction in digital projects.

For this research, I implemented digital projects in a content-based advanced language course and found them effective. In the future, I plan to incorporate similar projects in our lower-level language courses that place more emphasis on the learning of form and function. Research questions that require further investigation include "Is PBL equally effective in more form-focused language courses?" as well as "Is PBL more challenging to students with much more limited language skills?" and "How can instructors better implement and assess PBL?" Ideally, if this kind of project also works well for lower-level courses, instructors would be able to implement such assignments across different levels. Consequently, because students only need to learn the logistics of technology tools once, this practice would reduce the barrier to using technology-mediated PBL throughout their studies.

References

Beckett, G. H. (1999). Project-based instruction in a Canadian secondary school's ESL classes: Goals and evaluations. Unpublished doctoral dissertation, University of British Columbia.

Beckett, G. H. (2002). Teacher and student evaluations of project-based instruction. *TESL Canada Journal*, 19(2), 52–66. https://doi.org/10.18806/tesl.v19i2.929

Beckett, G. H., & Miller, P. C. (2006). *Project-based second and foreign language education: Past, present, and future*. Greenwich, CT: Information Age Publishing.

Beckett, G. H., & Slater, T. (2005). The project framework: A tool for language and content integration. *English Language Teaching Journal*, 59, 108–116. https://doi.org/10.1093/eltj/cci024

Beckett, G. H., & Slater, T. (2018). Technology-integrated project-based language learning. In C.A. Chapelle (Ed.), *The encyclopedia of applied linguistics* (pp. 1–8). Hoboken, NJ: John Wiley & Sons. https://doi.org/10.1002/9781405198431.wbeal1487

Beckett, G. H., Slater, T., & Mohan, B. A. (2019). Philosophical foundation, theoretical approaches, and gaps in the literature. In G. H. Beckett & T. Slater (Eds.), *Global perspectives on project-based language learning, teaching, and assessment* (pp. 3–22). New York: Routledge. https://doi.org/10.4324/9780429435096-1

Blake, R. (2016). Technology and the four skills. *Language Learning & Technology*, 20(2), 129–142.

Blyth C. (2018). Immersive technologies and language learning. *Foreign Language Annals*, 51(1), 225–232. https://doi.org/10.1111/flan.12327

Calogerakou, C., & Vlachos, K. (2011). Films and blogs: An authentic approach to improve the writing skill: An intercultural project-based framework in the senior high state school. *Research Papers in Language Teaching and Learning*, 2(1), 98–110.

Carpenter, J., & Matsugu, S. (2019). Translanguaging in projected-based language learning. In G. H. Beckett & T. Slater (Eds.), *Global perspectives on project-based language learning, teaching, and assessment* (pp. 49–68). New York: Routledge. https://doi.org/10.4324/9780429435096-3

Chappelle, C., & Jamieson, J. (2008). *Tips for teaching with CALL: Practical approaches to computer-assisted language learning*. White Plains, NY: Pearson Education.

Charge, N. J., & Giblin, K. (1988). Learning English in a video studio. *English Language Teaching Journal*, 42(4), 282–287. https://doi.org/10.1093/elt/42.4.282

Chen, Mo., & Hirch, R. (2019). A research-based framework for assessing technology-infused PBLL. In G. H. Beckett & T. Slater (Eds.), *Global perspectives on project-based language learning, teaching, and assessment* (pp. 224–243). New York: Routledge. https://doi.org/10.4324/9780429435096-12

Coleman, J. (1992). Project-based learning, transferable skills, information technology and video: *Language Learning Journal*, 5, 35–37. https://doi.org/10.1080/09571739285200121

Condliffe, B. (2016). *Project-based learning: A literature review* (White Paper). San Rafael, CA: Lucas Education Research.

Cope, B., & Kalantzis, M. (2013). Multiliteracies: New literacies, new learning. In M. R. Hawkins (Ed.), *Framing languages and literacies: Socially situated views and perspectives* (pp. 104–135). New York: Routledge.

Darling-Hammond, L., Barron, B., Pearson, P. D., Schoenfeld, A. H., Stage, E. K., Zimmerman, T. D., Cervetti, G. N., and Tilson, J. L. (2008). *Powerful learning: What we know about teaching for understanding*. San Francisco, CA: Jossey-Bass.

Dooly, M., & Sadler, R. (2016). Becoming little scientists: Technologically enhanced project-based language learning. *Language Learning & Technology*, 20(1), 54–78.

Dressler, R., Raedler, B., Dimitrov, K., Dressler, A., & Krause, G. (2019). Project-based learning in the advanced German class: Integrated content and language learning. In G. H. Beckett & T. Slater (Eds.), *Global perspectives on project-based language learning, teaching, and assessment* (pp. 69–84). New York: Routledge. https://doi.org/10.4324/9780429435096-4

Egbert, J., Hanson-Smith, E., & Chin-chi Chao. (2007). Introduction: Foundations for teaching and Learning. In J. Egbert & E. Hanson-Smith (Eds.), *CALL environments: Research, practice, and critical issues*, 2nd edition (pp. 1–15). Alexandria, VA: TESOL.

Eyring, J. L. (1989). Teacher experience and student reponses in ESL project work instruction: A case study. Unpublished doctoral dissertation, University of California, Los Angeles.

Fang, X., & Warschauer, M. (2004). Technology and curriculum reform in China: A case study. *TESQL Quarterly*, 38, 301–323. https://doi.org/10.2307/3588382

Felix, U. (2008). The unreasonable effectiveness of CALL: What have we learned in two decades of research? *ReCALL*, 20(2), 141–161. https://doi.org/10.1017/S0958344008000323

Ford, A., & Kluge, D. (2015). Positive and negative outcomes in creative project-based learning: Two ELF projects. *Academia, Literature, and Language*, 98, 113–154.

Foss, P., Carney, N., McDonald, K., & Rooks, H. (2007). Project-based learning activities for short-term intensive English programs. *Asian EFL Journal*, 20, 1–19.

Foster, P. (2009). Task-based language learning research: Expecting too much or too little? *International Journal of Applied Linguistics*, 19(3), 247–263. https://doi.org/10.1111/j.1473-4192.2009.00242.x

Fried-Booth, D. L. (2002). *Project work*, 2nd edition. New York: Oxford University Press.

Gardner, D. (1995). Student-produced video documentary provides a real reason for using the target language. *Language Learning Journal*, 12(1), 54–56. https://doi.org/10.1080/09571739585200451

Gleason, J., & Link, S. (2019). Using the knowledge framework and genre pedagogy for technology-enhanced form-function project-based language learning. In G. H. Beckett & T. Slater (Eds.), *Global perspectives on project-based language learning, teaching, and assessment* (pp. 204–213). New York: Routledge. https://doi.org/10.4324/9780429435096-11

Godwin-Jones, R. (2014). Games in language learning: Opportunities and challenges. *Language Learning & Technology*, 18(2), 9–19.

Golonka, E. M., Bowles, A. R., Frank, V. M., Richardson, D. L., & Freynik, S. (2014). Technologies for foreign language learning: A review of technology types and their effectiveness. *Computer Assisted Language Learning*, 27(1), 70–105. https://doi.org/10.1080/09588221.2012.700315

Haines, S. (1989). *Projects for the ESL classroom: Resource materials for teachers*. Walton-on-Thames, UK: Nelson.

Hedge, T. (1993). Project work. *English Language Teaching Journal*, 47(3), 276–277. https://doi.org/10.1093/elt/47.3.275

Henry, J. (1994). *Teaching through projects*. London: Kogan Page.

Hong, Z. W., Huang, Y. M., Hsu, M., & Shen, W. W. (2016). Authoring robot-assisted instructional materials for improving learning performance and motivation in EFL classrooms. *Educational Technology & Society*, 19(1), 337–349.

Hsieh, L. W. K. (2012). Technology supported PBL in a Taiwanese university oral communication course: A case study. Unpublished doctoral dissertation, Alliant International University, San Diego, CA.

Jordan, R. R. (1997). *English for academic purposes: A guide and resource book for teachers*. Cambridge: Cambridge University Press. https://doi.org/10.1017/CBO9780511733062

Kessler, G. (2018). Technology and the future of language teaching. *Foreign Language Annals*, 51(1), 205–218. https://doi.org/10.1111/flan.12318

Kobayashi, M. (2004). A sociocultural study of second language tasks: Activity, agency, and language socialization. Unpublished doctoral dissertation, University of British Columbia, Vancouver.

Kuo, A. C., Sutton, P. S., Wright, E., & Miller, B. K. (2019). Altering the view of language instruction in project-based learning: Examining bilingual teachers' unit design experience. In G. H. Beckett & T. Slater (Eds.), *Global perspectives on project-based language learning, teaching, and assessment* (pp. 244–262). New York: Routledge. https://doi.org/10.4324/9780429435096-13

Lam, Y., & Lawrence, G. (2002). Teacher-student role redefinition during a computer-based second language project: Are computers catalysts for empowering change? *Computer Assisted Language Learning*, 15(3), 295–315. https://doi.org/10.1076/call.15.3.295.8185

Lee, H. Y., Lim, C. (2012). Peer evaluation in blended team project-based learning: what do students find important? *Educational Technology & Society*, 15(4), 214–224.

Lee, M. M. T., Li, B. K. W., & Lee, I. K. B. (1999). *Project work: Practical guidelines*. Hong Kong: Hong Kong Institute of Education.

Legutke, M., & Thomas, H. (1991). *Process and experience in the language classroom*. New York: Longman.

Marsh, C. (1989). Some observations on the use of video in the teaching of modern languages. *British Journal of Language Teaching*, 27(1), 13.

Mohan, B., & Beckett, G. H. (2003). Functional approach to content-based language learning: Recasts in causal explanations. *Modern Language Journal*, 87, 421–432. https://doi.org/10.1111/1540-4781.00199

Papandreou, A. P. (1994). An application of the projects approach to EFL. *English Teaching Forum*, 32(3), 41–42.

Pearson, J. (1990). Putting pupils in the picture. *Language Learning Journal*, 2, 71–72. https://doi.org/10.1080/09571739085200541

Puntambekar, S., and Hubscher, R. (2005). Tools for scaffolding students in a complex learning environment: What have we gained and what have we missed? *Educational Psychologist*, 40(1), 1–12. https://doi.org/10.1207/s15326985ep4001_1

Reinders, H., & White, C. (2016). 20 years of autonomy and technology: How far have we come and where to next? *Language Learning & Technology*, 20(2), 143–154.

Salpeter, J. (2005). Telling tales with technology. *Technology and Learning*, 25(7), 18–24.

Slater, T., Beckett, G. H., & Aufderhaar, C. (2006). Assessing project-based second language and content learning. In G. H. Beckett & P. C. Miller (Eds.), *Project-based second and foreign language education: Past, present, and future* (pp. 241–262). Greenwich, CT: Information Age Publishing.

Spolsky, B. (1989). *Conditions for Second Language Learning*. Oxford: Oxford University Press.

Stoller, F. L. (2012). Project-based learning: A viable option for second and foreign language classrooms. *KOTESOL Proceedings 2012*, 37–48.

Terrazas-Arellanes, F. E., Knox, C., & Walden, E. (2015). Pilot study on the feasibility and indicator effects of collaborative online projects on science learning for English learners. *International Journal of Information and Communication Technology Education*, 11(4), 31–50. https://doi.org/10.4018/IJICTE.2015100103

Thomas, M. (2017). *Project-based language learning with technology: Learner collaboration in an EFL classroom in Japan*. New York: Routledge. https://doi.org/10.4324/9781315225418

Van den Bergh, V., Mortelmans, D., Spooren, P., Van Petergem, P., Gijbels, D., & Vanthournout, G. (2006). New assessment modes within project-based education: The stakeholders. *Studies in Educational Evaluation*, 32, 345–368. https://doi.org/10.1016/j.stueduc.2006.10.005

Van Lier, F. (1996). *Interaction in the language curriculum: Awareness, autonomy, and authenticity*. New York: Longman.

Vinogradova, P. (2011). Digital storytelling in ESL instruction: Identity negotiation through a pedagogy of multiliteracies. Unpublished doctoral dissertation, University of Maryland Baltimore, Baltimore, MD.

Zhao, J., & Beckett, G. H. (2014). Project-based Chinese as a foreign language instruction: A teacher research approach. *Journal of the Chinese Language Teachers Association*, 49(2), 45–73.

About the Author

Kai Xie is an Assistant Professor of Japanese at Kenyon College. She received her PhD in Japanese literature from the University of Washington and specializes in Sino-Japanese comparisons and interactions. She also holds a master's degree in Japanese linguistics from Beijing Foreign Studies University. As a teacher of Japanese language, literature, and culture, she is interested in pedagogy, especially the use of technology in language and culture learning.

7 Project-Based Learning for Content and Language Integrated Learning and Pluriliteracies: Some Examples from Italian Schools

Letizia Cinganotto

1 Introduction

Project-based learning (PBL) is a constructivist method that aims to enhance group work and social interaction to solve problems, develop students' thinking skills and co-construct knowledge (Kapp, 2009; Tamin & Grant, 2013). Projects which students are assigned to work on generally involve the whole class or even the school or the community in which they live, connecting the school with the world beyond its walls (Kolodner et al., 2003; Markham, 2011). PBL can be adjusted to all areas of knowledge and different types of learning and implies learning by doing, so that students can solve problems, develop creative and collaborative skills, and research relevant issues (Bell, 2010; Blumenfeld et al., 2011). Thomas (2017) highlights the evolution from task-based to project-based language learning underlining how it may help reshape and rethink teaching practices by promoting a better understanding of both learner interaction in his/her specific cultural contexts and the role of technology in language learning. Tamin & Grant (2013) highlight the following features of PBL:

- it is a student-centered approach as students are the real protagonists both in terms of language and in terms of content: they need to negotiate and co-construct knowledge, reach consensus and work together towards a common goal, which is generally an artifact, that could be paper (poster or wallpaper) or digital (PowerPoint presentation, webtool, booklet, blog etc);
- the teacher generally acts as a facilitator, mediating and moderating the different activities, and actively helps when needed;

- projects are generally related to subject content already known to the students or content they need to investigate further; when this happens in a foreign language, it can be considered as an effective way to implement CLIL methodology (Content and Language Integrated Learning);
- when assigned in a foreign language, projects are generally explained and illustrated to other groups, to the class, the school, or sometimes even to the community and this may help enhance fluency and improve language proficiency, especially for oral skills. (Vaca Torres & Gómez Rodríguez, 2017)

Arising from the above, the following dimensions can be identified as integral to PBL:

- a challenging problem, based on subject content or real-life issues;
- a public product, that could be a performance, a digital poster, a video, or a display;
- co-construction of knowledge and development of skills such as 21st-century skills (critical thinking, problem-solving, creativity, communication, collaboration, self-management);
- students as protagonists of the different choices (how to work in a group, which media to choose, which final output);
- feedback from the teacher and peer feedback to help them improve their work.

Kessler (2013) highlights the need for language teachers and educators to construct opportunities for learners to engage in meaningful interactions in environments allowing them to benefit from their peers. He argues that it is important to consider and foster our students' contribution to the participatory culture, enhancing an equal balance of opportunity and responsibility. Project-based learning may represent an effective way for learners to become aware of their active role in the participatory culture, learning with and from their peers.

Bell (2010) describes PBL as an innovative approach that can lead our students to improve their learning through inquiry and collaborative research, developing a wide range of skills crucial to success in the 21st century. Allison (2018: 4) highlights how "traditional, teacher-centered instructional approaches too often limit offering students the opportunity to work together and acquire 21st century skills of communication, collaboration, creativity, and critical thinking." PBL can help overcome this traditional, top-down way of delivering lessons, in favor of more active, interactive, and student-centered teaching techniques.

2 PBL for CLIL and Pluriliteracies

CLIL (Cinganotto, 2018; Cinganotto & Cuccurullo, 2019; Coyle, Hood, & Marsh, 2010) is a dual-focus approach aiming at developing language proficiency and content mastery at the same time. It is becoming an increasingly popular approach for language learning and content acquisition. Introduced as compulsory in Italy since 2010, it entails a wide range of student-centered active and interactive techniques and strategies. PBL is one of the methods most commonly adopted by CLIL teachers. According to Mehisto, Frigols, & Marsh (2008: 12) when dealing with subject content in a foreign language through CLIL, the following criteria should be taken into account:

- grade-appropriate levels of academic achievement in subjects taught through the CLIL language;
- grade-appropriate functional proficiency in listening, speaking, reading, and writing in the CLIL language;
- age-appropriate levels of first language competence in listening, speaking, reading, and writing;
- an understanding and appreciation of the cultures associated with the CLIL language and the student's first language;
- the cognitive and social skills and habits required for success in an ever-changing world.

The aforementioned criteria should also be considered when planning a PBL pathway, as language and content challenges should be well balanced with the aim to activate the students' thinking skills accordingly. In fact, language competences and content knowledge are perfectly interwoven in project-based learning, according to the following steps:

- a driving question or problem to be solved;
- specific learning goals students need to reach;
- exploration of the driving question, by applying important ideas in the subject;
- collaborative activities to find a solution;
- scaffolding with the use of learning technologies and webtools;
- production of artifacts or other tangible products as representative of the solution found and the learning outcomes.

A wider interpretation of CLIL, going beyond the well-known 4Cs framework (Coyle, 2005) of *Content, Cognition, Culture, and Communication* has recently been promoted by the Graz Group at the European Centre of Modern Languages (ECML), through a project entitled "Pluriliteracies Teaching for Deeper Learning" (PTL), in which the author is involved as a member of the consultancy team. The PTL model stems from the idea that integrating subject content and language to communicate in the background of a cultural scenario appears not to be enough for our students: it is necessary to guide them to be "pluriliterate," that is to become highly competent in a wide range of areas, which they need to master in order to meet the challenges of the 21st century.

At the core of the model lies the idea that deeper learning of both subject and language and the development of transferable knowledge do not happen separately from learning academic content and from the development of language competences. On the contrary, interweaving all these dimensions may prepare our students to become life-long learning citizens in our contemporary society. The PTL model is based on a holistic approach fostering the integration of four dimensions, which represent the major components of deeper learning ecologies:

1. (co)-constructing knowledge, which refers to the collaborative and cooperative processes involved in learning;
2. ("languaging" for) demonstrating understanding, referring to the verbal and nonverbal expression of thoughts, intentions, and knowledge;
3. learner mindset, involving the emotional and cognitive sphere of the learner;
4. mentoring learning, including the role of the teacher as a facilitator and coach.

The learner is the real protagonist of the ecology of this type of approach, helping him/her develop 21st-century skills, such as critical thinking, creativity, effective communication, and responsibility. As Do Coyle in the latest video of the PTL model states (Meyer, Coyle, & Schuck, 2019), "mastering discipline specific ways of constructing and communicating knowledge is the most effective way for learners to develop transferable knowledge and problem solving skills." PBL may represent an effective way to foster all four dimensions of the model.

2.1 (Co)-Constructing Knowledge

Constructing knowledge requires activating cognitive strategies and procedures in order to retain facts, notions, and concepts, and to recognize, manipulate, and possibly apply them to other contexts. Moreover, factual and conceptual subject-specific skills and strategies are needed to solve tasks, which can be more or less linguistically demanding or cognitively demanding (Coyle, 2005). Careful planning of the balance between linguistic demands and cognitive demands is crucial for deeper learning. Task-based learning and task-based language teaching (Nunan, 2004; Willis & Willis, 2007) provide learners with the opportunity to use the target language for the completion of meaningful tasks: the focus is on the authentic use of language for genuine communication, especially when communication refers to subject content as in CLIL. Constructing meaning in collaboration with peers can help deeper learning, as peer learning and peer feedback can reduce the levels of anxiety and avoid disappointment. As Piccardo & North (2019: 174) have argued: "One important aspect of the development of autonomy is giving learners the opportunity to co-construct meaning together in collaborative tasks, rather than seeing them only as individual speaker/listeners." Collaborative tasks and projects can take advantage of the strengths of each group member, raising individual motivation to work for the success of the group. This mutual help may impact deep learning in terms of both language competence and content acquisition.

Project-based learning takes advantage of task-based learning as students work to complete a project over an extended period of time that engages them in solving a real-world problem or answering a complex question. They demonstrate their knowledge and language competence by developing a public product or presentation for a real audience. As a result, students develop deep learning as well as critical thinking, creativity, and communication skills in the context of doing an authentic, meaningful project. As suggested by Krajcik & Shin (2014: 276), "in project-based learning, students engage in real, meaningful problems that are important to them and that are similar to what scientists, mathematicians, writers and historians do. … A project-based classroom allows students to investigate questions, propose hypotheses and explanations, argue for their ideas, challenge the ideas of others and try out new ideas."

2.2 "Languaging" for Demonstrating Understanding

The concept of "languaging" (Swain, 2007) emerged from Vygotsky's sociocultural theory of mind and refers to the natural expression of ideas, intentions, thoughts made visible through written or oral language, considered as not just a means of social communication, but a tool of the mind which mediates our thinking and cognition. It is the process of making and shaping knowledge through language. Collaborative dialogues through peer interaction and activities in their first, second, or third language can help students to show what they know, what they learn, what they want to learn, in a progressive continuum and development of both the thinking and the learning process. According to Swain, "languaging" to another, with another, or with one's self, can present us with new understanding and new insights. The activity domains depicted by the Graz Group's pluriliteracies model are the following:

- *Doing*: manipulating content, making investigations, research, experiments;
- *Organizing* and describing content through a multimodal approach;
- *Explaining* the content acquired through "languaging";
- *Arguing* and defending one's own position through evidence, facts and figures found and learnt.

While co-constructing and manipulating knowledge expressed through "languaging," progression occurs in the students' ability to extract information critically from different texts, or produce more and more complex oral, written, or digital texts or outputs, for different purposes in the appropriate register, mode, and style.

The Common European Framework of Reference for languages (CEFR) and the recent Companion Volume to the CEFR (Council of Europe, 2020) suggested a new model of language activity, shifting from the four-skill approach (listening, speaking, reading, writing) to the four modes of communication: Reception, Production, Interaction, Mediation, which refer to a more dynamic and meaningful use of the language which people currently make, facilitating collaborative interaction, transparent activities in specific contexts, activating content schemata and discourse organization appropriate to the specific genre (Piccardo & North, 2019). The four modes of communication include receptive and productive skills, highlighting mediation as a crucial socio-pragmatic dimension, which involves the ability to mediate among different texts, contents, and contexts and among different users.

A pluriliteracies approach may foster progression in the mastery of the language for the different genres through the different communication modes. Cognitive Discourse Functions (CDFs) (Dalton-Puffer, 2013, 2016) are the way we use the language (discourse) to express functions and intentions and perform acts. The pluriliteracies approach is aimed at helping learners become literate in their subjects, being able to use CDFs at increasingly complex levels.

Table 7.1 (adapted from Dale & Tannen, 2012) includes examples of tasks and languaging related to the different skills in Bloom's taxonomy (1994): cognitive skills and functions are well matched with discourse (words and questions), showing the close link between cognition and languaging during the performance of a certain task. Project-based learning in a foreign language is a very fruitful way to foster languaging and thinking (LOTs, or Lower Order Thinking skills and HOTs, or Higher Order Thinking skills, according to Bloom's taxonomy) at the same time, as shown in Table 7.1 where 'Create' is the last and more demanding step of the process entailing the production of an artifact as tangible output of PBL and involving a wide and complex use of the language for expressing knowledge, emotions, feelings, functions and for describing artifacts or products.

Table 7.1. Cognition and "Languaging" (adapted from Dale & Tannen, 2012)

Skill	Question	Words	Task
Remember	Can learners remember?	Tell, recall, repeat, list	Tell me Pythagoras' theorem
Understand	Can learners explain?	Describe, explain, paraphrase	Tell me what you observed during the experiment
Apply	Can learners use the information in another situation?	Demonstrate, dramatize, illustrate	How can we interpret these graphs? Make a poster to provide advice, illustrations, etc.
Analyze	Can learners break the information into parts and see relationships?	Compare, contrast, criticize	What is the relationship between oil production and consumption?
Evaluate	Can learners justify a position?	Argue, judge, evaluate	Design a questionnaire for our class to evaluate and assess our work during the project
Create	Can learners create new products?	Construct, create, design	Create a lighting circuit for a greenhouse

2.3 Learner Mindset

The impact of well-being and mindset on deeper learning is crucial and that is why the pluriliteracies model includes affective factors, learner engagement, mastery-orientation, and reflection as fundamental dimensions of the learning process. In PBL the learners feel comfortable as they can work with their peers, decreasing the affective filter and the fear of being observed and assessed individually by the teacher. There is a strong motivation in PBL, which triggers enthusiasm, the will to learn and to achieve common goals, and it has an important impact on deep learning. As Piccardo (2014: 18) points out, the mental context is as important as the external context in the learning process: "it filters and interprets the external context or situation. And the form that this interpretation or perception takes will depend on many different factors: physical, cultural, practical, cognitive, affective, emotional, etc." In order to foster deeper learning, it is essential to distinguish among three constructs often assumed as identical (Järvelä & Renninger, 2014): interest, motivation, and engagement. Interest can be triggered for learners in all the different phases, until the later ones, where they can start to make connections among concepts and contexts. However, some particular triggers are always needed for interest.

Motivation refers to a broader concept and involves different factors related to the environment and to the cognitive and affective spheres. However, while interest seems to be always motivating, what is motivating may not be of interest. Engagement includes socio-emotional and cognitive aspects of the learning environment, involving expectations, interests, and motivation, and plays a crucial role in self-regulating behavior, goals, and tasks. Reflection and meta-cognition play an important role in the learner mindset, therefore it is important to foster them. According to Winnie & Azevedo (2014: 63), meta-cognition is defined as "cognition where the information on which a learner operates describes features of cognition" and the following steps can be distinguished:

- *meta-cognitive monitoring*, that is awareness of meeting particular standards for a certain kind of knowledge;
- *meta-cognitive control*, getting input from meta-cognitive monitoring to generate a reaction and action in that direction;
- *self-regulated learning*, collecting different instances of meta-cognitive monitoring and meta-cognitive control to adapt thinking and engage in complex tasks with a high level of awareness.

According to Zimmerman (2001), self-regulation represents the self-directive process transforming the learners' mental abilities into task-related skills. Self-regulation involves self-reflection before, during, and after an action or performance: it is fundamental for a learner to be guided through this process, until a progressively autonomous reflection and full awareness of the outcomes of the different learning experiences for students' own personal growth is reached. A teacher's feedback and peer feedback on a project produced by a group of students can play an important role in improving students' own meta-cognitive understanding of the learning process. PBL can guide the learner towards a deeper and deeper awareness of his/her meta-cognitive and learning strategies, in order to meet his/her needs and constantly improve.

2.4 Mentoring Learning

In PBL as well as in the PTL model, the teacher acts as a facilitator, a mentor, or a coach within a student-centered approach. Among the tasks of a successful teacher the following can be mentioned: design, scaffolding, feedback, and assessment. During the teaching process, teachers should take into account several aspects, such as the students' learning needs, level of competence, affective factors, and literacy in the various subjects. Scaffolding and feedback are two other fundamental aspects in the mentoring role of the teacher. According to Van Lier (2007), scaffolding can take place at three levels:

- *macro*: planning over a certain period;
- *meso*: planning the single steps of a task;
- *micro*: guiding moment-to-moment interactional work.

According to Reiser & Tabak (2014: 45) "a central idea in scaffolding is that the work is shared between the learner and some more knowledgeable other or agent. Scaffolding enables not only the performance of a task more complex than the learner could handle alone, but also enables learning from that experience." Therefore, scaffolding is crucial and teachers should find an appropriate strategy to scaffold language competence and content acquisition in the different steps of the PBL pathway.

3 Focus on Feedback

Feedback on a project produced by a group of students is a crucial part of the monitoring process and is described by Wiggins (2012) as characterized by seven qualities, in particular:

- *goal-referenced*: feedback must provide goal-related information, referring to the aims of the corrective interventions suggested;

- *tangible and transparent*: there should be visible reactions to certain actions, such as attentive listening, concentration, or on the contrary, laughing, lack of attention, etc.;
- *actionable*: it should not be generic or abstract, but include concrete actions to perform;
- *user-friendly*, not too technical, but easily comprehensible for the learners, avoiding embarrassment;
- *timely*, as if it takes too long to provide feedback, it may be useless as the learner is not fully engaged in the task any longer;
- *ongoing*: this is the main feature of formative assessment, providing the opportunity to reshape and adjust certain tasks over time;
- *consistent*, that is, trustworthy: the learner should feel he/she is on the same page as the teacher.

Austin's butterfly (see: https://www.youtube.com/watch?v=hqh1MRWZjms) is a good example of constructive peer feedback: it is about first-grade students who want to help one of their friends, Austin, take a scientific illustration of a butterfly through multiple drafts toward a high-quality final product. The children want to provide meaningful feedback about the drawing of the butterfly done by one of their peers, without being "mean"; feedback coming from a friend can be felt as true and genuine more than that coming from the teacher, even if this implies repeating the same action again and again. The example shows the transformational power of models, critique, and descriptive feedback to improve student work.

Praise and encouragement should be essential components of feedback in PBL, which should not only be supportive, but also work-specific, providing specific information on the strengths and weaknesses of a performance, encouraging students to think for themselves (Scrivener, 2012). Therefore, it could be useful to ask for clarification, reformulation, and follow-up questions, fostering further language production. Mistakes can represent a good opportunity to reflect, but "offline" intervention after the interaction can be preferable to "online" correction during the performance itself, which may interrupt the flow of the discussion and impact fluency.

According to Hattie (2009), satisfactory formative feedback is one of the greatest contributors to student success. Hattie highlights the impact of feedback on visible learning and places it in the zone of desired effect, together with classroom discussion, response to intervention, direct instruction, and teacher clarity and credibility, which are perceived as essential qualities and values for a teacher. Therefore, feedback is placed in the zone of desired effect, as it can deeply impact the learning process and make it effective and long-lasting.

4 The Role of Technologies in PBL

Teaching with technologies (e.g., web-based learning, one-on-one laptops), mentoring, co- or team teaching are considered developmental effects by Hattie (2009), which can foster deeper learning both in terms of subject literacy and language competence. CALL, or Computer-Assisted Language Learning (Thomas, Reinders, & Warschauer, 2012) is considered "normalized" (Bax, 2003) by 21st-century students, the so-called "screenagers" (Rushkoff, 2006); in fact, students are constantly exposed to a screen (their smartphone or any other device) to communicate informally with their peers and to interact with the outer world in general.

PBL can reap a lot of benefits from the use of technologies: digital tools and multimedia artifacts are highly recommended in PBL, as students can easily interact and collaborate in groups and use technologies for their final product or digital artifact. According to Meyer, Coyle, & Schuck (2018: 29), "digital media and educational technologies must form an integral part of a deeper learning environment because of their potential to significantly increase learner engagement by establishing deeper connections between learners and their learning environment through a process of customization and individualization. Web 3.0 and its associated technologies make it possible to customize elements considered to be highly indicative of successful subject language learning." The aforementioned quotation from the authors of the "pluriliteracies" model underlines the importance of making the connection between digital technologies and classroom learning, identifying the criteria according to which a specific added value to learning is recognized.

The different activity domains provided by the pluriliteracies model as indicated above may be enhanced and facilitated thanks to the use of technologies and can be effective in PBL, for example:

- *Doing*: students can carry out research, webquests, or other learning activities using repositories or websites suggested by the teacher or discovered by themselves;
- *Organizing*: content knowledge can be organized or categorized with the help of maps or timelines, using specific webtools;
- *Explaining*: concepts and content can be explained and shown through the use of webapps for presentations;
- *Arguing*: their own position can be defended mentioning documents or sources found on the internet or through specific webtools for engaging classroom discussion or simulating debates.

In project-based learning an important role is played by the so-called "cognitive tools" (Kennedy & McNaught, 2001), webtools, or software allowing learners to collect, visualize, and share data and information, to collaborate with peers, to develop multimedia documents, to provide feedback, and to share and critique the ideas of others.

Learning technologies and webtools may facilitate the teacher's work in planning and assessing PBL: tools such as "Learning Designer," created by Laurillard at University College London, or "RubiStar" can help create lesson designs and rubrics in a very easy way, adapting existing templates or creating new projects depending on specific needs. A wide range of webtools for presentation, for creating graphs and maps, or for simulating phenomena or experiments in Physics or Chemistry, such as "PhET Simulations," can help students in the process of co-constructing and languaging their knowledge.

As far as feedback is concerned, technologies can help considerably: screen-capture software, such as Jing or Camtasia, can capture the screen while the teacher is providing feedback to a collective or individual piece of written work. Moreover, features similar to "Google Comments" or "Kaizena" allow teachers to leave feedback through voice recordings. Once the program has been added and the teacher has gained access to the document, the student's writing can be added to a group that will allow both the teacher and student to access any feedback left at any time.

Using e-feedback (Ho, 2015) can alleviate the limitations of face-to-face communications such as time and place; in fact, there are only so many hours in a given school day and with constant distractions popping up in the classroom, teachers need the time to focus and formulate their thoughts. By utilizing e-feedback, the quality of feedback can improve with this added time outside of the classroom.

Technologies may help design effective deep learning ecologies, including all the different languages and language varieties typical of our multiethnic, multicultural and multilingual classes. Through a pluriliteracies approach we can go beyond CLIL, aiming at "an understanding of CLIL as 'fusion' [which] implies a multi-perspective view on both language and content, which, taken together, should help us understand the fusion of language and content" (Dalton-Puffer et al., 2010: 289). Using PBL in a pluriliteracies class, 21st-century learners can be guided to be literate in the different subjects of the curriculum (history, physics, music, etc.) from a multilingual perspective, including L1, L2, L3, the lingua franca or the language of schooling, and enhancing at the same time the development of transversal skills such as critical thinking, problem-solving, creativity, collaboration, and communication.

5 Examples of PBL in Italy

In Italy CLIL has been mandatory in all upper secondary schools since 2010 and the Ministry of Education, in cooperation with INDIRE (National Institute for Documentation, Innovation and Educational Research), has been fostering school projects aimed at planning and implementing CLIL modules with the use of technologies (Langé & Cinganotto, 2014). In fact, CLIL is mandatory in the last year of all upper secondary schools where a subject or at least modules of a subject (STEAM or humanistic subjects) must be delivered through a foreign language according to CLIL methodology (Cinganotto, 2016). The Italian CLIL teacher is the subject teacher who has to be specifically trained via a university post-graduate course on CLIL methodology and language courses aimed at achieving a C1 level of language competence in the foreign language. The recent Council of the European Union Recommendation on a comprehensive approach to the teaching and learning of languages (2019) mentioned CLIL in Italy as an example of inclusive and democratic approach, as it is delivered in all classes, even if the students are generally mixed abilities; in some countries students need to pass a language test in order to be admitted to a CLIL course. PBL has also been encouraged as an effective strategy for implementing CLIL with ICT as students may experiment with CLIL by engaging in collaborative activities.

In the school year 2015–16 Italian school networks were given funds by the Ministry of Education to finance and support schools working with PBL. As a specific example, 62 upper secondary schools and 63 comprehensive schools (primary and lower secondary schools) were funded for their involvement with one or more classes in PBL. This activity led to the following outputs produced by the students: 106 PowerPoint presentations; 85 videos; 84 pdf documents; 60 assessment grids; 50 multimedia platforms; 31 interactive games; 9 Wikis; and 18 blogs. The most common foreign language in all the different projects was English (133 projects), followed by French with 27 projects, and German and Spanish with 9 and 5 projects respectively. An interesting finding arising from the initiative was the cooperation between language teachers and subject teachers in PBL (the so-called "CLIL Team" recommended by the Ministry of Education). Indeed, in 106 of the projects, they stated that they managed to cooperate effectively.

Some of the projects were analyzed in detail as case studies, investigating all the main features and steps, highlighting objectives accomplished and outputs produced. Some examples of these projects will be mentioned here as interpreted by the schools from a PBL perspective (Cinganotto, 2017).

Within the framework of the "CLIL4ALL" E-CLIL project, one of the schools decided to create an e-book about the city of Lucca (see http://www.piaggia.it/eclil) in Tuscany, presenting some buildings and monuments in English through visual inputs, videos, texts, and quizzes to check learning. The project was aimed at exploring some of the most important places in Lucca and describing them in English. This project allowed the students to explore their city and discover artistic features they probably had not yet discovered, using the foreign language to express artistic and historical content.

In another instance, a project in CLIL and art was undertaken: a real art exhibition was organized within a virtual gallery and a 3D environment was created (see: www.comprensivosantostefanoisa12.it). Entering the virtual gallery, visitors could appreciate the paintings and learn more about them, clicking on them to read the explanations provided by the students.

Another example of a CLIL and art project was carried out by some primary school classes engaged in analysing Kandinsky's works, identifying their main components: shapes, lines, and colours (https://epic2016.wordpress.com/emozioni-colori-e-ritmo-nellarte-e-nella-musica/). The students were guided to understand the message Kandinsky wanted to convey connecting art and music, especially to express one's own feelings and emotions. In the final project, the children produced a poster imitating Kandinsky's painting technique. The students were actively engaged in the project, leading them towards a progressive appreciation of the works of art. In this case no digital tools were used but a more traditional approach to art underpinned the project.

At the end of the school year a questionnaire was delivered to the heads of all the schools involved in these initiatives (62 upper secondary schools and 63 comprehensive schools), in order to collect the teachers' comments and ideas on the use of PBL in their schools. Each school head was asked to appoint the teacher who had coordinated the CLIL project to complete the questionnaire.

The data from the questionnaire were collected and analyzed according to "Framework Analysis" (Ritchie et al., 2014). One teacher's comments highlighted the importance of PBL for CLIL as an authentic and effective way to educate future European citizens since it helps build intercultural knowledge and vision, develop intercultural communication skills, and improve language skills and oral communication skills:

> The main didactic purpose is to promote the ability to acquire knowledge through a foreign language. This type of ability will be

> valuable for our students who will live in the global village created by the new information technologies (Internet); it will also be very useful for them as future European citizens, who must be able to communicate and operate in at least two Community languages. The key factor of the CLIL project is to acquire new knowledge on a subject that does not in itself involve language teaching, learning a foreign language through its use. The methodologies and strategies used are often linked to the area of the subject in question, the content of which guides the activities. The multidisciplinary approach can offer a variety of benefits: – it builds an intercultural knowledge and vision – it develops intercultural communication skills – it improves language skills and oral communication skills.

The strengths and weaknesses of PBL for CLIL were highlighted by the participants, as briefly mentioned below. The following strengths emerged from the data, as the PBL and CLIL approach was seen as leading to:

- collaboration among language teachers and subject teachers;
- greater exposure to the language;
- development of language skills;
- development of soft skills;
- collaboration among students and teachers;
- attention to multiculturalism and internationalization;
- innovation in teaching;
- promotion of e-skills for teachers and students;
- interest and involvement of students;
- a vertical curriculum.

Several of the more extended comments from the teachers elaborated on these strengths as follows:

> Extensive research work, sharing of good practices, use of real cases, replicability of the model, variety of materials used, organization of different group work, use of new technologies with attractive layout and close to the world of young people.
>
> Links with other similar projects for purposes, objectives and target groups (Web Generation 2.0), in particular with regard to the use of new technologies and the IWB, as well as projects for in-depth study.
>
> Methodological strategies, means and tools for problem-solving, use of multimedia equipment (computer, IWB, video camera).

The impact on the students' performance and on the improvement of their skills in English and in the use of ICT.

The students felt stimulated to work together with their peers to reach common goals.

Use of an innovative methodology that allows competence-based learning; continuous interaction among teachers and pupils; research group activities; intercultural exchanges.

The use of the eTwinning platform is strategic: having a specific space available to everyone, where everyone could share their work and, above all, their thoughts and experiences, has given a great boost to the activities and has allowed a much more productive organization of work.

Particularly interesting was the material produced by the students for the project, through the use of ICT: even the most reluctant students got involved showing a great enthusiasm.

Soft skills have been promoted through team work. The students were able to experience the role of producers and co-authors of digital content to be disseminated in a protected wiki environment, living in this way an absolutely new and rewarding experience for them. All the materials produced are the result of a synergic action of co-design and co-production among students, teachers and external experts.

The following weaknesses were highlighted, including insufficient time; inadequate funds; inadequate level of language proficiency of DNL (subject) teachers; and resistance of some teachers to change. Teachers also reported several challenges, including lack of technical equipment (internet equipment) of some schools; lack of experts in CLIL methodology; teachers of non-linguistic disciplines with no certification in English; difficulty in documenting the work due to the hostility or indifference of some teachers not willing to cooperate; weak digital competencies of some teachers and need for training; low tendency to use multimedia tools in daily teaching activities; and lack of experience with cooperative learning and PBL.

6 Discussion

Although technologies are generally strictly related to project-based learning, in the literature there have been relatively few empirical reports of technology-infused project-based teaching and learning (Beckett & Slater, 2018).

This statement was confirmed by the teachers involved in the study, highlighting strengths and weaknesses of PBL for CLIL often linked to the digital literacy of the teachers: some of them had generally higher levels of digital skillsets, while others were reluctant to innovate in their teaching practices and emerge from their comfort zone.

PBL, cooperative learning, peer learning, and multimedia learning could be time-consuming and demanding for a middle-aged teacher used to his/her own usual techniques and teaching strategies. Students often possessed higher levels of digital literacy or digital confidence and this may also have been perceived as a challenge for some teachers who did not like to be seen to "fail" or to appear "inexperienced" in front of their learners. Other problems connected with PBL can be linked to weak infrastructure and equipment in some Italian schools and to the need for teacher training on innovation and digital-based teaching techniques.

Despite all these weaknesses, the majority of the teachers involved in the study felt positive about PBL and were eager to embrace innovation in language learning and CLIL. Several identified a wide range of benefits from adopting PBL with their students in terms of participation and engagement, but also in terms of the potential to improve learning outcomes, with reference to both language competence and content acquisition. These findings can confirm the added value of PBL in second and foreign language learning, as highlighted in the literature (Beckett & Miller, 2006).

The comments and reactions of the majority of the teachers seemed to confirm findings from previous studies (Thomas & Reinders, 2015) in that PBL is perceived as an effective way to foster task-based learning by assigning authentic tasks in a foreign language, leading to the production of a tangible output in the shape of a project, often involving students in collaborative activities with their peers, producing outstanding multimedia products in some cases (Willie, 2001). PBL can help to position students at the center of the learning process, resulting as effective and successful in terms of language development and subject content acquisition. Through PBL students can feel they are the real protagonists of their choices, as they can be the authors of digital content and artifacts which have been collaboratively made by the groups.

7 Conclusion

The chapter began by identifying the conceptual framework related to PBL for language learning and CLIL and subsequently underlined several of the most important benefits in terms of students' learning outcomes. In particular, the link between PBL and PTL (Pluriliteracies Teaching for Deeper Learning), a model defined by the Graz Group at ECML, where the author is a member of the consultancy team, was investigated and explored, with particular reference to the four dimensions provided by the model. The focus on "pluriliteracies" to foster deeper learning and transferable skills, both in languages and in subject content, represents a wider interpretation of CLIL methodology and there is the potential that it can be enhanced through the use of PBL.

The second part of the chapter highlighted several examples of PBL in Italian schools, reporting on some of the teachers' comments and reactions to the approach with reference to its strengths and weaknesses via questionnaire in school year 2015–16. PBL was perceived as potentially beneficial as a methodology for language learning. Both CLIL and pluriliteracies were considered helpful approaches to overcome old-fashioned, top-down models of schooling and to encourage a more active and student-centered form of teaching and learning in the Italian context.

References

Allison, J. M. (2018). Project based learning to promote 21st century skills: An action research study. *Dissertations, theses, and masters projects*. Paper 1530192564. Retrieved from http://dx.doi.org/10.25774/w4-m5xm-wc95

Bax, S. (2003). CALL – Past, present and future. *System*, 31, 3 28. https://doi.org/10.1016/S0346-251X(02)00071-4

Beckett, G. H., and Miller, P. C. (2006). *Project-based second and foreign language education: Past, present, and future*. Greenwich, Connecticut: Information Age Publishing.

Beckett, G. H., & Slater, T. (2018). Project-based learning and technology. In J. I. Liontas & M. DelliCarpini (Eds.), *The TESOL encyclopedia of English language teaching*. Hoboken, NJ: Wiley Blackwell. https://doi.org/10.1002/9781118784235.eelt0427

Bell, S. (2010). Project-based learning for the 21st century: Skills for the future. *The Clearing House*, 83(2), 39–43. https://doi.org/10.1080/00098650903505415

Bloom, B. S. (1994). Reflections on the development and use of the taxonomy. In K. J. Rehage, L. W. Anderson, & L. A. Sosniak (Eds.), *Bloom's taxonomy: A forty-year retrospective. Yearbook of the National Society for the Study of Education*. Chicago: National Society for the Study of Education.

Blumenfeld, P. C., Soloway, E., Marx, R. W., Krajcik, J. S., Guzdial, M., & Palincsar, A. (2011). Motivating project based learning: Sustaining the doing, supporting the learning. *Educational Psychologist*, 26(4), 369–398. https://doi.org/10.1080/00461520.1991.9653139

Cinganotto, L. (2016). CLIL in Italy: A general overview. *Latin American Journal of Content and Language Integrated Learning*, 9(2), 374–400. https://doi.org/10.5294/laclil.2016.9.2.6

Cinganotto, L. (2017). Language for art in a CLIL curriculum: Some case examples from Italian school projects. *Humanising Language Teaching*, 19(4). Retrieved from https://old.hltmag.co.uk/aug17/mart04.htm

Cinganotto, L. (2018). *Apprendimento CLIL e interazione in classe*. Roma: Aracne.

Cinganotto, L., & Cuccurullo, D. (2019). *Techno-CLIL. Fare CLIL in digitale*, I Quaderni della Ricerca n. 42. Torino: Loescher.

Council of Europe. (2020). Common European Framework of Reference for Languages (CEFR). Companion Volume. Retrieved from https://rm.coe.int/common-european-framework-of-reference-for-languages-learning-teaching/16809ea0d4

Council of the European Union. (2019). *Council recommendation on a comprehensive approach on teaching and learning languages*. Retrieved from https://ec.europa.eu/education/education-in-the-eu/council-recommendation-improving- teaching-and-learning-languages_en

Coyle, D. (2005). *Planning tools for teachers*. Retrieved from https://www.unifg.it/sites/default/files/allegatiparagrafo/20-01-2014/coyle_clil_planningtool_kit.pdf

Coyle D., Hood P., & Marsh, D. (2010). *CLIL: Content and Language Integrated Learning*. Cambridge: Cambridge University Press.

Dale, L., & Tannen, R. (2012). *CLIL activities*. Cambridge: Cambridge University Press.

Dalton-Puffer, C. (2013). A construct of cognitive discourse functions for conceptualizing content–language integration in CLIL and multilingual education. *European Journal of Applied Linguistics*, 1(2), 216–253. https://doi.org/10.1515/eujal-2013-0011

Dalton-Puffer, C. (2016). Cognitive discourse functions: Specifying an integrative interdisciplinary construct. In T. Nikula, E. Dafouz, P. Moore, & U. Smit (Eds.), *Conceptualising integration in CLIL and multilingual education*. Bristol: Multilingual Matters. https://doi.org/10.21832/9781783096145-005

Dalton-Puffer, C., Nikula, T., & Smit, U. (Eds.). (2010). *Language use and language learning in CLIL classrooms*. Amsterdam: John Benjamins.

Hattie, J. (2009). *Visible learning: A synthesis of over 800 meta-analyses relating to achievement*. London & New York: Routledge. https://doi.org/10.4324/9780203887332

Ho, M.-C. (2015). The effects of face-to-face and computer-mediated peer review on EFL writers' comments and revisions. *Australasian Journal of Educational Technology*, 31(1), 1–15. https://doi.org/10.14742/ajet.495

Järvelä S., & Renninger, K. A. (2014). Designing for learning: Interest, motivation and engagement. In K. Sawyer (Eds.), *The Cambridge handbook of the learning sciences* (pp. 668–686). Cambridge: Cambridge University Press. https://doi.org/10.1017/CBO9781139519526.040

Langè, G., & Cinganotto, L. (2014). *E-CLIL per una didattica innovativa*, I Quaderni della Ricerca n. 18. Torino: Loescher.

Kapp, E. (2009). Improving student teamwork in a collaborative project-based course. *College Teaching*, 57(3), 139–143. https://doi.org/10.3200/CTCH.57.3.139-143

Kennedy, D., & McNaught, C. (2001). *Computer-based cognitive tools: Description and design*. Norfolk, VA: Ed Media, Vitelli Eds.

Kessler, G. (2013). Collaborative language learning in co-constructed participatory culture. *CALICO Journal*, 30(3), 307–322. https://doi.org/10.11139/cj.30.3.307-322

Kolodner, J. L., Camp, P. J., Crismond, D., Fasse, B., Gray, J., Holbrook, J., Puntambekar, S., & Ryan, M. (2003). Problem-based learning meets case-based reasoning in the middle-school science classroom: Putting learning by design into practice. *The Journal of the Learning Sciences*, 12(4), 495–547. https://doi.org/10.1207/S15327809JLS1204_2

Krajcik, J. S., & Shin, N. (2014). Project-based learning. In K. Sawyer (Ed.), *The Cambridge handbook of the learning sciences*. Cambridge: Cambridge University Press.

Markham, T. (2011). Project-based learning: A bridge just far enough. *Teacher Librarian*, 39(2), 38–42.

Mehisto, P., Frigols, M. J., & Marsh, D. (2008). *Uncovering CLIL*. London: Macmillan.

Meyer, O., Coyle D., & Schuck, K. (2018). Learnscaping: Creating next-gen learning environments for pluriliteracies growth. In J. Buendgens-Kosten & D. Elsner (Eds.), *Multilingual computer assisted language learning* (pp. 18–38). Bristol: Multilingual Matters. https://doi.org/10.21832/9781788921497-004

Meyer, O., Coyle D., & Schuck, K. (2019). PTL video. Retrieved from https://www.youtube.com/watch?v=ogxvMpDjtEU

Nunan, D. (2004). *Task-based language teaching*. Cambridge: Cambridge University Press. https://doi.org/10.1017/CBO9780511667336

Piccardo, E. (2014). *From communicative to action-oriented: A research pathway*. Retrieved from https://transformingfsl.ca/wp-content/uploads/2015/12/From-Communicative-To-Action-Oriented_Theory-into-Practice.pdf

Piccardo, E., & North, B. (2019). *The action-oriented approach*. Bristol: Multilingual Matters. https://doi.org/10.21832/PICCAR4344

Reiser, B. J., & Tabak, I. (2014). Scaffolding. In K. Sawyer (Ed.), *The Cambridge handbook of the learning sciences*. Cambridge: Cambridge University Press. https://doi.org/10.1017/CBO9781139519526.005

Ritchie, J., Lewis, J., Nicholls, C. M., & Ormston, R. (2014). *Qualitative research practice: A guide for social science students and researchers*. London: Sage.

Rushkoff, D. (2006). *ScreenAgers: Lessons in chaos from digital kids*. New York: Hampton Press.

Scrivener, J. (2012). *Classroom management techniques*. Cambridge: Cambridge University Press.

Swain, M. (2007). Languaging, agency and collaboration in advanced second language proficiency. In H. Byrnes (Ed.), *Advanced language learning: The contribution of Halliday and Vygotsky* (pp. 95–108). London: Continuum.

Tamim, S. R., & Grant, M. M. (2013). Definitions and uses: Case study of teachers implementing project-based learning. *Interdisciplinary Journal of Problem-Based Learning*, 7(2), 72–101. https://doi.org/10.7771/1541-5015.1323

Thomas, M. (2017). *Project-based language learning with technology: Learner collaboration in an EFL classroom in Japan*. London: Routledge. https://doi.org/10.4324/9781315225418

Thomas, M., & Reinders H. (2015). *Contemporary task-based language teaching in Asia*. London: Bloomsbury.

Thomas, M., Reinders H., & Warschauer M. (2012). *Contemporary computer-assisted language learning*. London: Bloomsbury Academic.

Vaca Torres, A. M., & Gómez Rodríguez, L. F. (2017). Increasing EFL learners' oral production at a public school through project-based learning, *PROFILE*, 19(2), 57–71. https://doi.org/10.15446/profile.v19n2.59889

Van Lier, L. (2007). Action-based teaching, autonomy, and identity. *International Journal of Innovation in Language*, 1, 46–65. https://doi.org/10.2167/illt42.0

Wiggins G. (2012). *Seven keys to effective feedback: Feedback for learning*. Retrieved from http://www.ascd.org/publications/educational-leadership/sept12/vol70/num01/Seven-Keys-to-Effective-Feedback.aspx

Willie, S. L. (2001). *Project-based learning with multimedia*. San Mateo County Office of Education.

Willis, D., & Willis, J. (2007). *Doing task-based teaching*. Oxford: Oxford University Press.

Winnie, P. H., & Azevedo, R. (2014). Meta-cognition. In K. Sawyer (Ed.), *The Cambridge handbook of the learning sciences*. Cambridge: Cambridge University Press.

Zimmerman, B. J. (2001). Theories of self-regulated learning and academic achievement: An overview and analysis. In B. J. Zimmerman & D. H. Schunk (Eds.), *Self-regulated learning and academic achievement: Theoretical perspectives* (pp. 1–65). London: Springer.

About the Author

Letizia Cinganotto is a researcher at INDIRE (National Institute for Documentation, Innovation and Educational Research) in Rome, Italy. She holds a BA in foreign languages, MAs in ELT, eLearning, and multimedia learning, and a PhD in synchronic, diachronic, and applied linguistics. She is a member of different working groups and scientific committees on CLIL and languages, both at national and international level. Her main research areas are language learning and teaching, CLIL, technology-enhanced learning, school innovation, and teacher training. She is a member of the ECML "pluriliteracies" consultancy team.

8 Project-Based Learning via ePortfolios: Integrating Web 2.0 Tools into Higher Education World Language Classes

Rebecca L. Chism and Evan W. Faidley

1 Introduction

The environment conducive to language acquisition is comprised of numerous elements, including educational activity (Swain, Brooks, & Tocalli-Beller, 2002; van Compernolle & Williams, 2013), social mediation (Lantolf, 2000; Wertsch, 2007; van Compernolle & Williams, 2013), knowledge construction (Lantolf, 2000; Tocaimaza-Hatch, 2015), and interaction (Hall, 1995; Warschauer, 1998; Lantolf, 2000), amongst others. Knowledge construction in particular allows for learners to associate the written or spoken symbol of the target language with its appropriate role and function. Project-based learning, based on student inquiry and critical process, can offer a learning scenario for such construction to take place. As multimedia and computer-mediated communication and collaboration (CMC) are common and prolific amongst 21st-century learners, the researchers were interested in exploring how project-based learning in the form of electronic portfolios (ePortfolios) could be incorporated into a university's intermediate-level world language class. Project-based learning is considered an ideal "strategy for weaving technology standards and skills together with language" (Shrum & Glisan, 2016: 417). The present study seeks to investigate how electronic ePortfolios can be used for knowledge construction within the context of project-based learning and foreign language education (Beckett, 2006).

The idea of using an ePortfolio derived from conversations in the academic unit at a comprehensive, research, public institution in the Midwest of the United States about orienting students towards several end-of-semester objectives. ePortfolios are considered an example of project-based learning in the following ways. First, self-authorship was outlined as an essential part of the redesign of course content. Rather than reading, remembering, and regurgitating grammar and vocabulary, students were encouraged to experience scaffolding – using previously learned tenses, syntax, and vocabulary – to recreate new ideas about specific topics. Simultaneously, students would engage in project-based, or action-based learning in which "learners' hearts, bodies, and senses" (Finkbeiner, 2000: 255) would constitute their involvement and investment in their second language (L2) acquisition. The second objective was communication practice. Rather than merely hoping that students would communicate with each other in French both in and out of the classroom, assignments were designed to ultimately end up as reflective artifacts (Barrett, 2001) on the ePortfolio (e.g., partner conversations and personal compositions) that facilitated instructor-student and student-student dialogue with new and previously learned French. Lastly, an objective for the ePortfolio was to encourage learning and growth in computer-based collaboration and design. Enhancements in multimedia skills can contribute to marketability and employability of an individual and show that they are multifaceted in website development, as well as active and resilient in language learning. The following research questions were considered:

1. *What are the implications of implementing ePortfolios in a university-level intermediate world language course through project-based learning?*
2. *In what ways can ePortfolios provide opportunities for linguistic and cultural knowledge construction in the target language?*

2 Review of the Literature

This section explains how project-based learning with ePortfolios can serve as the setting for knowledge construction, as supported by a constructivist framework. Airasian & Walsh (1997) presented constructivism as an epistemic perspective to knowledge development, explaining that it is not an instructional approach per se, but rather an understanding of how knowledge is formed, from external experiences and observations to internalized sensemaking. From this viewpoint, language serves as the primary means to create, negotiate, and solidify knowledge and meaning. According to Soviet psychologist Lev Vygotsky (1978), language is seen as a key tool for the integration of thought and practice. Biggs (1996) supported this balance of physical and metaphysical interactions, having posited that "learners arrive at meaning by actively selecting, and cumulatively constructing, their own knowledge, through both individual and social activity" (p. 348).

2.1 Sociocultural Theory

Sociocultural theory suggests that the development of language, thought, and behavior is learned and is dependent on interactions with more-capable others. Ultimately, these interactions are internalized and subconsciously impact one's day-to-day thought and behavior. Sociocultural theory combines the social environment with cognition (Atkinson, 2002; Swain et al., 2002), thus connecting "social context and individuals' psychological development" (Sabet, Tahiri, & Pasand, 2013: 1894). According to Lantolf (2000), the following four basic principles underlie [Vygotskian] sociocultural theory: (a) knowledge is constructed, (b) development cannot be separated from its social context, (c) language is mediated, and (d) language plays a central role in mental development. In other words, sociocultural theory regards human mental functioning as a mediated process that is organized by artifacts, activities, and concepts (Lantolf, 2000; Vygotsky, 1978). Lantolf (2000) highlighted the significance of interaction within social contexts for developing human cognitive ability. Generally, learners within the sociocultural framework are treated as active meaning-makers and problem-solvers in their process of learning; the greater emphasis being on that learning which stems from interaction and negotiations of meaning within a group of individuals in the language learning context. This concept is epistemologically opposed to Krashen's (1985) notion of language learners being "independent language-processing devices with a set of predefined individual differences that alternatively support or constrain the processor" (Kinginger, 2001: 421). Sawyer (2002) touched upon these epistemological tensions in the area of sociocultural theory, noting that

> learning involves a transformation of the social practices of the entire group, and thus cannot be reduced to an analysis of what any one participant in the group does or knows … sociocultural method focuses on situated social practices, and denies that one can study individuals or social contexts separately. (p. 284)

Airasian & Walsh (1997) reminded us that while the construction of knowledge by learners is presumed, one must also consider what exactly is constructed and whether it aligns with the course objectives. That is, while constructivism can provide a framework for study, it does not encompass all that is involved with the act of knowing. For instance, Deng, Li, & Lu (2018) sought to understand how first-year teacher education students in a

Hong Kong university employed Web 2.0 tools, particularly wikis, in support of group work. The results showed a disconnect between the instructor's intention for use of the wikis and the students' use of them. The alignment of learning and instructional outcomes must take into consideration the environment, activities, and evaluation of learners to maintain intent and organization of knowledge construction.

Language serves as a tool of development mediated by its cultural context. The Vygotskian perspective is fundamentally concerned with "the thesis that the development of human cognitive functions proceeds from the social or interpsychological plane to the individual or intrapsychological plane, with the use of symbolic, socioculturally developed tools, the most important of which is language" (Sabet et al., 2013: 1894). Writing, in particular, is considered to be "one of the most important and challenging skills which involves a complicated process of generating ideas and translating them into written symbols" (p. 1893). Within sociocultural theory exists the idea of the zone of proximal development (ZPD), which Lantolf (2000) defined as "the difference between what a person can achieve when acting alone and what the same person can accomplish when acting with support from someone and/or cultural artifacts" (p. 17). Turuk (2008) also added to the understanding of ZPD by its "higher level of potential development as determined through problem solving under adult guidance or in collaboration with more capable peers" (p. 249). The ZPD has become an area of research in and of itself in that the prescribed interactions between instructor and student are no longer considered the only relationship in the learning process. The positioning of expert, either singular or collective, and novice in the act of negotiation and the role of the environment in ameliorating knowledge provides a more holistic and realistic model to investigate (Reichert & Liebscher, 2012). This type of dyadic interaction engages all participants to use language as a tool of mediation and subsequent internalization.

Scaffolding, per Vygotsky's perspective, is necessary for growth in the ZPD of the learner (Lantolf, 2000). The correlation between the level of competence and the level of challenge progresses in a positively skewed fashion to where the learner will ultimately be able to achieve an objective independently. Scaffolding provides the means of support for progression, which can occur as students ask questions and support one another in their abilities (Smith, 2007). In addition, in this type of environment, the learner may feel more engaged and motivated to learn, encouraging him or her to take on challenges through deep learning and discovery to the point of autonomy and realization of the objective. Hatch (1978) argued that conversations serve as the basis of language learning and evolution of "how to carry out conversation and that syntactic constructions develop out of conversation" (as cited in Foley, 1994: 101). In a mutual scaffolding situation, as provided in de Guerrero & Villamil's (2000) study, the expert supports the learner in the construction of phrases with no syntax error(s) whereupon the learner [receiver] recognizes these structures, which, in turn, leads to their appropriate use.

Dillenbourg (1999) cautioned that collaborative learning is neither a single mechanism nor a method but rather a "situation in which particular forms of interaction among people are expected to occur, which would trigger learning mechanisms, but there is no guarantee that the expected interactions will actually occur" (p. 5). Collaborative learning aims to provide scaffolding through social interaction either among students or between students and an instructor; it essentially assists students in advancing through the ZPD, defined as: "the distance between the actual developmental level as determined by independent problem solving and the level of potential development as determined through problem solving under adult guidance or in collaboration with more capable peers" (Vygotsky, 1978: 86). Simply put, "collaborative learning means working together towards a common goal" (Giannopoulos, 2015: 176–177). Placing collaborative learning into the context of second language acquisition, the exchange of ideas makes the negotiation of meaning possible (Pica, 1994; Yang, 2016).

By nature, collaborative learning highlights the interdependence between individuals and the social process in co-constructing knowledge in social settings (Warschauer, 1998). In turn, this creates opportunities to develop students' cognition when actively communicating with more proficient peers and thereby expanding their conceptual potential (de Guerrero & Villamil, 2000). DiNitto (2000) wrote that successful scaffolding depends on numerous factors, including students' prior knowledge, understanding of the task, and underlying values and beliefs about teaching and learning, amongst others. Gonulal & Loewen (2018) reminded us that applying scaffolding techniques effectively can be challenging. That is, they go beyond mere support; they are dependent upon collaboration as well as a priori understanding of where students are in their ZPD. As such, not all students respond to scaffolding equally; thus, preparation for the transfer of responsibility for learning to the student needs to be specific to the learner.

Project-based learning entered into the educational field in the later part of the 20th century as a means to make learning more student-centered and meaningful and in response to the need for the development of critical thinking skills in students (Kokotsaki et al., 2016). Poonpon's study (2011) investigated the implementation of project-based learning in a language classroom to encourage learners to apply their language skills and knowledge of their specific field of study in order to complete a task. The study inquired into how project-based learning may enhance their four skills of English (i.e., listening, speaking, reading, and writing). Using a semi-structured interview, the researchers elicited students' opinions and qualitatively analyzed the responses, finding that such an approach was effective in enhancing the learners' English skills. Another study conducted by Gibbes & Carson (2014) investigated project-based language learning at a university in Ireland using Activity Theory (Leontiev, 1978), a derivative of Vygotsky's (1997) concept of instrumental activity connecting the external world with human beings' internal worlds. Mixed results in learning outcomes displayed inequities in the amount of effort put forth in project completion, perceived lack of time due to community and regulation mediation of the project, and the level of capability to meet project module outcomes by assessing performance in the target language.

2.2 Computer-Mediated Learning with Web 2.0 Tools

Warschauer (1998: 133) viewed "interaction as socialization, interaction as speech activity, and interaction as apprenticeship." Interaction encompasses sociocultural perspectives as it pertains to language learning in computer-mediated communicative learning environments (CMC). Socialization in CMC offers electronic, virtual communication as its derivative, showcasing a normative behavior in the 21st century (Edwards, 2014; Slavkov, 2015). In addition, "the possibility of using computer-mediated communication as a vehicle for expressive talk should be beneficial to self-regulation" (Warschauer, 1998: 134). Students may take the time and effort necessary to compose electronic communications without interrupting other participants, supporting self-regulation. St. John & Cash (1995) proposed a model that is integrable, where intermediate-high learners in German, as identified according to the American Council on the Teaching of Foreign Languages (ACTFL) proficiency guidelines (see Table 8.1), systematically studied new vocabulary and phrases via e-mail communications. The researchers found that this type of linguistic engagement supported language learners in their second language development as they received, interpreted, and utilized language systems (e.g., syntax, semantics), resulting in their ability to become more fashioned contributors in both face-to-face and asynchronous online interactions (Warschauer, 1995; Swain et al., 2002).

With the proliferation of interactive computer-mediated communication and learning, the use of online forums, particularly Web 2.0 tools, allows students to virtually engage with others and has become a common trend in language learning (Fornara & Lomicka, 2019; Lee, 2010; Liu et al., 2015; Wang & Vásquez, 2012). In terms of practical utility, Web 2.0 tools allow "users to work together to construct a knowledge base" (Giannopoulos, 2015: 177). Compared to the Web 1.0 concept where users would glean information from sources from the internet, Web 2.0 orients the user to interact and engage with the resources; "people have become active participants and content creators" (p. 177), thus creating opportunities for them to share and create content of their own. This shift in user interaction rather than transaction signifies a dynamic orientation shift, whereby democratic participation and technical skills become more accessible (Collis & Moonen, 2008).

Table 8.1. ACTFL Proficiency Standards, adapted from "ACTFL Proficiency Levels," by The American Council on the Teaching of Foreign Languages (ACTFL), 2012

Distinguished	Can reflect on a wide range of global issues and highly abstract concepts, use persuasive hypothetical discourse, and tailor language to a variety of audiences
Superior	Can support opinion, hypothesize, discuss topics concretely and abstractly, and handle linguistically unfamiliar situation
Advanced (high, mid, low)	Can narrate and describe in all major time frames and handle a situation with a complication
Intermediate (high, mid, low)	Can create with language, ask and answer simple questions on familiar topics, and handle a simple situation or transaction
Novice (high, mid, low)	Can communicate with formulaic and rote utterances, lists, and phrases

The subsequent transformation from the static Web 1.0 experience has allowed students to access and customize "platforms for sharing and joint content creation" (Kluhal, Gybas, & Kostolányová, 2016: 83); however, these tools are accompanied by evident limitations. Wang & Vásquez's (2012) meta-analytic review of Web 2.0 tools and second language learning identified several disadvantages. For example, learners' frustrations in distinguishing standard and nonstandard forms of the foreign language from an authentic blog environment (Lee, 2006) and wanting to develop oral communication skills from vlogs in lieu of growth in reading and writing in the target language (Pinkman, 2005). Language learners may also need support by the instructor on how to navigate and effectively interact with other learners online (Dippold, 2009; Ducate & Lomicka, 2008). Ultimately, the instructor or curriculum developer must evaluate the usefulness of such Web 2.0 tools (see Table 8.2) and decide if they can effectively serve as a means to achieve learning objectives (Nemec, 2011).

2.3 Utilizing ePortfolios

Technological advancements in web-based applications have become more prominent amongst higher education institutions. The integration of ePortfolios into the curriculum is seen to "have a greater potential to alter higher education at its very core than any other technology application we've known thus far" (Rhodes, 2011: 7). Rhodes's statement is bold but makes sense when we understand what constitutes an ePortfolio. Lorenzo and Ittelson (2005: 2) define ePortfolios as "a digitized collection of artifacts including demonstrations, resources, and accomplishments that represent an individual, group, or institution." This digitalization of artifacts has the potential to provide empirical proof of how students choose to represent their learning and can document their progression. The use of ePortfolios affords students flexibility and accessibility in their learning (Blackley, Bennett, & Sheffield, 2017; Ngui, Pang, & Hiew, 2020) as well as the ability to customize the aesthetic and structure of their virtual dossier.

Table 8.2. Examples of Web 2.0 Tools

Category	Examples
Aggregators	Aggie, RSS Reader, WikiNews
Bookmark Managers	Diigo, Google Bookmarks, One Note
Classroom Tools	Animoto, Engrade, Slideshare
Collaboration	Mindomo, Skype, Twiddla, Webex
Course Management	Blackboard Learn, Google Classroom, Moodle
Office Suites	Google Docs, ThinkFree
Public Content Management	Google Sites, Weebly, WordPress
Social Media	Facebook, Pinterest, Twitter
Storage	Google Drive, Scribd, Symbaloo

This notion of personalization through a virtual portfolio includes using and/or manipulating blank and preset templates where students upload and present content. Through a project-based lens, a shift from transactional, prescribed instruction to transformational, interactive occurs to boost encouragement of students' motivation, resource access, and construct of knowledge (Frank, Lavy, & Elata, 2003).

Compared to the physical, traditional portfolio that showcases personal and professional achievements, an ePortfolio permits the creator to share more content, to address a larger audience, and to experience greater autonomy and accessibility. Paper-based portfolios are typically comprised of written material (i.e., essays and journals), whereas ePortfolios may encompass a wider variety of examples of student work, including clips, audio-visuals, and links. All of these elements, as shareable online, can reach a larger audience if desired; an ePortfolio can be constructed as public content, thus available for the world to see and from which others may learn and be inspired. Apart from limitations of internet access, the navigation of building an ePortfolio as an online hub of ample resources and artifacts, and ensuring student safety and confidentiality, an ePortfolio is indeed portable, timeless, and accessible via the World Wide Web (Barrett, 2006; Cambridge, 2010), and may serve as one's method of personal branding (Lukkarinen, 2019).

According to Goldsmith (2007), ePortfolios can enhance students' learning as well as assess learners authentically; the nature of the requirements that a student must demonstrate displays not only the autonomy and individuality of the learner (Gonzalez, 2009), but also their engagement in learning. In regard to second language acquisition, "students can become the owners of their language learning and recognize that learning has to also occur outside the classroom" (Yastibas & Yastibas, 2015: 5). Even though a final product is valuable to the learner, the integration of project-based ePortfolios as a means to assess language learning represents the learning process (Garthwait & Verrill, 2003). During this simultaneously autonomous, yet interactive process, students can participate in the continuous cycle of feedback, reflection, and adjustment via-a-vis their ePortfolios. As with paper portfolios, ePortfolios can be used to display accomplishments or to serve as an interactive platform between online users and their posted content. Yastibas & Yastibas (2015) identify the characteristics of a quality ePortfolio: (a) authenticity, (b) controllability, (c) communication, (d) dynamics, (e) personalization, (f) integration, (g) multipurpose, (h) multisource, (i) motivation, and (j) reflection. To ensure these qualities are present, one of several ways is to include communicative approaches such as vlogs (Hung, 2011) and typed blogs (Goodwin-Jones, 2003), amongst others. The social elements required to stimulate conversation, whether it be via recorder-webcam or spontaneous commentary, privilege the learner to become even more invested by not only responding to posed questions or prompts, but by sparking deeper connections. In addition to the aforementioned advantages of ePortfolios, their cost to learning ratio is advantageous (Grossek, 2009). Walti (2004) viewed ePortfolios as "available tools that are low cost (or free) and low technology" (p. 161). Online portfolios can also attract different manifestations that can be adapted for each learner. This supports the initiatives to economize student expenses by using available online formats.

This study explores the implications of implementing ePortfolios as a project-based tool of construction within a higher education setting. Through the framework of Vygotsky's sociocultural theory, concepts such as the ZPD, scaffolding, and collaborative learning are considered in the investigation of the use of the Web 2.0 tool *Weebly* as the ePortfolio medium. Through the users' interaction via computer-mediated communication and collaboration (CMC), a learner-centered discourse community governed by virtual exploration and communicative autonomy emerged, showcasing the use of language and discourse functions that went beyond the traditional foreign language classroom setting. Inspired by "open educational resources," or OERs (McMurtrie, 2017: 2), this study explores the use of ePortfolios to as a means to encourage a deeper integration of knowledge construction, guided by the following research questions:

1. *What are the implications of implementing ePortfolios in a university-level intermediate world language course through project-based learning?*
2. *In what ways can ePortfolios provide opportunities for linguistic and cultural knowledge construction in the target language?*

3 Methodology

For this study, both quantitative and qualitative data provided multiple sources of information to evaluate constructive learning in language and cultural knowledge. Apart from descriptive statistics, a basic interpretive qualitative research design was implemented through an interpretive paradigm for qualitative data collection and analysis. Merriam (2002) posited that interpretive research leads to understanding the perspectives of people through a lived phenomenon. This qualitative research method is deemed most useful in understanding students' construction of linguistic and cultural knowledge while interacting with content and peers through the creation of an ePortfolio. Framed around an underlying framework of project-based learning and Giannopoulos's (2015) implementation of *Weebly* in exploring a history topic, this study seeks to add to the research literature in constructive language learning and curriculum design in higher education.

3.1 Participants and Data Collection

This study took place in Spring 2018 in a 15-week intermediate French-level class at a comprehensive, research, public institution in the Midwest of the United States. Participants of the survey were undergraduate students (n=18) enrolled in the course to fulfill university degree requirements. The sample consisted of 11 (61%) female and seven (39%) male students. Undergraduate class statuses were reported at one (6%) first-year, seven (39%) second-year, five (28%) third-year, and five (28%) fourth-year or higher. Twelve (67%) students reported their race as Caucasian while four (22%) reported as African American, one (6%) as Asian, and one (6%) as Hispanic/Latinx. Representation of academic programs among participating students was diverse: biological sciences (17%), computer science (11%), history/political science (11%), humanities (22%), mathematics (17%), psychological sciences (11%), and undeclared (11%). Using purposive sampling (Merriam, 2002; Wiersma & Jurs, 2009) of undergraduate students enrolled full-time at the institution in an intermediate French-level course to complete graduation requirements, these participants were recruited from this course since it was in its pilot phase as part of updating and innovating the curriculum. Every student had access to a portable device to access online material and *Weebly*. All students gave implied consent upon beginning the end-of-semester 15-item Qualtrics survey used to collect data to ascertain their perceptions of project-based learning and the implementation of ePortfolios.

3.2 Procedures

On the first day of class, the instructor explained that the course would not be using a traditional textbook nor a traditional learning management system (LMS) to submit and evaluate work, but rather a *Weebly*. *Weebly* is a website creator that allows users to create and design websites, blogs, and other displayed and/or interactive environments for other users without requiring HTML coding. "Weebly is an attractive tool because of its 'drag and drop' management and the given prerogative to cloud hosting, options available for domain names, and customized designs" (Giannopoulos, 2015: 178). This website development platform is free for users with additional online features available to premium members. Overall, *Weebly* is an intuitive website development tool that is user-friendly, available in fun designs via templates or from customization tools for blank sites, and ultimately ideal for students to create an ePortfolio. A sample entry page is displayed in Figure 8.1. This new course structure required an updated curricular approach; traditional summative assessments of chapter tests and a high traffic of quizzes were replaced with additional writing assignments spaced out during the semester as well as recorded conversations to demonstrate French speaking and conversation skills. Students would actively customize and post assignments and resources to the learning module's respective page in their ePortfolios as a means of assessment of ongoing language use in written and audio-visual formats. The instructor utilized an analytic rubric specific for each formative assessment throughout the whole semester.

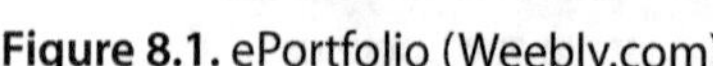

Figure 8.1. ePortfolio (Weebly.com)

Students attended in-class sessions each week in accordance with the section's scheduled meeting times, aimed for students to develop intercultural communication skills that would inform language and cultural learning. While each student engaged with content and peer-interaction in the target language, an overarching course objective focused on students' competencies in connecting and comparing their respective languages and cultures to those of the Francophone world. The instructor of the course would facilitate conversation and writing opportunities among the students as a result of having read, watched, or heard authentic resources for that class.

The course consisted of four modules, each ranging three to four weeks in length: family and friends; food; school and work; and leisure (see

Appendix for a sample course schedule). These themes revolve around building students' grammatical and cultural knowledge bases from previous French courses and preparing them to engage with specific topics that pertain to them individually. Though students discussed these general topics in and out of class, they also related the topic to their personal and/or professional experiences and elaborated on how they react, think, and feel in French. Per module, this level of engagement took the form of not only written, submitted, and corrected writings that would be later posted into their individual ePortfolio, but also through a four- to five-minute dyadic or triad video-recorded conversation of an assigned topic; culture-focused initial blogs ending with an engaging question on which fellow students would comment with at least three to four substantive sentences; one- to two-minute monologue vlogs reacting to cultural differences between francophone countries and the United States (e.g., talking about personal family values compared to learned family values in France); an accumulated vocabulary list of at least 10 newly-learned terms with personal definitions and a student-created phrase that demonstrated understanding of the word (e.g., *bouffer* [to eat] – *chercher un burger à MacDo* [to get a burger at McDonald's]; *Avant que mon pote et moi ayons assisté au match, nous avions bouffé du fast-food* [Before my friend and I attended the game, we had eaten a quick meal of fast-food meal]); and at least two additional resources not provided from the curriculum that the student found useful in learning more about that module.

3.3 Data Analysis

Descriptive coding (Saldaña, 2016) was employed to summarize themes that emerged from students' responses to Likert scale and open-ended survey questions. The decision to analyze the data as such was based on the hope that there would be common themes throughout the content of the entirety of the dataset. To improve inter-rater reliability (Armstrong et al., 1997), the researchers read and analyzed the data independently prior to meeting to discuss each researcher's respective findings in surfaced themes as discovered through descriptive coding. Coding the content revolved around common statements and words repeated throughout the dataset, then directly related to the research questions. Once each researcher had reviewed their data, both researchers came together to discuss similar and any outlier themes. To maintain credibility and dependability during the data analysis process, the researchers acknowledged research bias through researcher reflexivity and disconfirming evidence (Creswell & Miller, 2000).

4 Results and Discussion

Both descriptive quantitative and qualitative data are addressed to respond to the research questions. A 5-point Likert scale (1=Strongly Disagree to 5=Strongly Agree) was used to ascertain students' perspective on language comfortability in communicating about the modular topics, as well as identify students' learning of cultural comparisons between self and French culture (see Table 8.3).

Table 8.3. Student Perceptions of ePortfolio Assignments

Selected Statements of the Survey	Mean
Logistics	
1. I prefer not to have a textbook for this course because other material helps me learn.	4.6
Linguistic and Cultural Knowledge	
2. The course made me more aware of cultural differences in the American and Francophone worlds. [Cultural Knowledge]	4.3
3. As a result of the **Family/Friends module**, I feel like I can comfortably speak/write about my family and friends in French. [Linguistic Knowledge]	4.2
4. As a result of the **Family/Friends module**, I recognize cultural differences between my culture and French culture in regard to family and friends. [Cultural Knowledge]	4.4
5. As a result of the **Food module**, I feel like I can comfortably speak/write about food-related topics that interest me. [Linguistic Knowledge]	4.3
6. As a result of the **Food module**, I recognize cultural differences between my culture and French culture in regard to food. [Cultural Knowledge]	4.4
7. As a result of the **School/Work module**, I can comfortably speak/write about school- and work-related topics in French. [Linguistic Knowledge]	4.3
8. As a result of the **School/Work module**, I recognize cultural differences between my culture and French culture regarding school and work. [Cultural Knowledge]	4.6
9. As a result of the **Leisures module**, I can comfortably speak/write about leisure-related topics in French. [Linguistic Knowledge]	4.2
10. As a result of the **Leisures module**, I recognize cultural differences between my culture and French culture regarding leisure. [Cultural Knowledge]	4.3

4.1 Open Educational Resource Cost-Efficiency

The creation of an online community within a university-level course sometimes occurs within an LMS, supplemented with additional material that students need to purchase (e.g., textbooks, reference texts). Contemporary higher education best practices are now taking concerns in student expenses into account, leading to changes in attitudes and attention to equitable student learning, such as cost efficiency (Kaatrakoski, Littlejohn, & Hood, 2017; Walti, 2004). From the quantitative survey results, students demonstrated a high level of agreement ($\bar{x}$=4.6) in not having a textbook in their intermediate-level French course, but rather using other resources to engage in constructing linguistic and cultural knowledge. One student's comment highlights the appreciation for the depth that was offered by using an ePortfolio in lieu of a traditional textbook:

> I really enjoyed not having a textbook for this class. I feel as though when we had the online work I bs'd my way through it and didn't learn anything. It was just repeating exactly what was in the book and I didn't learn anything. This class I learned way more about how to actually speak the language and what is pertinent in the French culture not just what book French says.

4.2 Growth in Constructing Linguistic and Cultural Knowledge

Descriptive coding was used to explore the open-ended responses from the survey. The researchers did find discursive reference to various key concepts associated with sociocultural theory. These concepts were the ZPD, scaffolding, computer-mediated communication and collaboration, and intercultural knowledge.

Students did acknowledge growth within their ZPD. One student noted:

> I really enjoyed that we got to revisit a topic we were exposed to in 101 and 102. It helped me to feel more confident in what I was doing but by going deeper into the topic I was still able to learn much more about the topic as well as cultural differences, which we had only barely touched on previously.

In this instance, the student writes of deeper understanding or knowledge construction in this context. Wells (1999: 127) identified three important characteristics that give scaffolding its educational features:

1. The conversational nature of the learning discourse by which the learners construct their knowledge,

2. The importance of the categories of activities in which knowledge is embedded, where scaffolding emerged as one of the ways that this movement within the ZPD occurred, and
3. The role and type of the teaching artifacts that mediate the process of knowing.

Identifying the usefulness of teaching artifacts and guidance from the [instructor] expert, another student wrote:

> During the school and work module, at first I thought it was going to be tricky to talk about. However [the instructor] is always wonderful giving us a basic outline to go off of. School was actually kind of interesting to talk about because everyone comes from a different educational background and I think that is great!

The graphic organizer of a basic outline provided by the instructor and the subsequent discussion that took place demonstrates scaffolding as a means to encourage knowledge construction.

> Leisures was such a fantastic topic also! I love to travel and it is so amazing to share my experiences with others, as well as receiving feedback from other students where they have been! One day I would absolutely love to travel to France and what keeps me wanting to go is whenever I hear others talk about how much fun they had on their trip and all the beautiful sights to see and delicious food to eat!

4.3 Engaging in Computer-Mediated Community Learning

Students generally viewed the implementation of ePortfolios favorably. In an effort to establish an online community through an OER (*Weebly*), this study echoes the importance of social capital in reference to a stock of active, voluntary connections among people (Cohen & Prusak, 2001). Putnam (2001), a large contributor to the understanding and integration of social capital, serves as a driving framework in establishing a virtual learning community (Daniel, Schwier, & McCalla, 2003). As an embedded learning opportunity while creating an ePortfolio, students have the opportunity to integrate their reflections that not only align with course requirements, but also in their life-wide learning (Chen, 2009). Life-wide learning – advanced learning from formal contexts (i.e., university courses) through community engagement (Cambridge, 2008) – is an incentive of creating a community and a sense of working together while sharing tangible evidence of progress. One student wrote:

> I like the portfolio a lot! I think it is a great way to put all of our work together and see our progress. I did not like the video blogs because I felt as though I was just reading a script because I was too nervous to just speak. I think commenting on others blog posts is great because it makes us feel like a whole class. I like the additional resources because they give the topic more personal depth.

The computer-mediated communication and peer collaboration feature was highly supported by the students: 57% indicated that their work in small groups facilitated their learning. The students enjoyed sharing real and relevant information about themselves with their peers:

> I loved talking about my family and where I come from. My town is not very big and so coming to this university is quite the experience. Also, I love to learn about other individuals and their families. I am a people person to the max. In addition, I think it is a great idea to share who your best friend is or why they are. This helps you understand why you care about them the way you do and why you are best friends with one another.

Another wrote:

> This was a great module. I liked learning about my future profession and what it would be called. I liked learning how to discuss the classes I am taking with other students. This was a well taught module and it really kept my interest.

One of the stronger aspects of student perceptions of knowledge construction was that of intercultural competence (see Table 8.3). Many comments from the students addressed this particular content area:

> I liked the cultural comparisons about family punishments and upbringings. I felt like I took something away and that stands out to me. I feel comfortable talking about family and friends in French, that was probably the easiest causerie to do, so that was a good initial start for those.

Another stated:

> Diversity among students is wonderful because it makes it that more interesting to learn about one another. Work was even a good topic to touch basis on because there are some students who bust their butts during the school year, just to pay their bills. I love learning about peoples' jobs because I like to know how their work environment differs from mine.

A third commented:

> I found it very interesting on how the schools/workplaces cooperate with their students/employees. What they do, how they react, the benefits given. It was a big cultural difference compared to America.

One pondered:

> I was intrigued how this module would play out when introduced to us at the beginning of the semester as it is so vast. I really enjoyed it, more than I thought I would, as it was more centered on us as people and not just cookie cutter leisures. The cultural differences here really shined through and were quite thought provoking as it not only taught us about the differences between nations but it also caused us to reflect on our own ideas, which I would really like to applaud you [the instructor] for.

4.4 Learners' Feedback on Thematic Modules and ePortfolios

The implementation of ePortfolios in this intermediate French course was the first time such an instrument had been used in this setting. As a result, the researchers were especially interested in suggestions from students. First, because of the unfamiliar format, it is helpful for the instructor to explicitly go over and model expectations. One student offered:

> My biggest issue with the first module was that I was a little confused by the syllabus for the blog part of this module. It might be beneficial to go over exactly what is needed for the blog when going over the first module.

Also, the issue of time was brought up by several students. One of the survey open-ended responses concluded:

> I wish that this module would have been given more time. This was a fun experience getting to discuss my free time with my classmates. The longer that this class has gone on, the more and more it feels less like work when I'm having a conversation with my classmates. By the final class I was able to tell jokes in French with the same timing that I have in English (which was my main goal for the class). I think this was a good topic to end on, but could have been given a little more room to blossom.

The modules themselves enticed students to go even further in their construction of knowledge. For instance,

> I found this to be the most informative module in this course. I really learned a lot about the French culture in both school and work. The second redaction (where we created a CV français) was my favorite redaction of the course! I would love to see the course go a little more in depth with talking about our own work experiences so that if I were to go to France one day, I could more efficiently communicate about work.

Some students noted that the four modules were too condensed and expedited, thus unable to truly grab a hold and make sense of the language and culture. Heckendorn (2002) explains that project-based learning requires much more time to complete, thus optimizing the end-product and learning experience of the student.

Several students voiced an inconvenience and challenge in their attempt to make sense of integrated artifacts in French. For example, one student shared, "The articles, videos, songs [about family and friends] were too advanced for our level. I did not feel that I learned anything from this module." While echoing the remarks of Dippold (2009) and Ducate & Lomicka (2008) on their research findings of students needing assistance in navigating advanced technology such as Web 2.0 tools, one student's remark on vlogs stressed,

> Written blogs helped because they were active application of the reading materials and lectures. Video blogs were good in the sense of helping us with our speaking, but without active feedback, I think it was something I did to fulfill the assignment but not to learn from.

As a result of these suggestions, the researchers propose several modifications to the implementation of ePortfolios after its pilot introduction. One recommendation includes fewer modules (and accompanying assignments) so that there is more time to go more in-depth with the topic. There should be a conscious effort to align all of the assignments so that one scaffolds the next. For instance, the short writings can be used to help prepare the student for the vlog. The length of the vlogs should be reduced to two to three minutes to facilitate more natural and spontaneous conversation, followed by instructional guidance on how to react to video blogs more constructively (e.g., video responses).

5 Conclusions, Limitations, and Future Studies

The current study has explored the implications of implementing project-based learning through ePortfolios in a university-level world language course. In sum, ePortfolios proved to be a viable and popular instrument for students and for assessment of their projects (Gülbahar & Tinmaz, 2006). Through the use of student-driven projects central to the curriculum (Thomas, 2000), participating students appreciated the cost-effectiveness of not having to buy a textbook and not having to come to a designated place for their work. Future uses of ePortfolios should be careful as instructors are charged with explaining expectations for usage while navigating projects as a means to construct knowledge and promote an interactive community of learners. The assignments in each module should be used as a means to scaffold linguistic and cultural themes. Content should be within the zone of proximal development of intermediate-low to intermediate-mid language learners as outlined by ACTFL. Intermediate students should be given numerous reasons to personally connect to the material and its presentation. Mutual peer collaboration should be promoted in ways that are real and relevant. ePortfolios provide opportunities for such linguistic and cultural knowledge construction in the target language as supported by the responses to the survey. Of particular note, ePortfolios in this instance strengthened the students' intercultural awareness and appreciation.

The current study has focused on the area of knowledge construction with ePortfolios; suggestions for further research could address other factors in language acquisition such as instances of social mediation and interaction. An additional study could highlight aspects of individual portfolios in addition to the survey. Test scores, writing samples, or other examples of student work could also serve as empirical evidence of knowledge construction in linguistic and cultural knowledge. A follow-up study could make the suggested changes to see their impact.

In conclusion, language learning has evolved in the sense of how teachers engage materials and the students. In a digital age, students have become more susceptible to engaging in online learning and constructing knowledge through a virtual realm (Gülbahar & Tinmaz, 2006). Through project-based learning, in particular using ePortfolios as an assessment tool, students showcase their observed second language learning. Additionally, they practice and become familiar with their autonomous, self-regulated interaction with digital material and with others in a collaborative, computer-mediated platform like *Weebly*. Growth in written and oral communications via website development affords students the opportunity to enhance their growth not only as language learners, but also as contributors to a virtual environment, thus preparing them to rightfully participate in both online and real-world societies.

Appendix

Sample Course Calendar (First Module: Family/Friends)

CALENDRIER DU COURS				
Module	**Semaine**	**Séance**	**En classe**	**Devoirs**
1 La famille et les amis	1	1	Introduction au cours *** Regardez le programme chez vous	Devoir court 1
		2	Écoutons les interviews d'autres personnes sur la rue (video) *** Partageons nos propres perceptions de la famille (en jeu, en groupes)	Devoir court 2 *** Lisez l'article sur la famille française
	2	3	Discutons l'article que vous avez lu (Il ne faut pas tout comprendre, mais utilisez les questions qui vont vous guider!)	Regardez le podcast sur la famille en ligne *** Devoir court 3
		4	Échangeons nos idées sur les différences culturelles entre: la France, l'Espagne et les États-Unis *** Commençons à aborder le sujet de l'éducation positive	Lisez l'article en ligne sur la bonne/mauvaise education
		5	Approfondissons notre compréhension de l'éducation positive	Devoir court 4 *** Lisez l'article sur les styles parentaux en ligne *** Regardez la vidéo en ligne ---------------------------------- DATE LIMITE pour les points de bonus pour votre première version du portfolio (*Accueil* et *Mon Profil*) cette séance
	3	6	Citons des exemples personnels à propos des rapports parent-enfant	Regardez le vidéoclip de l'amitié (Les paroles sont disponibles en ligne avec la vidéo.)

		7	Parlons de l'amitié et des amis: Qu'est-ce que ça veut dire? *** Analysons les paroles de la chanson	Reregardez et finissez l'analyse de la chanson *** Rédaction 1
1 La famille et les amis	3	8	Finissons l'analyse des paroles *** Persistons à en découvrir: Que feriez-vous pour votre meilleur(e) ami(e)? (C'est une bonne idée de noter les mots que vous ne connaissez/comprenez pas.)	Lisez l'article sur le concept d'un(e) meilleur(e) ami(e) *** Devoir court 5 *** Conversation entre partenaires
	4	9	Trouvons le sens d'un(e) vrai(e) ami(e), en commençant à vous écouter (1 minute à l'oral)	Créez des questions d'entrevue à poser à quelqu'un(e) en classe (Considérez à écrire des questions qui vous donneront un sens de leur vie et de leurs intérêts)
		10	Lions d'amitié avec quelqu'un en classe: Vous vous entendriez bien?	Rédaction 2
		11	Parlons des amis ET de la famille. Y-a-t-il un équilibre entre les deux?	Apportez votre ordinateur pour bosser votre portfolio
	5	12	Terminons le module et travaillons sur les éléments du portfolio	Faites référence à la grille de portfolio (EN ANGLAIS: Everything for Module 1 is to be posted on your *Famille/Amis* page, including corrected redactions, conversation, blogs, your comments on other students' blog posts, your personal dictionary/definitions, and other resources with logic.)

NOTE: Branding of the university and its learning management system have been removed for confidentiality purposes.

References

Airasian, P., & Walsh, M. (1997). Constructivist cautions. *The Phi Delta Kappan*, 78(6), 444–449.

American Council on the Teaching of Foreign Languages. (2012). *ACTFL proficiency guidelines 2012*. Retrieved from https://www.actfl.org/sites/default/files/guidelines/ACTFLProficiencyLevels11x17withFunctions_0.pdf

Armstrong, D., Gosling, A., Weinman, J., & Marteau, T. (1997). The place of inter-raterreliability in qualitative research: An empirical study. *Sociology*, 31(3), 597–606. https://doi.org/10.1177/0038038597031003015

Atkinson, D. (2002). Toward a sociocognitive approach to second language acquisition. *The Modern Language Journal*, 86(4), 525–545. https://doi.org/10.1111/1540-4781.00159

Barrett, H. C. (2001). Electronic portfolios. In *Educational technology; An encyclopedia*. https://electronicportfolios.com/portfolios/encyclopediaentry.htm

Barrett, H. C. (2006). Using electronic portfolios for classroom assessment. *Connected Newsletter*, 13(2), 4–6.

Beckett, G. H. (2006). Project-based second and foreign language education. In G. H. Beckett, & P. C. Miller (Eds.), *Project-based second and foreign language education: Past, present, and future* (pp. 3–16). Charlotte, NC: Information Age Publishing.

Biggs, J. (1996). Enhancing teaching through constructive alignment. *Higher Education*, 32, 347–364. https://doi.org/10.1007/BF00138871

Blackley, S., Bennett, D., & Sheffield, R. (2017). Purpose-built, web-based professional portfolios: Reflective, developmental and showcase. *Australian Journal of Teacher Education*, 42(5), 1–16. https://doi.org/10.14221/ajte.2017v42n5.1

Cambridge, D. (2008). Audience, integrity, and the living document: eFolio Minnesota and lifelong and lifewide learning with ePortfolios. *Computers & Education*, 51, 1227–1246. https://doi.org/10.1016/j.compedu.2007.11.010

Cambridge, D. (2010). *E-portfolios for lifelong learning and assessment*. San Francisco: Jossey-Bass.

Chen, H. (2009). Using ePortfolios to support lifelong and lifewide learning. In D. Cambridge, B. Cambridge, & K. B. Yancey (Eds.), *Electronic portfolios 2.0: Emergent research on implementation and impact* (pp. 29–35). Sterling, VA: Stylus.

Cohen, D., & Prusak, L. (2001). *In good company: How social capital makes organizations work*. Boston, MA: Harvard Business School Press.

Collis, B., & Moonen, J. (2008). Web 2.0 tools and processes in higher education: Quality perspectives. *Educational Media International*, 45(2), 93–106. https://doi.org/10.1080/09523980802107179

Creswell, J. W., & Miller, D. L. (2000). Determining validity in qualitative inquiry. *Theory into Practice*, 39(3), 124–130. https://doi.org/10.1207/s15430421tip3903_2

Daniel, B., Schwier, R., & McCalla, G. (2003). Social capital in virtual learning communities and distributed communities of practice. *Canadian Journal of Learning and Technology*, 29(3), 113–139. https://doi.org/10.21432/T21S4R

de Guerrero, M. C. M., & Villamil, O. S. (2000). Activating the ZPD: Mutual scaffolding in L2 peer revision. *The Modern Language Journal*, 84(1), 51–68. https://doi.org/10.1111/0026-7902.00052

Deng, L., Li, S. C., & Lu, J. (2018). Supporting collaborative group projects with Web 2.0 tools: A holistic approach, *Innovations in Education and Teaching International*, 55(6), 724–734. https://doi.org/10.1080/14703297.2017.1321494

Dillenbourg, P. (1999). What do you mean by collaborative learning? In P. Dillenbourg (Ed.), *Collaborative-learning: Cognitive and computational approaches* (pp. 1–19). Amsterdam: Elsevier.

DiNitto, R. (2000). Can collaboration be unsuccessful? A sociocultural analysis of classroom setting and Japanese L2 performance in group tasks. *The Journal of the Association of Teachers of Japanese*, 34(2), 179–210. https://doi.org/10.2307/489553

Dippold, D. (2009). Peer feedback through blogs: Student and teacher perceptions in an advanced German class. *ReCALL*, 21(1), 18–36. https://doi.org/10.1017/S095834400900010X

Ducate, C. L., & Lomicka, L. L. (2008). Adventures in the biosphere: From blog readers to blogwriters. *Computer Assisted Language Learning*, 21(1), 9–28. https://doi.org/10.1080/09588220701865474

Edwards, S. (2014). Towards contemporary play: Sociocultural theory and the digital consumerist context. *Journal of Early Childhood Research*, 12(3), 219–233. https://doi.org/10.1177/1476718X14538596

Finkbeiner, C. (2000). Handlungsorientierter Unterricht (Holistic and action-oriented learning and teaching). In M. Byram (Ed.), *Routledge encyclopedia of language learning and teaching* (pp. 255–258). London: Routledge.

Foley, J. (1994). Key concepts in ELT: Scaffolding. *ELT Journal*, 48(1), 101–102. https://doi.org/10.1093/elt/48.1.101

Fornara, F., & Lomicka, L. (2019). Using visual social media in language learning to investigate the role of social presence. *CALICO Journal*, 36(3), 184–203. https://doi.org/10.1558/cj.37205

Frank, M., Lavy, I., & Elata, D. (2003). Implementing the project-based learning approach in an academic engineering course. *International Journal of Technology and Design Education*, 13, 273–288. https://doi.org/10.1023/A:1026192113732

Garthwait, A., & Verrill, J. (2003). E-portfolios: Documenting student progress. *Science and Children*, 40(8), 22–27.

Giannopoulos, D. (2015). Italian presence in the Dodecanese 1912–1943: Teaching a history topic in Weebly environment. *Procedia Computer Science*, 65, 176–181. https://doi.org/10.1016/j.procs.2015.09.106

Gibbes, M., & Carson, L. (2014). Project-based language skills: An activity theory analysis. *Innovation in Language Learning and Teaching*, 8(2), 171–189. https://doi.org/10.1080/17501229.2013.793689

Goldsmith, D. J. (2007). Enhancing learning and assessment through e-portfolios: A collaborative effort in Connecticut. *New Directions for Student Services*, 119, 31–42. https://doi.org/10.1002/ss.247

Gonulal, T., & Loewen, S. (2018). Scaffolding technique. In J. I. Liontas (Ed.), *The TESOL encyclopedia of English Language Teaching* (Vol. 1, pp. 1–5). New York: John Wiley & Sons, Inc. https://doi.org/10.1002/9781118784235.eelt0180

Gonzalez, J. A. (2009). Promoting students' autonomy through the use of the European Language Portfolio. *ELT Journal*, 63(4), 373–382. https://doi.org/10.1093/elt/ccn059

Goodwin-Jones, B. (2003). Emerging technologies: Blogs and wikis: Environments for on-line collaboration. *Language Learning & Technology*, 7(2), 12–16.

Grosseck, G. (2009). To use or not to use web 2.0 in higher education? *Procedia Social and Behavioral Sciences*, 1(1), 478–482. https://doi.org/10.1016/j.sbspro.2009.01.087

Gülbahar, Y., & Tinmaz, H. (2006). Implementing project-based learning and e-portfolio assessment in an undergraduate course. *Journal of Research on Technology in Education*, 38(3), 309–327. https://doi.org/10.1080/15391523.2006.10782462

Hall, J. K. (1995). "Aw, man, where you goin'?": Classroom interaction and the development of L2 interactional competence. *Issues in Applied Linguistics*, 6(2), 37–62.

Hatch, E. M. (1978). Discourse analysis and second language acquisition. In E. M. Hatch (Ed.), *Second language acquisition: A book of readings* (pp. 401–435). New York: Newbury House.

Heckendorn, R. B. (2002). Building a Beowulf: Leveraging research and department needs for student enrichment via project based learning. *Computer Science Education*, 12(4), 255–273. https://doi.org/10.1076/csed.12.4.255.8620

Hung, S. T. (2011). Pedagogical applications of vlogs: An investigation into ESP learners' perceptions. *British Journal of Educational Technology*, 42(5), 736–746. https://doi.org/10.1111/j.1467-8535.2010.01086.x

Kaatrakoski, H., Littlejohn, A., & Hood, N. (2017). Learning challenges in higher education: An analysis of contradictions within Open Educational Practices. *Higher Education*, 74(4), 599–615. https://doi.org/10.1007/s10734-016-0067-z

Kinginger, C. (2001). I + 1 ≠ ZPD. *Foreign Language Annals*, 34(5), 417–425. https://doi.org/10.1111/j.1944-9720.2001.tb02081.x

Klubal, L., Gybas, V., & Kostolányová, K. (2016). *Comparison of various forms of online instruction support*. Paper presented at Information and Communication Technologies in Education (ICTE-2016) (pp. 83–88). https://konference.osu.cz/icte/dokumenty/2016/proceedingsICTE2016.pdf

Kokotsaki, D., Menzies, V., & Wiggins, A. (2016). Project-based learning: A review of the literature. *Improving Schools*, 19(3), 267–277. https://doi.org/10.1177/1365480216659733

Krashen, S. (1985). *The input hypothesis: Issues and implications*. London: Longman.

Lantolf, J. P. (2000). *Sociocultural theory and second language acquisition*. Oxford: Oxford University Press.

Lee, J. S. (2006). Exploring the relationship between electronic literacy and heritage language maintenance. *Language Learning & Technology*, 10(2), 93–113.

Lee, L. (2010). Exploring Wiki-mediated collaborative learning: A case study in an elementary Spanish course. *CALICO Journal*, 27(2), 260–276. https://doi.org/10.11139/cj.27.2.260-276

Leontiev, A. (1978). *Activity, consciousness, personality*. New York: Prentice-Hall.

Liu, M., Abe, K., Cao, M. W., Liu, S., Ok, D. U., Park, J., & Sardegna, V. G. (2015). An analysis of social network websites for language learning: Implications for teaching and learning English as a second language. *CALICO Journal*, 32(1), 113–152. https://doi.org/10.1558/calico.v32i1.25963

Lorenzo, G., & Ittelson, J. (2005). An overview of e-portfolios. *Educause Learning Initiative*, 1–27.

Lukkarinen, A. (2019). Personal branding with an online portfolio in support of job search. Bachelor's thesis, Haaga-Helia University of Applied Sciences, Helsinki. https://www.theseus.fi/handle/10024/263709

McMurtrie, B. (2017, December 19). Use of free textbooks is rising, but barriers remain. *The Chronicle of Higher Education.* https://www.chronicle.com/article/Use-of-Free-Textbooks-Is/242086

Merriam, S. B. (2002). *Qualitative research in practice: Examples for discussion and analysis*. San Francisco: Jossey-Bass.

Nemec, P. B. (2011). Teaching tools, gadgets, and geegaws. *Psychiatric Rehabilitation Journal*, 35(2), 151–153. https://doi.org/10.2975/35.2.2011.151.153

Ngui, W., Pang, V., & Hiew, W. (2020). Designing and developing an e-portfolio for second language learners in higher education. *International Journal of Information and Education Technology*, 10(5), 362–366. https://doi.org/10.18178/ijiet.2020.10.5.1390

Pica, T. (1994). Research on negotiation: What does it reveal about second language learning conditions, processes and outcomes? *Language Learning*, 44(3), 493–527. https://doi.org/10.1111/j.1467-1770.1994.tb01115.x

Pinkman, K. (2005). Using blogs in the foreign language classroom: Encouraging learner independence. *The JALT CALL Journal*, 1(1), 12–24. https://doi.org/10.29140/jaltcall.v1n2.r2

Poonpon, K. (2017). Enhancing English skills through project-based learning. *The English Teacher*, 40, 1–10.

Putnam, R. D. (2001, December 19). The prosperous community: Social capital and public life. *The American Prospect*. https://prospect.org/infrastructure/prosperous-community-social-capital-public-life/

Reichert, T., & Liebscher, G. (2012). Positioning the expert: Word searches, expertise, and learning opportunities in peer interaction. *The Modern Language Journal*, 96(4), 599–609. https://doi.org/10.1111/j.1540-4781.2012.01397.x

Rhodes, T. L. (2011, January/February). Making learning visible and meaningful through electronic portfolios. *Change*, 43(1), 6–13. https://doi.org/10.1080/00091383.2011.538636

Sabet, M. K., Tahiri, A., & Pasand, P. G. (2013). The impact of peer scaffolding through process approach on EFL learners' academic writing fluency. *Theory and Practice in Language Studies*, 3(10), 1893–1901. https://doi.org/10.4304/tpls.3.10.1893-1901

Saldaña, J. (2016). *The coding manual for qualitative researchers*, 3rd edition. Thousand Oaks, CA: Sage.

Sawyer, R. K. (2002). Unresolved tensions in sociocultural theory: Analogies with contemporary sociological debates. *Culture & Psychology*, 8(3), 283–305. https://doi.org/10.1177/1354067X0283002

Shrum, J., & Glisan, E. (2016). *Teacher's handbook: Contextualized language instruction*, 5th edition. Boston, MA: Cengage.

Slavkov, N. (2015). Sociocultural theory, the L2 writing process, and Google Drive: Strange bedfellows? *TESL Canada*, 32(2), 80–94. https://teslcanadajournal.ca/index.php/tesl/article/view/1209/1033

Smith, H. J. (2007). The social and private worlds of speech: Speech for inter- and intramental activity. *The Modern Language Journal*, 91(3), 341–356. https://doi.org/10.1111/j.1540-4781.2007.00584.x

St. John, E., & Cash, D. (1995). German language learning via email: A case study. *ReCALL*, 7(2), 47–51. https://doi.org/10.1017/S0958344000003931

Swain, M., Brooks, L., & Tocalli-Beller, A. (2002). Peer-peer dialogue as a means of second language learning. *Annual Review of Applied Linguistics*, 22, 171–185. https://doi.org/10.1017/S0267190502000090

Thomas, J. W. (2000, March). *A review of research on project-based learning.* http://www.bobpearlman.org/BestPractices/PBL_Research.pdf

Tocaimaza-Hatch, C. C. (2015). An analysis of Spanish L2 learners' orientation through activity theory. *Foreign Language Annals*, 48(3), 491–510. https://doi.org/10.1111/flan.12148

Turuk, M. C. (2008). The relevance and implications of Vygotsky's sociocultural theory in the second language classroom. *ARECLS*, 5, 244–262.

Van Compernolle, R. A., & Williams, L. (2013). Sociocultural theory and second language pedagogy. *Language Teaching Research*, 17(3), 277–281. https://doi.org/10.1177/1362168813482933

Vygotsky, L. S. (1978). *Mind in society: The development of higher psychological process*. Cambridge, MA: Harvard University Press.

Vygotsky, L. S. (1997). The method of reflexological and psychological investigation. In R. Rieber, & J. Wollock (Eds.), *The collected works of Lev Vygotsky* (Vol. 3, pp. 35–50). New York: Plenum Press. https://doi.org/10.1007/978-1-4615-5893-4_3

Walti, C. (2004). Implementing web-based portfolios and learning journals as learner support tools: An illustration. *Learner support in open, distance and online learning environments*, 9, 157–168.

Wang, S., & Vásquez, C. (2012). Web 2.0 and second language learning: What does the research tell us? *CALICO Journal*, 29(3), 412–430. https://doi.org/10.11139/cj.29.3.412-430

Warschauer, M. (1995). *Computer-mediated collaborative learning: Theory and practice*. Honolulu: University of Hawai'i, Second Language Learning Teaching & Curriculum Center.

Warschauer, M. (1998). Interaction, negotiation, and computer-mediated learning. In A. D. V. Daleguy & M. Svensson Lyon (Eds.), *Educational technology language learning: Theoretical reflection and practical applications* (pp. 125–136). Lyon, France: National Institute of Applied Sciences, Center of Language Resources.

Wells, G. (1999). *Dialogic inquiry: Towards a sociocultural practice and theory of education*. Cambridge: Cambridge University Press.

Wertsch, J. (2007). Mediation. In H. Daniels, M. Cole, & J. Wertsch (Eds.), *The Cambridge companion to Vygotsky* (pp. 178–192). Cambridge: Cambridge University Press. https://doi.org/10.1017/CCOL0521831040.008

Wiersma, W., & Jurs, S. G. (2009). *Research methods in education: An introduction*, 2nd edition. Boston, MA: Allyn & Bacon.

Yang, X. (2016). An analysis of discourses in CLT from sociocultural theory perspective. *Theory and Practice in Language Studies*, 6(1), 194–198. https://doi.org/10.17507/tpls.0601.25

Yastibas, A. E., & Yastibas, G. C. (2015). The use of e-portfolio-based assessment to develop students' self-regulated learning in English language teaching. *Procedia Social and Behavioral Sciences*, 176, 3–13. https://doi.org/10.1016/j.sbspro.2015.01.437

About the Authors

Rebecca L. Chism is an Associate Professor of Foreign Language Pedagogy and Pedagogy Coordinator in Modern and Classical Language Studies at Kent State University, Ohio, USA. She teaches undergraduate and graduate courses in second and foreign language teaching methods and approaches. Her research interests include best practices in teaching, pre- and in-service teacher preparation, differentiated instruction, and computer mediated communication.

Evan W. Faidley is a doctoral candidate of Higher Education Administration and the Graduate Student Career Liaison and Graduate Assistant for Graduate Studies at Kent State University, Ohio, USA. He also serves as an undergraduate and Upward Bound instructor of French, as well as a graduate adjunct instructor in Higher Education Administration. Evan has over four years of experience in designing and delivering different curricula among different higher education institutional types, focusing on identity, linguistic, and cultural development through learning French. His research interests include second language acquisition, French higher education, career development, socialization of postsecondary students, and first-generation college student transitions.

PART III

Project-Based Language Learning and Social Justice

9 Transcultural Language Learning through a Cinema and Social Justice Teletandem Program

Martha Guadalupe Hernández Alvarado and
Anton T. Brinckwirth

1 Introduction

This chapter reports on the design, implementation, and outcomes of a project-based language learning (PBLL) telecollaboration program delivered jointly by a full-time lecturer and researcher at the Linguistics Department of the Universidad Autónoma del Estado de Hidalgo, Mexico, and the language lab director at Virginia Commonwealth University in Richmond, Virginia, USA. Both course instructors' linguistic and pedagogical objectives were aligned to provide their learners with authentic language immersion opportunities. This involved transcultural learning through structured teletandem interactions, weekly tasks, and a final collaborative project completed in sessions conducted off-campus without the instructor's presence.

The project was planned as an action-research study to take place across three different cycles or academic terms: Fall 2018 (July–December 2018), Spring 2019 (January–July 2019), and Fall 2019 (July–December 2019). The research was driven by intensive observation, evaluation, reflection, and documentation of the specific factors that led to the successes and hindrances of the teletandem exchanges. The project's implementation in each cycle continually informed the practice of telecollaboration throughout this study and enhanced students' learning experience in both countries. The specific aims of the project were to:

1. Provide students from both countries with the opportunity to gain cultural and linguistic knowledge through instructor-guided teletandem sessions designed to address complex social issues

presented in films and the collaboration to carry out language tasks and a final project, conducted during and at the end of the program;
2. Gain practical knowledge and experience in telecollaboration and identify ways to improve the efficacy of the practice of teletandem while increasing the number of students to benefit from its culturally and linguistically enriching palette of opportunities.

The research questions guiding the study were:

1. To what extent did the telecollaboration exchanges benefit students in terms of language and cultural learning?
2. What issues were identified that adversely impacted the student experience of teletandem?
3. What steps were taken and deemed necessary to resolve or mitigate these problems?
4. To what extent were the implemented strategies effective in enhancing the student learning experience?

2 Overview of the Research

2.1 Project-Based Language Learning (PBLL)

According to Mont & Masats (2018), the promotion of student-centered and competency-based practices in education entails adopting project-based syllabi. It encourages students to take an active role in their learning process and collaborate successfully with others to solve real-world challenges. As the authors explain, problem-solving tasks require students to harness their linguistics, interpersonal, intercultural, and cognitive abilities.

For Patton (2012: 13), "project-based learning refers to students designing, planning, and carrying out an extended project that produces a publicly exhibited output such as a product, publication or presentation." Even though teachers' approach to TBLL may be different, the British Council (2013, as cited in Thomas, 2017: 25) identifies four common elements to all project-based activities/classes/courses: (1) a central topic which all the activities drive and which drives the project towards a final objective; (2) access to means of investigation to collect, analyze, and use information; (3) plenty of opportunities for sharing ideas, collaborating, and communicating; and (4) a final product, often produced using technologies, in the form of posters, presentations, reports, videos, webpages, blogs, among others.

Dooly, Masats, & Mont (2012) state that project-based learning is an ideal tool for teachers to get students "to connect the dots" between content, language use, knowledge construction, and the development of 21st-century skills. In the context of telecollaboration, in particular, Mont & Masats (2018) argue that projects are powerful tools for developing inter-cultural competence among students from different places, giving them the opportunity to see the world from someone else's perspective.

Based on their telecollaborative project design experience, Mont & Masats (2018) suggest a series of steps for teachers to engage in PBLL tele-collaborative practices. Some of these steps involve: searching for a partner, scheduling virtual online meetings to plan together, setting SMART goals, deciding on the project outcomes, posing interesting driving questions, arranging a variety of structured tasks, choosing appropriate tools, preparing students for collaboration, providing continuous support, and deciding what and how to assess. Mont & Masats (2018) perceive planning and assessment as two complex tasks on which the project's success or failure relies. Consequently, it is vital that partner-teachers are equally motivated and committed to implementing PBLL telecollaborative programs.

2.2 Defining Telecollaboration

Online intercultural exchange (OIE), also referred to widely as telecollaboration, denotes, in the words of Lewis & O'Dowd (2016:3), "the engagement of groups of students in online intercultural interaction and collaboration with partner classes from other cultural contexts or geographical locations under the guidance of teachers or trained facilitators." This form of learning, as O'Dowd (2016a) states, has been called by many names depending on the educational context and the pedagogical focus of its practitioners. Examples of these names, as listed by O'Dowd (2016a), include e-tandem (O'Rourke, 2007), internet-mediated intercultural foreign language education (Belz & Thorne, 2006), Collaborative Online International Learning (COIL) (Rubin, 2016), virtual exchange (Helm, 2016), and teletandem (Telles, 2015; Telles & Vassallo, 2006; Vassallo & Telles, 2006). For this chapter, the terms online intercultural exchange (OIE), telecollaboration, and teletandem will be used interchangeably.

2.3 Principles of Teletandem

According to Vassallo & Telles (2006), teletandem exchanges should be guided by three main principles:

1. Languages should not be mixed: each session should consist of two parts, and each should be devoted to the practice of only one of the languages. This principle ensures that both students can communicate in the language in which they are proficient, particularly when trying to attain communicative goals that are too difficult or challenging in the target language.
2. Reciprocity: teletandem partners should take turns in acting both as a student of the target language and as a linguistic expert of the language in which each of them is proficient. As stated by Brammerts & Calvert (2003), this form of learning involves free and mutual exchange of knowledge about language and culture; therefore, both partners should benefit equally.
3. Autonomy: both partners are free to decide what, when, where, and how to study and how long they wish to do it. This principle can be interpreted differently, depending on the context in which teletandem is carried out – as part of a program in a school or university (institutional teletandem) or as a mutual agreement between individuals (independent teletandem).

Telecollaboration partners learn autonomously and are responsible for managing their learning. A teletandem language partnership is reciprocal and mutually beneficial. Students must support one another during the learning process. For a telecollaboration partnership to be successful, both learners need to be prepared and committed to setting learning goals and collaborating with their teletandem partner to achieve them. As cited in Cavalari & Aranha (2016), goal-setting is vital for motivation, a continuation of partnerships, and for the learning process itself (Cavalari, 2009, 2010; Kami, 2011; Luz, 2012; Silva, 2012).

Telles & Vassallo (2006) explain that teletandem learning can be differentiated from "mere and ordinary *chatting* mingled with corrections of grammar and lexicon" (p. 194) in two ways: (1) teletandem sessions must finish with a debriefing activity where participants reflect on the form, lexicon, and the interaction that took place during the exchange; and (2) even though the focus of teletandem is on oral production and reception, reading and writing skills can also be practiced to write accounts on the themes discussed between one session and the next.

2.4 Integrating Telecollaboration into Higher Education

Telecollaboration can be implemented in a school or university (institutional teletandem) or as a mutual agreement between individuals (independent teletandem). According to Brammerts (2002, 2003, as cited in Cavalari, 2018: 420), within institutional teletandem, telecollaboration can be carried out by learners as an individual complementary practice (non-integrated to a particular course), or it can be integrated into the foreign language curriculum for only one of the learners that participate in the exchange (semi-integrated) or for both learners (integrated).

Institutionally integrated teletandem (iiTTD) is defined by Aranha & Cavalari (2014, as cited in Cavalari & Aranha, 2016: 329) as a series of teletandem sessions that are embedded in regular lessons in a way that lessons feed and are fed by teletandem practice. For Motteram & Sharma (2009), the procedures that characterize such integration involve: (1) preparing students for iiTTD in practical and theoretical terms; (2) blending teletandem interactions and the course syllabus; and (3) implementing assessment procedures that include self-assessment, peer-assessment, and assessment by the instructor.

However, practitioners may encounter some barriers during the implementation of telecollaboration exchanges. Based on his research on practices of telecollaboration in higher education in Europe, O'Dowd (2013) identifies the following challenges for practitioners: time necessary to set and run exchanges; difficulties in integration and assessment due to institutional requirements; lack of pedagogical knowledge about how to run and integrate exchanges; teachers' lack of e-literacies and required technological knowledge; and difficulty in finding appropriate partners.

Helm (2015) found similar barriers which she classified as: time issues; lack of institutional interest, recognition, and funding; tech issues including access and teacher e-literacies; organization and size of student groups; too much of a novelty and need for pedagogic training; the need for dedicated staff; challenges in assessment or awarding of credits; difficulties in finding partners; relationship with a partner; lack of student time, motivation, and language competence; and finally, institutional constraints.

To overcome some of the problems mentioned above, O'Dowd (2013) proposes a set of strategies. These include: (1) building-up reliable and steady partnerships; (2) raising awareness and prestige of the telecollaborative exchange in the local institution and beyond; (3) using and blending telecollaboration creatively to adapt to local institutions' needs; (4) achieving credit or recognition for the students' telecollaborative work, and; (5) linking telecollaboration to broader international activity. Further, O'Dowd (2013: 53) points out that "in order for a teacher to regularly and successfully integrate online exchange into the classroom and into their institution, the activity needs to be valued and acknowledged by both teachers and the institution."

2.5 The Role of Tasks in Telecollaboration

O'Dowd & Waire (2009) claim that although there is a wide range of interpretations of what a task is in the context of second language learning, there seems to be a consensus that a task is a meaning-centered activity that is based on a learner's communicative needs and related to the real world (Levy & Stockwell, 2006). In Müller-Hartmann's own words, "historically, tasks and task design have always played an important role when designing Online Intercultural Exchanges (OIEs)" (2016: 32). According to O'Dowd & Waire (2009), telecollaborative tasks generally involve different linguistic and cultural communities, which result in the possibility of opportunities for negotiation of meaning and the exploration of different cultural perspectives. In this respect, Lätsch (2017) argues that:

> Tasks in the context of online tandem learning have to serve as a means to prepare, build up, and structure communication. They have to activate the prior knowledge of topics relevant in a tandem session and vocabulary that can be used in a specific context and according to the task object. Tasks also have to take into account the spontaneous character of language production and provide the learners with enough language material to converse fluently. (p. 59)

O'Dowd & Waire (2009) classify language tasks into three main categories that reflect the type of communicative activity that is involved in each case: (1) information exchange tasks, (2) comparison and analysis tasks, and (3) collaborative tasks. The most appropriate type of task should be selected or designed based on the context in which teletandem learning occurs, and the students' learning needs. However, Lätsch (2017) argues that rather than imposing a specific task, it is best to provide a variety of tasks and let learners decide.

According to O'Dowd (2016b), practitioners can adopt a strong or a weak approach to task design when coordinating telecollaboration projects. This decision will generally depend on the context in which telecollaboration is to be implemented, the project itself, course goals, student needs, and language proficiency. An OIE model that focuses on superficial communicative themes and lacks opportunities for collaboration, reflection, and critical evaluation, is a weak approach to telecollaborative design. Conversely, a strong approach employs tasks that promote social justice and intercultural citizenship, active collaboration, and participants' self-reflection.

2.6 Cinema, Social Justice, and Teletandem

As O'Dowd & Waire (2009) assess, the learning outcomes of telecollaborative exchanges have varied considerably. They demonstrated how online intercultural collaboration could contribute to the development of diverse areas such as learner autonomy (Schwienhorst, 2000), linguistic accuracy and fluency (Kinginger & Belz, 2005; O'Rourke, 2005; Ware & O'Dowd, 2008), intercultural awareness (Müller-Hartmann, 2000; O'Dowd, 2006; Ware, 2005), online intercultural skills (Belz & Müller-Hartmann, 2003; O'Dowd & Ritter, 2006), and electronic literacy (Hauck, 2007).

However, few studies have explored the pedagogical possibilities of blending cinema, social justice, and institutional integrated teletandem (iiTTD) into a PBLL telecollaboration program. Castillo-Scott (2018) conducted such a study with a partner school in Chile over two semesters to promote linguistic skills and address sociocultural issues among two student groups: the first, comprised of students majoring and minoring in Spanish at a Southeastern US university; and the second, a group of Chilean science and engineering students at a Chilean university.

While Castillo-Scott's project significantly informed the design and implementation of the present study, it was clear to us, as researchers, from the onset that there is no unique or best approach to PBLL telecollaborative practices. Each initiative is unique and needs to be adapted to the educational context in which it takes place, the program and course goals, and the students' learning needs.

Research studies on the use of films in language learning have revealed that films contribute to develop students' intercultural awareness and promote multilingualism (Herrero & Vanderschedlen, 2019). According to student perceptions, through cinema, they can learn colloquial English in real-life contexts and be exposed to a wide range of native speakers with different accents and dialects (Seferoğlu, 2008). Learners consider films authentic means of language learning that can help them improve their language skills and increase their cultural awareness (Albiladi, Abdeen, & Lincoln, 2018).

Castillo-Scott (2018) also states that research has provided evidence of the benefits of social justice-oriented practices for learners: students are better prepared to actively participate in a multicultural and multilingual society (Da Cruz, 2017); students develop social responsibility that makes them better participants in the world (Pratama, 2016); and students gain a better understanding of international issues as well as get interested in contributing to a better world (Kip, 2005).

Castillo-Scott (2018) paired students based on their shared interdisciplinary interests. She also provided them with guidelines that included topics, due dates, partners' contact information, and grading criteria, and suggested Web 2.0 tools and uploading procedures. Students engaged in online communication with their partners through teletandem sessions conducted outside-of-class once a month, four in total for the academic term. Students were asked to video-capture the sessions and upload them to their learning management system (LMS) for assessment. Both instructors assigned the topics of discussion for three of the sessions, and each group of students had their own set of topics according to their course goals and material. The interactions were mainly based on the social issues presented in the selected films. The fourth session was reserved for the teletandem partners to negotiate a topic of their choice.

Castillo-Scott (2018) reported that the students' perceptions of the project were overwhelmingly positive. The students considered the teletandem project an excellent opportunity to speak with native speakers of the target culture and collaborate to mentor their oral language skills. As a result of teletandem, students developed their linguistic skills, expanded their intercultural competence, and improved their confidence to interact with native or competent speakers of the target language. They viewed telecollaboration as a useful language learning technique and demonstrated they had become aware of the similarities and differences of sociopolitical issues in both countries.

On the other hand, some students reported having difficulties with the programs used to record sessions and upload them to the LMS. Other learners experienced communication problems with their teletandem partners, mainly in the context of not responding to their emails, not completing the sessions, or dropping the course. Another difficulty some students faced was the lack of vocabulary when interacting with their partners. To solve the challenges described above, Castillo-Scott (2018: 271) suggests the following:

1. Provide technical support to students throughout the program.
2. Allow flexibility to work with another partner when this need arises.
3. Prepare a list of vocabulary related to each social issue and a list of most used colloquial expressions in each target culture and disseminate it to students.
4. Remind students of the learning goals of each session.
5. Prepare students well before the meetings.
6. Hold additional open topics for students to choose from.

6. Be more flexible with the outcomes of sessions when assessing student's video-recorded sessions.

Castillo-Scott (2018) concludes that even though the sessions are carried out independently by students outside of class, it is the instructor's responsibility to ensure that they are carried out in a manner that enables students to glean the most from the opportunity.

3 Methodology

As language instructors and teletandem practitioners with 18 years of combined experience, we view teletandem as a viable strategy for students to have structured immersion and practice in the L2 with a native speaker. We also see advantages and disadvantages to delivering teletandem as a lab supplement for students in traditional language courses, or as an assigned extracurricular activity. However, there is still a wide variance in student impact and learning outcomes. The specific aims of the project were to:

1. Provide students from both countries with the opportunity to gain cultural and linguistic knowledge through instructor-guided teletandem sessions designed to address complex social issues presented in films and the collaboration to carry out language tasks and a final project, during and at the end of the program;
2. Gain practical knowledge and experience in telecollaboration and identify ways to improve the efficacy of the practice of teletandem while increasing the number of students to benefit from its culturally and linguistically enriching palette of opportunity.

3.1 Research Design

We employed an action research methodology appropriate for collecting and analyzing data to identify problems, make necessary adjustments, implement optimal solutions, and repeat the process. Our study meets the characteristics of action research as it was concerned with the identification and resolution of problems in a specific context; it was carried out collaboratively; and it was aimed at improving the current state of affairs within the educational context in which it was carried out (Burns, 2010). However, given the small population sample and the study's low internal validity, the results would not be generalizable.

We began the study with the idea that this would be an action research study with an array of mixed methods for data collection. We used an ethnographic/phenomenological approach to interpret and report the findings. Ethnography enabled us to integrate ourselves into the project to draw conclusions and make assertions about the implementation process. Phenomenology made it possible to focus on the students' teletandem experiences to shed light on the program's impact and effectiveness.

As language instructors, we wanted to optimize the telecollaboration experience for our students. As researchers, we focused on identifying problems and implementing solutions to resolve them by:

- observing teletandem implementation closely;
- identifying problems, particularly recurring errors;
- classifying errors, types of impediments, and technical failures;
- applying repetitive experimentation, identifying optimal solutions; and
- implementing change.

3.2 Research Questions

The study was ultimately concerned with finding ways to ensure that students would benefit from an optimized teletandem product. We were completely aware of specific problems that have been deemed by other teachers and students as impediments and hindrances to the teletandem implementation process. In line with the research aims, the research questions were:

- To what extent did the teletandem exchanges benefit students in terms of language and cultural learning?
- What issues were identified as trouble areas that could adversely impact a teletandem session?
- What steps were taken and deemed as necessary to resolve or mitigate these complexities?
- To what extent were the implemented strategies effective in enhancing the student learning experience?

3.3 Research Instruments

The gold standard for telecollaboration should be determined by those closest to its implementation and use – the instructors, facilitators, and students who can experience teletandem directly. These participants will develop the most informed opinion through positive and negative experiences and outcomes and by making significant observations.

Various data collection methods were therefore employed, including program evaluation questionnaires, student journals, student VoiceThread reflections in the LMS, video-recorded sessions, and an array of artifacts: images, video WhatsApp text logs, as well as our observations of student performance as teletandem facilitators.

Student journals were employed by UAEH students to keep a record of their learning process. Learners wrote their journals based on the course instructor's prompts, which asked them to express their perceptions of the teletandem program's effectiveness to develop their linguistic and cultural learning, the problems they faced in the process, and suggestions to improve the program. During each telecollaboration session, students documented their learning process and were encouraged to reflect on the overall experience.

At VCU, students used the VoiceThread application, integrated with the institution's LMS, *Blackboard*, to make brief voice recordings to express comments, opinions, and suggestions for improving teletandem at both institutions. Students also used VoiceThread to communicate with the instructor at critical intervals in the course. Through the VoiceThreads, students at VCU were able to tell the instructor how their sessions were going, how they were getting along with their partners, and generally convey thoughts and concerns about the sessions, the themes, and the final project.

The questionnaires consisted of 10 Likert scale items on the pedagogical value of teletandem for language and cultural learning, audio and video quality, and collaboration among partners. The brief questionnaire did not have the depth necessary to examine student attitudes and perspectives about teletandem, or to measure target language improvement and performance. Still, it gave students a voice and informed the researchers to make future decisions on the processes, contexts, and tools used in the program.

Finally, video-recorded sessions, images, videos, WhatsApp text logs, and our observations of student performance as teletandem facilitators were collected to document the implementation process, enabling us to identify and resolve problems, provide the necessary support to students, and make future decisions to improve the student experience of teletandem. Table 9.1 shows the research instruments employed to answer the research questions.

Table 9.1. Relationship between Research Questions and Data Collection Instruments

Research question	Data collection instruments
1. To what extent did the teletandem exchanges benefit students in terms of language and cultural learning?	Student journals Evaluation questionnaires
2. What issues were identified to impact the student experience of teletandem adversely?	Student journals Evaluation questionnaires Student VoiceThread reflections in the LMS Video-recorded sessions Researchers' observations
3. What steps were taken and deemed as necessary to resolve or mitigate these problems?	Artifacts: images, video, WhatsApp text logs Researchers' observations
4. To what extent were the implemented strategies effective in enhancing the student learning experience?	Student journals Evaluation questionnaires Student VoiceThread reflections in the LMS Video-recorded sessions Researchers' observations

3.4 Research Participants

We perceived our students not as research subjects, but as research participants. We were also participants and had a comprehensive view of all the sessions through each academic term cycle. Each semester, two groups from each university participated in the teletandem program. We used convenience sampling to select participants; that is to say, all students enrolled in our respective courses participated in the study. Despite their being linguistically and culturally different, students had many things in common: their age, academic interests, and L2 skill levels.

The UAEH students were pre-service English teachers in their second year of study. They were between 20 and 24 years of age and generally had proficiency in the B1–B2 range per the Common European Framework of Reference for Languages (CEFR). They did teletandem in the context of a learning autonomy class to become familiar with another learning mode where they could practice their language skills and learn autonomously with a partner's support. The size range of both classes in each term was 15–29 students. Table 9.2 shows the total number of students at both institutions that participated in the teletandem program in each term.

Table 9.2. Population Sample per Class in Each Term

	Cycle/Term 1 Fall 2018	Cycle/Term 2 Spring 2019	Cycle/Term 3 Fall 2019	Total
UAEH	39 (22+17)	51 (29+22)	39 (24+15)	129
VCU	36 (18+18)	40 (20+20)	36 (18+18)	112
Total	75	91	75	241

Note. The difference in the number of students in each group during each cycle meant the instructors had to make special partnering arrangements to ensure that every student had a partner.

The VCU student groups consisted of undergraduate students, mostly between 18 and 25 years of age, from various majors and backgrounds, including Spanish. Their reason for taking a 300-level Spanish Film and Conversation course was to fill part of the language requirement for their major of study or to use it toward a major or minor in Spanish. The VCU students generally had a Spanish proficiency level in the range of B1–B2 per the CEFR scale and within the range of intermediate-mid and intermediate-high per the ACTFL Proficiency Guidelines.

3.5 Project Design: Context, Processes, and Tools

Before this study, we had already developed an awareness of the connection between teletandem and international education, but we began to see other connections. One of the more compelling links had to do with principles of diversity, equity, and inclusion. Combining these tangentially relevant concepts brought an element of global citizenship to the teletandem construct that enriched students and instructors, too.

Our agreement required us to commit to a teletandem program that was mutually beneficial, completely neutral, and reciprocal. The idea was to create a safe learning space where both cultures were welcomed and could coexist without one being dominant over the other. Practicing foreign languages in teletandem brings all of the elements of sharing culture, tradition, identity, and perspective.

At the end of the teletandem program, students were required to work on a final project collaboratively. The assignment was to select a film not previously discussed and develop compelling written summaries for the selected film. The learning objective was to allow both students to write about the films and help one another edit and polish them. The UAEH students wrote a film critique in English, and the VCU students wrote a narration in Spanish for a 3-minute video montage they were required to produce for their final project. The assignments were different, but the target language (L2) immersion needs and goals were the same.

Before this study, we had already developed an awareness of the connection between teletandem and international education, but we began to see other connections. One of the more compelling links had to do with principles of diversity, equity, and inclusion. Combining these tangentially relevant concepts brought an element of global citizenship to the teletandem construct that enriched students and instructors, too.

We wanted to produce a teletandem program that was mutually beneficial, completely neutral, and reciprocal. The idea was to create a safe learning space where both cultures were welcomed and could coexist without one being dominant over the other.

At the end of the teletandem program, students were required to work on a final project collaboratively. The assignment was to select a film not previously discussed and develop compelling written summaries for the selected film. The learning objective was to allow both students to write about the films and help one another edit and polish them. The UAEH students wrote a film critique in English, and the VCU students wrote a narration in Spanish for a 3-minute video montage they were required to produce for their final project. The assignments were different, but the target language (L2) immersion needs and goals were the same.

3.5.1 Scheduling

Scheduling is a significant part of the implementation process. Basic knowledge of technology-enhanced event planning is required for any teacher or facilitator who might be contemplating telecollaboration. Behind every good teletandem program is an excellent scheduling system. The number of teletandem sessions offered during any given academic term depends on how well the partnered schools' academic calendars align. The UAEH term starts earlier and lasts longer. The one-hour time difference was not a problem, but US and Mexican holidays and Daylight Saving Time could all potentially limit the number of sessions scheduled.

Despite the differences in academic calendars between the universities, there was enough pedagogical value in teletandem to justify the allocation of a total of 8 to 10 telecollaboration sessions each term. The challenges of working around the schools' different academic calendars, national holidays, and other factors prevented us from having more than 6 lab sessions during most semesters. However, we felt that 10 sessions per term were more appropriate; therefore, some sessions were assigned as off-campus activities. We also wanted to see how students would communicate with their partners and carry out their meetings without the instructor present.

Students carried out the final sessions outside of class for two reasons:

1. To ensure flexibility in the second half of the term;
2. To create a natural flow that increased student confidence and autonomy with each session, enabling student pairs to manage their final project sessions.

We set all of the dates for on-campus teletandem to take place during class. At VCU, these dates were entered into the language center's primary calendar, a public calendar visible to VCU students and other stakeholders. For off-campus sessions, a timeframe was provided so that students could negotiate the days and times to meet with their partners.

3.5.2 The social justice themes

The social justice themes included illegal immigration, mistreatment, objectification of women, marginalization of indigenous peoples, gang violence, human trafficking, government corruption, and other topics relevant to Mexico and the United States. We were careful when addressing the topics as we did not want the sessions to become heated debates. Instead, we encouraged tolerance and respect for diversity in cultural and political beliefs. The instructors informed students that intolerant acts and gestures would not be not permitted.

The VCU instructor used a textbook titled *Cinema for Spanish Conversation*, 4th Edition (Gill, Smally, & Haro, 2014) as a basis for the films selected and presented. All but one of the movies came from this textbook. The level of Spanish, the selection of films, and depth of critical analysis were appropriate for B1–B2 learners (CEFR) and intermediate-low to intermediate-mid (ACTFL) undergraduate college students.

At the UAEH, the instructor only used the book as the basis for task design. Still, learners were encouraged to do their own research regarding the theme of each film and the language (specific vocabulary) that could be used for the interaction with their partners.

3.5.3 Telecollaborative task design

Following some of the characteristics for adopting a robust approach to telecollaborative task design (O'Dowd, 2016b), the tasks designed for the teletandem program reflected themes of social justice. They were intended to inform learners about real-world problems and promote intercultural citizenship, collaboration, and cultural self-reflection and evaluation.

Each teletandem session was carefully coordinated with task-based learning objectives. The tasks took the form of information exchange and comparison and analysis to guide learners to identify and discuss cultural perspectives and influences and give a critical analysis of the social themes in each country. The instructors were careful to connect the tasks to the film themes. Table 9.3 shows the recommendations of O'Dowd (2016b) on task design and how we integrated these concepts in the Cinema and Social Justice Teletandem Program.

Table 9.3. Building Strong Telecollaborative Task Design: Activities Integrated in the Social Justice-Themed Teletandem Sessions

O'Dowd's Recommendations	UAEH-VCU Teletandem Sessions – Cinema and Social Justice
Tasks reflect themes of social justice and intercultural citizenship.	Each on-campus lab session required students to complete communicative tasks regarding social justice issues relevant to the US and Mexico, culturally, linguistically, and socio-politically. Students collaborated on a final project, a trans-lingual review of a film through teletandem. VCU students reflected on teletandem experiences with VoiceThreads.
Tasks engage students in active collaboration together.	Tasks came mainly in the form of conversations, but students were required to exchange ideas and discuss similarities and differences.
Tasks include stages of cultural self-reflection and critical evaluation.	The student reported back to the instructor on discussions through journaling activities (UEAH) and reflective VoiceThread recordings inside the LMS (VCU). Short entries after each session took shape after 6 or 7 sessions. Students were encouraged to reflect on the effectiveness of the pedagogy and the appropriateness of the technologies used. In the third cycle, more students were fixing their own audio signal routing issues in class.
Tasks avoid stereotyping and forced culture clash.	Students were encouraged to explore different perspectives objectively and use civil discourse tone when commenting on hot-button issues. Several sessions were held at the time the US president had made disparaging remarks about Mexico. This had relevance in the themes of discussion, particularly when addressing immigration issues. The students on both sides handled these matters with maturity and respect, a sign of global citizenship.

3.5.4 Optimizing the learner partnerships for teletandem

We used Google Forms to create and disseminate a 5-item questionnaire before the first session to match language partners by simple demographic criteria. We felt it was a factor in making optimal pairings and doing everything possible to ensure students feel comfortable and have an optimal experience. Students reported their:

1. self-assessed speaking and listening skills in the L2;
2. academic major and minor, and extracurricular interests;
3. gender preference (male or female partner);
4. personal interests.

This demographic data told us much about the participants and helped us make the most suitable matches from the learners in both groups. When pairings did not work out, we went back to the original data to make adjustments. By storing the information in the same secure shared folder, we created the flexibility to make quick adjustments. The first partner-pairing forms were used in 2018. The process and questionnaire have been refined since that time, showing vast improvement in terms of the student pairings with fewer requests to change partners.

3.5.5 Preparing students for the teletandem exchange

Both student groups were debriefed about the project before the exchanges took place. Due to our research goals' phenomenological nature, it was vital to inform students about the process in detail and answer their questions in advance. We felt it was our responsibility as instructors to disclose our intentions and goals thoroughly. Thus, telling students what to expect and teaching them how to identify signs of trouble, whether technical, pedagogical, or partner-related, helped us establish a culture of cooperation and mutual respect throughout the process.

3.6 Data Collection and Analysis

The instruments used to collect data were student journals, teletandem evaluation questionnaires, student VoiceThread reflections, screen-captured telecollaboration sessions, images, and videos of full lab sessions, and WhatsApp text logs. We mainly depended on our observations of live sessions and ongoing critical self-reflection processes concerning all of the methods, contexts, and tools used to design and implement teletandem. With 18 years of combined experience, our keen awareness of telecollaboration made our observations invaluable for this study. We analyzed data from the three cycles of teletandem programming for three academic terms: Fall 2018, Spring 2019, and Fall 2019.

Student evaluation questionnaires were analyzed statistically with the graphic and data output provided by Google Forms. Data from students' journals and VoiceThread reflections were coded and analyzed qualitatively. Learners wrote their journals and recorded their reflections based on the facilitators' prompts, which asked students to elaborate on aspects of teletandem included in the questionnaire. In both instruments, students expressed their perceptions about the telecollaboration program's effectiveness to develop their linguistic and cultural learning, problems they faced in the process, and suggestions to improve the project.

4 Findings and Discussion

4.1 Language Learning

Students indicated that teletandem had enhanced their language learning experience. As a result of the collaboration with their partners, they were able to improve their communication skills in numerous ways. Mostly, learners reported they had improved their speaking and listening skills and expressed their ideas in a spontaneous and authentic non-academic environment. The exchange strengthened their confidence to speak and their ability to communicate with native speakers. Students perceived that their pronunciation also improved as their partners had been their language models and helped them correct their pronunciation. Moreover, they increased their vocabulary range with words related to each social theme and with idioms, phrasal verbs, and colloquial expressions that are commonly used by native speakers. Students also benefited from the feedback provided by their peers, especially on their final projects, as partners suggested ways to improve their final projects by enriching the vocabulary used and improving the organization of ideas.

4.2 Cultural Learning

Students reported learning many new things about both cultures through discussions about the film themes proposed for the exchanges. The interaction helped them be more open-minded, increased their tolerance and respect for diversity, widened their perspective of the world, and contributed to eliminating stereotypes and previous misconceptions. It was a surprise for many students to learn that both countries faced poverty, inequity, discrimination. The teletandem program made participants more critical and raised their awareness of their own and their partners' country. It also increased their interest in the target language as they learned different aspects from the ones they usually gained in class. Mexican students perceived telecollaboration as an opportunity to learn cultural aspects of the language they will teach in the future as EFL practitioners.

This study's results are consistent with Castillo-Scott's (2018) findings. Students in both teletandem programs improved linguistic skills in the target language, developed their intercultural competence, and gained the confidence to communicate with native speakers. However, participants in our study had at least twice as many sessions (8–10) compared to the four sessions Castillo-Scott organized for her students, which could have contributed to their linguistic and cultural learning to a greater extent. The fact that Mexican students were studying to become EFL teachers and some VCU learners were heritage speakers of Spanish may have also helped them be more reflective and critical about similarities and differences between their partners' language and culture and their own.

4.3 Recurring Problems and Implemented Solutions

As teletandem facilitators, we took part in the physical and technical coordination of the implementation process. Most of the complications that disrupted the natural ebb and flow of a teletandem session in progress are recurring problems. Among these are the time-consuming nature of coordinating and delivering a quality session; difficulties in integration and assessment due to institutional requirements; lack of pedagogical knowledge about how to run and integrate exchanges; teachers' lack of e-literacies, and required technical knowledge; as well as difficulty in finding appropriate partners (Castillo-Scott, 2018; Helm, 2015; O'Dowd, 2013).

Helm (2015) acknowledges the enthusiasm for teletandem but points out that telecollaboration is not yet mainstream in higher education. Some of Helm's issues reported about telecollaboration programming, such as lack of institutional interest, lack of recognition and funding, lack of e-literacies among the faculty, were not problems in the UAEH-VCU Cinema and Social Justice Teletandem Program. However, observations made during the implementation process made us realize that Helm's points could be genuine hurdles for teachers contemplating a telecollaboration project at an institution that fits the profile associated with the issues mentioned above. Helm paints teletandem pedagogy as a novelty that still requires a dedicated staff, teacher training, and assessment mechanisms.

Cultural differences are also an essential factor because behavioral norms, expectations, canons of conduct, and professional behavior are considered. Today's youth and social media culture are also factors that ultimately play a part in the vast landscape of telecollaboration in high education.

Issues reported that are technical can generally be repaired or resolved quickly. Still, whenever an instructor has to troubleshoot a technical problem in the middle of a session, usually it means a student will lose precious learning time in the process. Planning for potential problems in advance can prevent these difficulties from ruining a session for whatever reason. Technical issues are far easier to resolve than implementation issues attributable to human error. We found that a good partnership is built on trust and respect; both lead to enhanced confidence. When solving problems jointly, both sides must be equally committed to and involved in finding permanent solutions. The recurring problems related to teletandem implementation experienced by students from both countries in the Fall 2018 VCU-UAEH program are reported in Table 9.4 and deiscussed in the sections below.

Table 9.4. Teletandem Implementation Problems Reported during Fall 2018, Classified and Categorized

Recurring technical problems	1. A reverberating echo in the headset impedes students' ability to listen clearly to their partner, amplifies room noise, and makes it difficult to hear partners. 2. The headsets are connected, but the audio is not working properly. 3. Internet service slows down (on certain computers) causing interruption of audio and video signals. 4. Zoom automatically shuts down early with three or more students with the limited free version. 5. Sessions automatically terminate.
Student-related issues	1. Late arrivals and absences at sessions held on campus (in a computer lab). 2. Students experience difficulty coordinating external sessions. 3. Students request a change of partner due to personality or skill-level mismatch.
Cooperation issues stemming from human and non-human factors	1. Partially misaligned academic calendars and varying holidays. 2. Daylight saving time. 3. Aligning the learning content (selected films, themes, social justice themes, global citizenship) to keep teletandem sessions flowing in a timely manner. 4. Having to switch a student partner-pairing.
Beyond our control	1. School closures due to natural disasters, extreme weather conditions, and other factors.

4.4 Technical Problems

At the core of the teletandem experience, few things are more important than the audio and video signals (Figure 9.1). They are paramount to the students' experience of a telecollaboration session. Students should not have to worry about equipment failing during a session or having a short session because of faulty devices. Troubleshooting and fixing audio problems during a session can be time-consuming and difficult given the room noise.

Figure 9.1. A UAEH-VCU Teletandem Session in Progress

Several factors can cause audio problems. There are cases when the headset cabling becomes faulty, and as a result, speaking and hearing during a session will become difficult, strained, and sometimes impossible. Therefore, the headsets used for teletandem in labs need to be high-performing and durable to withstand the wear-and-tear from being handled by students throughout the day, and not always gently.

In some other cases, the webcam's associated software takes over the operating system sound settings and turns itself on (mic input) without turning off the headset mic, which causes awful feedback. Because webcam mics are generally unidirectional, they will pick up the room noise, whereas a language lab headset or a special gaming headset will limit external noise. The headset problem can be a source of frustration for instructors who may not be versed in digital audio fundamentals. Today's computers can have multiple audio sources and inputs.

The VCU lab used Sanako SLH-07 headsets, a premium model designed to diminish excessive room noise in language labs while sharpening the microphone audio to cut through muddy and distorted background noise. There was an ample supply of new cables. However, at the UAEH, due to external factors that did not depend on the instructor, students used their Apple-style "earbuds" instead of the standard headset. In almost all sessions, VCU students complained that they had to strain to hear their UAEH partners well.

One of the solutions implemented to mitigate this problem was changing the Mexican students' seating arrangement to widen space between students in the lab and reduce excessive background noise. The instructor also encouraged students to use more appropriate headsets of their own (if they had them). Still, it was something that could not be implemented in all cases, being a public university. We were able to minimize the number of occurrences, but not eliminate them. It was a source of ongoing frustration for the instructors and students. We stress the importance of selecting the right model because the earphones and microphone are an essential component for quality interaction.

Another technical problem that participants encountered was related to bandwidth. A standard telecollaboration session for 20 students requires a generous amount of bandwidth that will need to transfer 20 or more standard high-definition video streams in real-time free of visible debris and other artifacts running out of Skype or Zoom. When sessions are corrupted by an unreliable service provider or limited service, it considerably affects communication between teletandem partners.

During the implementation of the telecollaboration program, some of the Mexican students complained about the limited service in the lab as many times this problem negatively impacted the interactions with their partners. Although we attempted to increase bandwidth during the telecollaboration exchanges, it was a factor that remained beyond the scope of the instructor's expertise.

The last technical problem students faced was related to the videoconferencing application itself. We used Skype during the first two years of exchanges and decided to change to Zoom Video Conferencing at the start of the third year. Zoom afforded new conveniences and provided a streamlined workflow that even non-techies could appreciate and master quickly.

Students in the study conducted by Castillo-Scott (2018) also experienced technical problems related to video recording and uploading programs, which could be easily solved by providing the necessary technical support. As discussed previously in this chapter, O'Dowd (2013) suggested raising awareness about telecollaborative exchange within the institution and beyond, so that teletandem programs are valued and acknowledged by students, faculty, and management.

4.5 Student-Related Problems

Late student arrivals and absences were also a recurring problem. When a student from either country was late for a session, usually their partner had already been paired with some else, which caused yet another problem. Students complained about partner changes because they could not follow up on a previous session or because they had already created a positive learning relationship with their original partner. Even though teletandem facilitators in both countries made students aware of the implications this problem had on their partners' motivation, it continued to be an issue in all of the academic terms observed. These types of scenarios occurred consistently in less than 20% of the sessions.

On the other hand, when students engaged in off-campus sessions with their partners, they reported having difficulties negotiating the date and time for the interactions as some of them worked or had other activities. The time difference between Mexico and the US (one or two hours) was not a factor in this problem's solution. In some cases, students contacted their partners but the latter did not respond, and as a result, they lost some motivation. We had to mediate these situations as the course instructors to reestablish contact or make other arrangements for all students to do their teletandem sessions.

Another student-related problem was caused by a switch in partners when a university student requested it or dropped the course. This issue could be reduced by disseminating the 5-item questionnaire to match language partners before the first session. However, we could not predict when a student might drop the course. Still, when that happened, we referred back to the questionnaire to find the best suitable partner(s) for the remaining student(s).

Castillo-Scott (2018) experienced the same communication problems with her students and recommended allowing flexibility to work with other partners if students lose contact with their originally-assigned partner.

The highest priority for sessions held in the lab during regularly-scheduled class hours is avoiding making students wait and lose precious learning time. The lab's technical problems are easily resolved by having additional computer stations configured, connected via Zoom to a non-used computer station, so that if trouble occurs, students can move to a standby computer bypassing the need to troubleshoot and fix technical problems during a session. At VCU, it was standard procedure to have at least one standby computer for every five students. When a technical issue could not be resolved within one or two minutes, the student would be moved to a standby computer.

4.6 Cooperation Issues Stemming from Human and Non-Human Factors

Recurring problems in this last category included misaligned academic calendars, daylight saving time differences, difficulties in aligning both courses' content, and lack of awareness of students who needed to switch partners. Regarding misaligned academic calendars and time differences, we did our best to adapt to our teaching context. This was achieved by scheduling the sessions according to our calendars so that sessions in the labs could occur when there was only a one-hour time difference between Mexico and the US. Off-campus sessions were specifically scheduled when there was a two-hour difference in daylight saving times in both countries.

Initially, we were uncertain whether it would be possible to create a mutually beneficial teletandem program for student groups that seemed to share only the need for L2 immersion. Despite this, both instructors contributed to design a telecollaboration program that suited their academic needs. Castillo-Scott (2018) also found this to be a problem in telecollaboration implementation and recommended three strategies to minimize it: reminding students of the learning goals of each session (as they might be different in the two classes); preparing students well before the meetings so that they know what to do and have everything they need for the session; and holding additional open topics for students to choose from.

Our students frequently expressed the desire to stray from the social justice themes to explore other topics such as cultural traditions, customs, national holidays, and tourist destinations. We encouraged students to explore non-relevant topics outside of class. We offered extra credit to students who proved they engaged in additional tandems beyond our classes' required sessions. It became common for students to send a screenshot with a timestamp of their external and extra-credit session to show proof of the session.

4.7 Beyond Our Control

These events are not necessarily recurring problems, but they cannot be predicted or controlled. We created an array of "Plan B" strategies that enabled us to run a relatively seamless telecollaboration program. Problems, errors, failures, glitches, and anomalies will eventually happen. The more prepared instructors are to mitigate commonly recurring problems to deliver quality telecollaboration sessions, the more successful the actual sessions will be, and the more likely that teachers and students will view teletandem as a useful, high-impact language and cultural learning experience.

5 Contributions, Limitations, and Recommendations for Further Research

5.1 Main Contributions

This study adds to the literature on the integration of cinema, social justice, and teletandem programs. Castillo-Scott's (2018) work influenced the study's design but did not alter the characteristics of our teaching styles and philosophies. We were able to implement and deliver 8–10 telecollaboration sessions per academic term, which contributed to our ability to synergize immersion opportunities and practice in the L2 and learn about the culture. Students reported they had improved their communication skills as they interacted with native speakers in a non-academic environment and benefited from the feedback provided by their partners. The teletandem exchanges enhanced student confidence, motivation, fluency, and pronunciation.

Students also developed their cultural learning by becoming aware of sociopolitical differences and similarities between the cultures, which is more of a perception that evolved with each discussion, each film, and social justice issue addressed. Students also reported having become more tolerant and respectful of diversity. The telecollaboration program contributed to the elimination of stereotypes and previous cultural misconceptions. The exchanges made students reflect on and evaluate their partners' as well as their own languages and cultures.

The most significant findings came in the form of growing awareness of teletandem as a collaborative practice among teachers in foreign institutions to connect students for language immersion and cultural learning in an environment that promotes social justice, intercultural citizenship, self-reflection, and critical evaluation. Our experience in implementing the teletandem project has made us more aware of our telecollaboration practices and their implications. It has also provided us with insight into possible ways in which our project could be improved in the future.

5.2 Limitations

Our way of practicing telecollaboration is unique to what we do as teachers, our circumstances, our UAEH-VCU partnership, our understanding of the contexts, tools, and processes of teletandem, and our vision for synergizing transcultural immersion and practice opportunities for our students. As course instructors, we were intrigued by the concept of telecollaboration and created many incarnations and versions of the processes, contexts, and tools of teletandem that were developed and implemented to connect with classrooms in foreign countries.

This is significant because this study concerns identifying areas needing improvement and making teletandem a more effective and useful learning investment. Although the study is context-specific, it offers an illuminating view of the instructors' collaboration process to carry out PBLL teletandem between the faculty and students at domestic and foreign institutions of higher education.

There were recurring problems that limited our ability to implement and explore telecollaboration as a pedagogical tool for students. Although some strategies were identified and implemented to mitigate these problems, their recurring nature caused frustration and demotivation in the students, instructors, and teletandem facilitators.

5.3 Recommendations for Further Research

The VCU and UAEH courses used in this study were vastly different in terms of discipline, content, and learning objectives, but the instructors found ways to align them around the themes and the learning objectives by designing a telecollaboration project that responded to their institutional contexts and academic needs. For future implementations of the teletandem program, it is recommended that the courses are better aligned, especially in terms of the requirements for the final projects in both courses. One way to do this could be by exploring the possibility of making the final project a simultaneously-delivered presentation. Each presentation would have at least one student in each of the two countries. The student pairs would simultaneously engage in synchronous communication with classmates and instructors in attendance to view their presentations.

Increasing the number of exchanges and allowing flexibility for the allocation of partners, timeframe for off-campus sessions, and learning outcomes could also contribute to better results in the implementation of teletandem projects. It is also recommended to facilitate more personalized counseling to partners in order to motivate them and support their learning process. At the same time, it is advisable to provide more opportunities for students to exercise their autonomy and give them more freedom to make decisions regarding the films and tasks used in the sessions.

Fostering a deeper commitment to teletandem in both institutions is necessary to continue building online communities for students and teachers. Making institutional authorities aware of the pedagogical value of teletandem practices could also result in more funding and support to facilitate the integration of telecollaboration projects into higher education and access to better equipment, resources, and reliable bandwidth.

As O'Dowd (2013) argues, an understanding of telecollaborative exchanges should not be reduced to the successful integration of online and classroom activities, as they need to involve a blend of OIE as a whole. When this is achieved, students, faculty, and management may be able join forces and successfully implement telecollaboration projects involving foreign institutions.

References

Albiladi, W. S., Abdeen, F. H., & Lincoln, F. (2018). Learning English through movies: Adult English language learners' perceptions. *Theory and Practice in Language Studies*, 8(12), 1567–1574. https://doi.org/10.17507/tpls.0812.01

Belz, J. A., & Müller-Hartmann, A. (2003). Teachers as intercultural learners: Negotiating German-American telecollaboration along the institutional fault line. *The Modern Language Journal*, 87(1), 71–89.

Belz, J. A., & Thorne, S. L. (2006). *Internet-mediated intercultural foreign language education*. Boston, MA: Thomson Heinle.

Brammerts, H., & Calvert, M. (2003). Learning by communicating in tandem. In T. Lewis & L. Walker (Eds.), *Autonomous language learning in tandem* (pp. 45–60). London: Academy Electronic Publications Limited.

Burns, A. (2010). *Doing action research in English language teaching: A guide for practitioners*. London: Routledge. https://doi.org/10.4324/9780203863466

Castillo-Scott, A. (2018). Teaching social issues through cinema and teletandem. *Revista do GEL*, 15(3), 257–278. https://doi.org/10.21165/gel.v15i3.2409

Cavalari, S. M. S. (2009). A auto-avaliação em um contexto de ensino-aprendizagem de línguas em tandem via chat. Doctoral dissertation, Universidade Estadual Paulista "Júlio de Mesquita Filho", São José do Rio Preto. Repositório Institucional UNESP.

Cavalari, S. M. S. (2010). A definição das metas e o processo de autoavaliação no contexto Teletandem. In A. M. Benedetti, D. A. Consolo, & M. H. Vieira-Abrahão (Org.), *Pesquisas em ensino e aprendizagem no Teletandem Brasil: línguas estrangeiras para todos* (pp. 329– 349). PLACE OF PUB: Pontes.

Cavalari, S. M. S. (2018). Integrating telecollaborative language learning into higher education: A study on teletandem practice. *BELT*, 9(2), 417–432. https://doi.org/10.15448/2178-3640.2018.2.31927

Cavalari, S. M. S., & Aranha, S. (2016). Teletandem: integrating e-learning into the foreign language classroom. *Acta Scientiarum: Language and Culture*, 38(4), 327–336. https://doi.org/10.4025/actascilangcult.v38i4.28139

Da Cruz, Z. J. (2017). Social justice-oriented teaching in the English language classroom: Perspectives and practices. Unpublished Master's thesis, Faculty of Teacher Education, School of Education University of Iceland. Skemman.

Dooly, M., Masats, D., & Mont, M. (2012). "Snoopy, go left!": Real activities of young language learners in virtual worlds. Paper presented at *APAC ELT Convention 2012: Solid learning for liquid times*. Universitat de Barcelona, Catalunya.

Gill, M. M., Smalley, D., & Haro, M. P. (2014). *Cinema for Spanish conversation*. 4th edition. Indianapolis: Hackett Publishing.

Hauck, M. (2007). Critical success factors in a TRIDEM exchange. *ReCALL*, 19(2), 202–223.

Helm, F. (2015). The practices and challenges of telecollaboration in higher education in Europe. *Language Learning & Technology*, 19(2), 197–217.

Helm, F. (2016). Facilitated dialogue in online intercultural exchange. In R. O'Dowd & T. Lewis (Eds.), *Online intercultural exchange: Policy, pedagogy, practice* (pp. 150–172). London: Routledge.

Herrero, C., & Vanderschedlen, I. (2019). *Using film and media in the language classroom: Reflections on research-led teaching*. London: Multilingual Matters. https://doi.org/10.21832/9781788924498

Kami, C. M. C. (2011). A motivação na aprendizagem de língua estrangeira via Teletandem. Master's thesis, Universidade Estadual Paulista "Júlio de Mesquita Filho", São José do Rio Preto. Repositório Institucional UNESP.

Kinginger, C., & Belz, J. (2005). Socio-cultural perspectives on pragmatic development in foreign language learning: Microgenetic and ontogenetic case studies from telecollaboration and study abroad. *Intercultural Pragmatics*, 2(4), 369–422.

Kip, A. C. (2005). Teaching for a better world: Global issues and language education. *Human Rights Education in Asian Schools*, 8, 41–52.

Lätsch, J. A. (2017). The notion of task in the context of online tandems. In H. Funk, M. Gerlach, & D. Spaniel-Weise (Eds.), *Handbook for foreign language learning in online tandems and educational settings* (pp. 53–64). Bern: Peter Lang.

Levy, M., & Stockwell, G. (2006). *CALL dimensions. Options and issues in computer-assisted language learning*. Mahwah, NJ: Lawrence Erlbaum.

Lewis, T., & O'Dowd, R. (2016). Online intercultural exchange and foreign language learning: A systematic review. In R. O'Dowd & T. Lewis (Eds.), *Online intercultural exchange: Policy, pedagogy, practice* (pp. 21–68). London: Routledge.

Luz, E. B. P. (2012). Variáveis influenciadoras da continuidade ou descontinuidade de parcerias de Teletandem à luz da teoria da atividade. Doctoral dissertation, Universidade Estadual Paulista, IBILCE, São José do Rio Preto. Repositório Institucional UNESP.

Mont, M., & Masats, D. (2018). Tips and suggestions to implement telecollaborative projects with young learners. In M. A. Dooly Owendy & R. O'Dowd (Eds.), *Teachers' experiences with transnational, telecollaborative language learning projects* (pp. 93–122). Bern: Peter Lang.

Motteram, G., & Sharma, P. (2009). Blending learning in a Web 2.0 World. *International Journal of Emerging Technologies & Society*, 7(2), 83–96.

Müller-Hartmann, A. (2000). The role of tasks in promoting intercultural learning in electronic learning networks. *Language Learning & Technology*, 4(2), 129–147. http://llt.msu.edu/vol4num2/ muller/default.html

Müller-Hartmann, A. (2016). A task is a task is a task is a task... or is it? Researching telecollaborative teacher competence development – The need for more qualitative research. In S. Jager, M. Kurek, & B. O'Rourke (Eds.), *New directions in telecollaborative research and practice: Selected papers from the second conference on telecollaboration in higher education* (pp. 31–43). Research-publishing.net. https://doi.org/10.14705/rpnet.2016.telecollab2016.488

O'Dowd, R. (2013). Telecollaborative networks in university higher education: Overcoming barriers to integration. *The Internet and Higher Education*, 18, 47–53. https://doi.org/10.1016/j.iheduc.2013.02.001

O'Dowd, R. (2016a). Emerging trends and new directions in telecollaborative learning. *CALICO Journal*, 33(3), 291–310.

O'Dowd, R. (2016b). Learning from the past and looking to the future of online intercultural exchange. In R. O'Dowd & T. Lewis (Eds.), *Online intercultural exchange: Policy, pedagogy, practice* (pp. 273–293). New York: Routledge.

O'Dowd, R., & Ritter, M. (2006). Understanding and working with "failed communication" in telecollaborative exchanges. *CALICO Journal*, 23(3), 623–642.

O'Dowd, R., & Waire, P. (2009). Critical issues in telecollaborative task design. *Computer Assisted Language Learning*, 22(2), 173–188. https://doi.org/10.1080/09588220902778369

O'Rourke, B. (2005). Form-focused interaction in online tandem learning. *CALICO Journal*, 22(3), 433–466.

O'Rourke, B. (2007). Models of telecollaboration (1): E(tandem). In R. O'Dowd (Ed.), *Online intercultural exchange: An introduction for foreign language teachers* (pp. 41–62). Cleveland: Multilingual Matters. https://doi.org/10.21832/9781847690104

Patton, A. (2012). *Work that matters: The teacher's guide to project-based learning*. London: Paul Hamlyn Foundation.

Pratama, H. (2016). Global education in English classroom: Integrating global issues into English language teaching. *International Journal of Social Science and Humanity*, 6(9), 719–722.

Rubin, J. (2016). The collaborative online international learning network. In R. O'Dowd & T. Lewis (Eds.), *Online intercultural exchange: Policy, pedagogy, practice* (pp. 263–272). London: Routledge.

Schwienhorst, K. (2000). *Virtual reality and learner autonomy in second language acquisition*. Unpublished Doctoral dissertation, Trinity College Dublin. TARA.

Seferoğlu, G. (2008). Using feature films in language classes. *Educational Studies*, 34(1), 1–9. https://doi.org/10.1080/03055690701785202

Silva, J. M. (2012). Projeto Teletandem Brasil: As relações entre as comunidades virtuais, as comunidades discursivas e as comunidades de prática. Master's thesis, Universidade Estadual Paulista "Júlio de Mesquita Filho", São José do Rio Preto. Repositório Institucional UNESP.

Telles, J. A. (2015). Learning foreign languages in Teletandem: Resources and strategies. *DELTA: Documentação de Estudos em Lingüística Teórica e Aplicada*, 31(3), 603–632. https://doi.org/10.1590/0102-445022647564373077

Telles, J. A., & Vassallo, M. L. (2006). Foreign language learning in-tandem: Teletandem as an alternative proposal in CALLT. *The ESPecialist*, 27(2), 189–212.

Thomas, M. (2017). *Project-based language learning with technology*. London: Taylor & Francis Ltd. https://doi.org/10.4324/9781315225418

Vassallo, M. A., & Telles, J. A. (2006). Foreign language learning in-tandem: Theoretical principles and research perspectives. *The ESPecialist*, 27(1), 23–59.

Ware, P. (2005). "Missed" communication in online communication: Tensions in a German-American telecollaboration. *Language Learning & Technology*, 9(2), 64–89. http://llt.msu.edu/vol9num2/ware/default.html

Ware, P., & O'Dowd, R. (2008). Peer feedback on language form in telecollaboration. *Language Learning & Technology*, 12(1), 43–63. http://llt.msu.edu/vol12num1/wareodowd/default.html

About the Authors

Martha Guadalupe Hernández Alvarado, MA, is a full-time teacher and researcher in the Linguistics Department at Universidad Autónoma del Estado de Hidalgo. She currently teaches courses on learning autonomy and teaching practice for the BA in English Language Teaching, a teacher preparation program for English teachers in Mexico.

Anton T. Brinckwirth is the Director of the World Studies Media Center at Virginia Commonwealth University (VCU). He has a PhD in Education (Instructional Leadership) from VCU. Dr Brinckwirth teaches Spanish through film and media and his primary teaching and research interests are Teletandem, Virtual Classroom, and Online International Exchange (OIE).

10 Stories, Communities, Voices: Revitalizing Language Learning through Digital Media within a Project-Based Pedagogical Framework

Jim Anderson and Vicky Macleroy

1 Introduction

It has long been recognized that language learning is most engaging when it is related to authentic content and tasks and involves the use of relevant tools. In its most developed form this means subject teaching through a foreign or second language (e.g., Content Based Instruction or Content and Language Integrated Learning). However, it is also used to refer to cross-curricular or thematic approaches led by a languages specialist sometimes in collaboration with a colleague from another subject area (Brown & Brown, 1998, 2003; Coyle, Hood, & Marsh, 2010; Curtain & Dahlberg, 2015; Grenfell, 2002). Project-Based Language Learning (PBLL), which has much in common with Task Based Language Teaching (TBLT), fits within this second category (Beckett & Miller, 2006; Beckett & Slater, 2019). Alongside these developments there have been rapid advances in the role played by digital media in language learning and the emergence of Web 2.0 has offered new ways of realizing the emphasis on interaction, learner agency, and identity negotiation, central elements within prevailing sociocultural and dialogic paradigms (Miller & McVee, 2012; Thomas, 2017; Thorne, 2013).

One of the most promising applications of digital media for language learning is digital storytelling which enables both the digital creation and sharing of stories using a range of digital tools including cameras, laptops, editing software, the World Wide Web, and online platforms (Anderson & Macleroy, 2016). It is fully consistent with a project-based approach since it requires a sequence of activities to be carried out within an overarching process of assemblage and design. It opens up a space for experimentation, for multimodal and potentially multilingual bricolage, for expanding life-worlds, and for developing voice. A language-and-culture learning dimension sits naturally within this extended semiotic field and the opportunity through subtitling to incorporate more than one language makes it possible for translingual and transcultural perspectives to be incorporated. Moreover, it involves a range of skills: cognitive and affective, critical and creative, social, technical, and aesthetic. Worth noting is that the technical dimension is fully integrated with, though subservient to, the story being constructed.

This chapter examines the Critical Connections: Multilingual Digital Storytelling Project (Goldsmiths, University of London) from the perspective of PBLL and the vision for language education which this represents. The project, initiated in 2012 with funding from the Paul Hamlyn Foundation, has supported young people in the UK and six other countries in creating and sharing multilingual digital stories across a range of languages and genres. It has been based on ongoing dialogue between teachers and researchers and this collaborative ethos has also informed the research approach adopted. We shall elaborate on this below and also summarize the range of findings made as the project has developed. In particular, we shall demonstrate how multilingual digital storytelling has enabled fully integrated and creative use of technology within a learner-centered, interdisciplinary PBLL approach. We shall further make clear issues encountered not least due to constraints imposed by institutional frameworks and policies.

2 PBLL in the Context of Post-Communicative Language Teaching, Multiliteracies, and CALL

As we have moved beyond the narrow instrumentalism of the communicative era (Kramsch, 2014), so thinking on language pedagogy has moved in various directions. Language learning is now understood as an inherently translingual and transcultural activity, a dialogue between self and other, in which we not only absorb new ways of naming the world but also discover new ways of being in the world (Byram, 1997; Kramsch, 2009; Phipps & Gonzalez, 2004; Rosi Solé, 2016). There is much fuller understanding that context, purpose, and negotiation of meaning are crucial to providing an engaging and supportive learning experience leading to deeper learning and higher levels of communicative competence. This is why, around the world, there has continued to be much interest both in Content and Language

Integrated Learning (CLIL) and in Task-based Language Teaching (TBLT) (Tsuchiya & Pérez Murillo, 2019; Wen & Ahmadian, 2019).

CLIL is an umbrella term which has been used, at one end of the spectrum, to refer to situations where a subject is taught by a subject specialist through the medium of a second language and, at the other, to cross-curricular and/or culture-based units of work typically delivered by a Languages specialist. Whatever form is practiced, a dual focus on content and language is required, which includes content encompassing concepts, information, and skills (Coyle, Hood & Marsh, 2010). Development of the academic language competence required to progress knowledge construction and meaning-making in the subject area concerned is one of the particular challenges here and remains a focus for research (Meyer et al., 2015).

In TBLT, whilst some importance is given to content, the main focus is on providing opportunities for learners to apply the language they are learning to "real-life" tasks (Bygate, 2016). The two approaches are similar, however, in favoring an analytic syllabus design, in other words one in which communicative needs take precedence over an artificially constructed sequence of linguistic items as in the traditional synthetic syllabus (Long & Crookes, 1992). Emerging from cognitive and interactionist perspectives, TBLT places the main emphasis on learner interaction and on the development of learner autonomy. Thus the onus is on students, both individually and collectively, to draw on their own linguistic and cognitive resources in working on tasks and to self-regulate the process.

Developing alongside TBLT and sharing a number of its features, PBLL, an offshoot from the broader concept of PBL, is viewed as a learner-centered, experiential, holistic, process-oriented, interdisciplinary approach which prioritizes active engagement with real-world issues within a supportive context drawing on the full range of semiotic resources available for meaning-making in a globalized world. Consistent with dialogic, collaborative, and creative approaches to learning, priority is given to learner agency and voice with outcomes being shared with local and global audiences (Beckett & Slater, 2019).

As indicated, many of these ideas and the notion of project work within the languages curriculum have been proposed over decades and have been built into cross-curricular work, as defined above, including work around literature and the arts more widely (Abdelhadi et al., 2019; Byram & Fleming, 1998; Legutke & Thomas, 1991; Psaltou-Joycey, Agathopoulou, & Mattheoudakis, 2014; van Lier, 2007). This involves a much more open and holistic approach to language-and-culture learning making it "a semiotic-ecological endeavor that focuses on the making and using of signs that are multisensory and multimodal" (van Lier, 2006: xiv). The promotion of learner autonomy involving group work has been seen as particularly beneficial within this model partly because it "provides students with a real purpose for the language use" but also because "in the exploration of themes and topics, the production of materials, and the general discussion of project management (who does what, why, how, when), it involves students in a wide range of interactions in the target language" (McGarry, 1995: 6–7).

What has altered this picture most significantly in the past two decades has been developments in digital media in the context of a globalizing world. Indeed the new social and cultural conditions engendered by the internet have brought about a fundamental shift in epistemological perspective from a monologic view based on the "transmission of true representations" to a dialogic one involving "participation in ongoing enquiry in an unbounded context" with an assumption that "meaning is never singular but always emerges in the play of different voices in dialogue together" (Wegerif, 2013: 3). Involved here are fluid and dynamic processes of meaning-making reflecting multiplicity, diversity, and challenges of shifting identities.

The implications of this for education and in particular for understandings of literacy were captured in the design model proposed by the New London Group and in its multiliteracies pedagogy integrating multicultural and multimodal strands (1996). Here communicative practices are viewed not just from a linguistic perspective, but in much broader semiotic terms taking into account the range of available resources for meaning-making and how these interrelate. Whilst limited in its impact on mainstream UK education thus far, the model recognizes that texts fall into different genres shaped by social context and by the audience for which they are intended. Pedagogically it foregrounds four interwoven knowledge processes: *experiencing* – working with the known and the new; *conceptualizing* – naming and making connections to theory; *analyzing* – viewing critically to expose underlying perspectives/ideologies; and *applying* – creative transformation (Cope & Kalantzis, 2013).

A related framework which gives greater weight to the digital dimension and in particular to rapidly developing web-based social practices, is the iPed model proposed by Mills & Levido (2011) which emerged from a longitudinal digital literacy intervention with socially disadvantaged and ethnically diverse students:

- Link – involving personal, cultural, and global perspectives (including use of web-based resources);
- Challenge – thinking critically, including judgment of authenticity and authority of web sources;

- Co-create – drawing on the affordances of Web 2.0 (with some teacher guidance) to "co-produce media for real audiences within and beyond the school";
- Share – gaining recognition through presentation to local and global audiences.

(Mills, 2015: 11–16)

The emphasis in multiliteracies pedagogy on learner agency and incorporation of students' backgrounds and experience is fundamental to the notion of "identity texts", the creative outcomes of projects orchestrated by the teacher which may be written, spoken, visual, musical, dramatic, or combinations in multimodal form (Cummins & Early, 2011: 3). Identity texts, including, for example, online magazines, (digitized) dual language storybooks, and digital films, open up a space for multiple languages, for cultural and aesthetic perspectives, and for collaborative knowledge generation. Use of technology, although not essential, can act as an "amplifier" both in the process of production and in dissemination. Importantly, particularly for minority background students, an identity text can promote deep learning and engagement because it "holds a mirror up to students in which their identities are reflected back in a positive light" (Cummins & Early, 2011: 3). Extending work in this area, in a recent study with Latino background learners in California, Vu, Warschauer, & Yim (2019) endorse the view of digital stories as identity texts pointing out how they can serve to bridge languages, cultures, generations, and communities.

Also foregrounding identity investment and empowerment, Darvin & Norton (2014) propose digital storytelling as a means of creating a Third Space for migrant learners where they can bring transnational literacies to life. Selecting from the range of available multimodal and multilingual resources for storytelling, migrant learners are "given an opportunity to become agents of their learning and authors of their own representation" enabling them to claim the "right to speak" (ibid.: 63).

In terms of Computer-Assisted Language Learning (CALL), it is evident that Web 2.0 has made a significant contribution to the growing interest in "social CALL" (Thomas, Reinders, & Warschauer, 2013: 5). Web 2.0 technology encompasses a range of tools such as blogs, podcasts, wikis, social networking sites (SNS), and digital sharing platforms enabling synchronous and asynchronous computer-mediated communication (CMC). It has extended opportunities for interaction, collaboration, personalization, and creativity, enhancing conditions for meaningful language output (Dooly, 2017; Wang & Vasquez, 2012) whereby, given appropriate levels of support, there can be a shift of emphasis from learners as consumers to producers of information (Bustamente, Hurlbut, & Moeller, 2012).

Digital storytelling is a technique greatly facilitated by the integrated use of Web 2.0 technology both in the creation and sharing of digital stories in any language or combination of languages. There has been a growing number of studies examining whether and how Web 2.0 technology can bring benefits for language learning. Concluding a major review (Parmaxi & Zaphiris, 2017: 713) report that "Web 2.0 technologies can support a wide range of skills, including collaborative learning, autonomous learning, and intercultural awareness." They also stress, however, that greater consideration needs to be given to how the use of technology fits within program design and planning.

Focusing more specifically on research into digital storytelling as a means of promoting language learning, there have been various studies related to foreign and heritage language learning as well as English as an Additional Language (See Anderson, Chung, & Macleroy, 2018). These have generally been small-scale exploratory studies, related to foreign language and English as a Second Language learning based on thematic units of work and largely consistent with principles underlying PBLL. Overall they have shown positive outcomes in relation to vocabulary development and memorization; oracy, in particular pronunciation, fluency, and expression; (multi) literacy skills, especially scaffolding of the (multimodal) composition process; creative and critical thinking; student-centered, collaborative learning; potential for combination with other art forms (process drama, visual art); building bridges between out-of-school learning (including encounters with popular culture) and in-school learning; engagement linked to learner agency, self-efficacy, a dynamic interaction with culture, and identity construction. Various issues have also emerged including how digital storytelling can best be integrated with institutional programs of study; a danger that technical concerns may divert attention from story development; and the importance of an appropriate pedagogical approach and the implications of this for teacher professional development.

3 The Critical Connections Project: Vision and Development

We move on now to examine in some detail the Critical Connections: Multilingual Digital Storytelling Project developed at Goldsmiths, University of London (initiated in 2012 and ongoing). The idea for the project grew out of concerns about trends in language and literacy education in the UK, in particular the failure, in an increasingly interdependent and interconnected world, to recognize the dangers of remaining culturally encapsulated and to engage constructively and critically with the digital media (Anderson & Obied/Macleroy, 2011). This has been reflected in a fragmented curriculum in which the study of other languages and cultures has not been adequately supported, in which children's home languages in particular have been consistently marginalized and devalued, and in which the affordances of the digital media have not always been harnessed in the most thoughtful and productive ways. It was our belief that multilingual digital storytelling could contribute to addressing both these issues and, in so doing, offer a vision for education which recognizes multiple sites of learning, local and global, and multiple ways of knowing.

Espousing an integrated and inclusive approach to language learning, this project has established an intercultural global learning network (Cummins, Brown, & Sayers, 2007) bringing together young people in the UK and in six other countries (Algeria, Cyprus, Luxembourg, Palestine, Taiwan, and the US) to create and share digital stories in bilingual version. It has involved students across primary and secondary age ranges, in mainstream and complementary sectors, learning over 15 languages. The term "complementary" school (also referred to as "supplementary," "mother tongue," or "community" school) is used here to refer to voluntary community-based schools which operate mainly at weekends. The languages include Arabic, Bengali, Bulgarian, Croatian, English (Mother Tongue, English as an Additional Language, English as a Foreign Language), Estonian, French, German, Greek, Hungarian, Mandarin Chinese, Portuguese, Spanish, Tamil, and Turkish. To make films accessible to as wide an audience as possible, they have been created bilingually with voiceovers in one language and subtitles in another (usually English). To give coherence to the project and to reinforce its cross-curricular nature, each year a broad theme has been established with a growing emphasis on issues of social justice and the environment, such as "Fairness," "Belonging," and "Our Planet." Within these themes, story ideas have been negotiated with students themselves drawing on their lifeworlds and interests and developing their sense of agency. This has led to work across a range of genres (drama, fantasy, science fiction, traditional tales, documentary) drawing on various digital media tools (cameras to capture still and moving images, stop animation and green screen software, and editing software). The multilingual digital stories created have been shared within classrooms and schools, across schools, at film festivals, and through the project website. At the film festivals students have come onto the stage to introduce their work before the showing of the film.

Critical Connections takes a holistic view of language learning, recognizing the significance of "ecologically valid contexts, relationships, agency, motivation and identity" (van Lier, 2010: 2). Figure 10.1 captures the multilayered and multidimensional nature of the model:

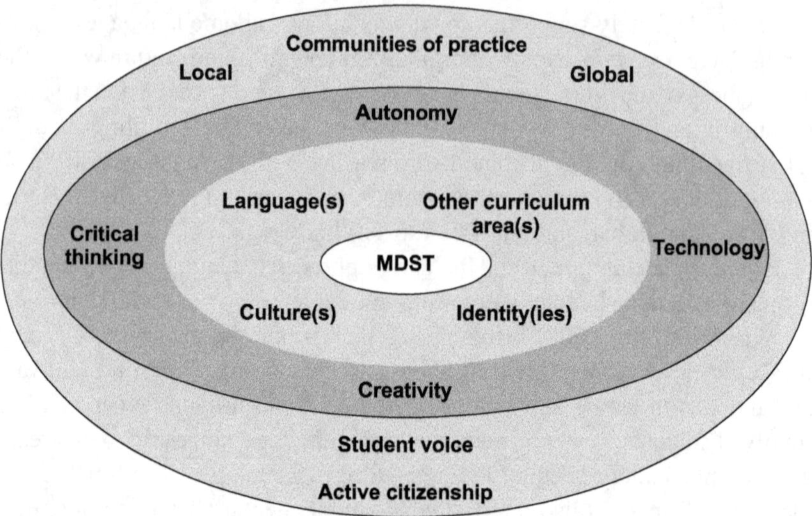

Figure 10.1. The Critical Connections Model for Multilingual Digital Storytelling

Central to the model is multilingual digital storytelling. The power of stories to move us at a personal level – emotionally, culturally, and intellectually – and thus to provide an engaging focus for language-and-culture learning has long been recognized (Anderson & Chung, 2011; Kirsch, 2016; Lucarevschi, 2016; Morgan & Rinvolucri, 1983; Sneddon, 2009). Moreover, the internal logic and mood of the story reflect important thematic and structuring elements in the composition process. The multilingual aspect brings to the forefront the range of languages in the project and the unique window on the world that each language represents. It also values linguistic repertoires and the porous boundaries between language varieties so that translanguaging is perceived as a natural and potentially productive communication strategy. The digital introduces an extended range of semiotic resources and facilitates collaborative modes of learning. It holds particular appeal for young people who have grown up in an all-pervasive and dynamic digital culture.

Moving out to the next circle in the diagram, we wanted to emphasize a view of language-and-culture learning as a translingual-transcultural process entangled with personal lifeworlds and identity investment. In tune with trends in post-communicative language teaching, we see this perspective as compatible with the focus on storytelling and with a cross-curricular perspective, particularly in relation to the arts (drama, visual arts, music, poetry, dance).

The third circle identifies four interrelated strands within the learner-centered pedagogical strategy proposed. As noted above, the use of technology is widely seen as a means of supporting learner autonomy both inside and outside the classroom. It can take multiple forms and bring both organizational and pedagogical advantages, including authenticity, interaction, situated learning, control, and empowerment (Herrero & Vanderschelden, 2019; Reinders & Hubbard, 2013). Web 2.0 has greatly extended the possibilities here enabling learners to perform a much more active and creative role in their learning, for example, through web authoring of different types. Creativity is about experimentation, self-expression, and the generation of new knowledge. It recognizes the importance of student agency and ownership in the learning process and how "co-creativity through dialogue" can be a key to engaging constructively with four p's of the digital world: "plurality, playfulness, participation, and possibilities" (Craft, 2012: 184). However, whilst creativity may imply freedom to explore it also involves the ability to think critically, for example through reviewing digital stories both in development and as final products according to criteria negotiated collaboratively. Computer applications such as VoiceThread and Kannu can play a valuable role in facilitating peer review across schools through text, audio or video means and have been used in the Critical Connections project. However, outcomes in this area have been mixed and this will be discussed further in the section on future implications.

Turning now to the outer circle, the model recognizes multiple sites of learning, local and global, and including online. Following the notion of "school as basecamp" (Paul Hamlyn Foundation and the Innovation Unit, 2010), it takes account of much wider contexts for (language-and-culture) learning in the modern world including funds of knowledge in the home and community (Gonzales, Moll, & Amanti, 2005) and the possibility, facilitated by digital technology, of participation in multilingual learning communities. In this way, it recognizes how digital storytelling can give students the confidence to make their voices heard and in so doing uncover "cultural alternatives" (Pennycook, 1997). In terms of language learning pedagogy this means moving beyond the "often empty babble of the communicative classroom" (ibid.) to an approach which engages seriously with students' lifeworlds and recognizes the discourses of power in which identities are entangled. Seen from this perspective multilingual digital storytelling becomes active citizenship in practice.

Taken as a whole, this pedagogical approach represents an integrated and coherent model for language-and-culture learning in which the digital media make an important contribution to the achievement of educational goals. It is fully consistent with a Project-Based Language Learning approach and the 21st-century skills which it seeks to support. As Table 10.1 illustrates, CALL is drawn upon to serve clearly defined pedagogical aims through the stages of a multilingual digital storytelling project. Underlying this is an assumption of students working collaboratively, both in and out of school, and sometimes remotely.

Table 10.1. Embedding CALL within the Critical Connections Pedagogical Framework

Stage in Process	Pedagogical Aim	Potential CALL Application
Pre-production	• Developing understanding of what makes a good digital story (content, skills, and language use) to inform film-making process and reviews of progress • Mindmapping ideas	• Viewing examples of digital stories online • Smartart/MindView (to support mindmapping) • Email/WhatsApp for group communication in and out of school
	• Planning • Drama and media activities around objects • Scripting (bilingual) and storyboarding	• Wordprocessing/digital template for storyboarding/digital sketches • Online dictionaries/Google Translate • Sharing amongst group members
	• Researching ideas • Exploring key questions	• Surfing the web for information • Sharing amongst group members via email/WhatsApp
Production	• Choosing digital tools • Multimodal composition (including camera shots and angles) • Filming, adding voiceover/soundtrack, adding subtitles • Peer review	• Filming equipment (cameras, tripods, laptops/iPads) • Software for creating and editing (Photostory 3, Moviemaker, iPad, Serif), animating (Zu3D), green screen (I Can Present 2, Serif Moviemaker) • Software for reviewing (VoiceThread, Kannu)
Post-production	• Reviewing and editing digital story • Presenting to a global audience • Archiving • Blogging	• Software for editing and adding credits (Photostory 3, Moviemaker, iPad, Serif) • Software for reviewing (VoiceThread, Kannu) • Wordpress, Vimeo

Whilst the educational vision for the project was clear, developing it in practice across very different settings and with teachers from different backgrounds and with different areas of expertise presented a significant challenge. A main strategy in addressing this was regular meetings between teachers and researchers. The space for dialogue and discussion was crucial to developing expertise and confidence in what for most represented a new approach to language teaching. A valuable outcome from this collaboration two years into the project was the creation of a *Handbook for Teachers* (Anderson, Macleroy, & Chung, 2014) bringing together ideas based on shared experience within the group. As has been found in PBLL generally, a clear structure is needed to guide work and this led to the development of a 10-stage framework for embedding multilingual digital storytelling within a thematic unit of work. Ways of addressing the dual focus on content and language and the range of scaffolding strategies required to achieve this are also covered. This includes language-specific terminology in Arabic, Chinese, and French related to the use of digital media in the classroom (Section 12 of *Handbook for Teachers*). As the project has progressed over the years, so the potential role of the arts in multilingual digital storytelling has become increasingly apparent. This has emerged particularly strongly where languages teachers have been able to collaborate with colleagues teaching drama, visual arts, dance, poetry, and music.

4 Research Methodology for the Critical Connections Project

Our research project was funded by the Paul Hamlyn Foundation (2012–2014) to re-engage young people with language learning through digital technology and develop teachers' skills in this area in both mainstream and complementary schools; it was re-funded by Paul Hamlyn (2015–2017) to build stronger connections between mainstream and complementary schools in the teaching of languages using digital media; and the latest phase of the project was funded by Language Acts and Worldmaking (2018–2020) to further develop language pedagogies linked with digital storytelling.

Our project combines PBLL with digital technology and it both confirms and extends research findings in the field of PBLL which report "improved language skills, content learning, real-life skills, sustained motivation, and positive self-concepts" (Stoller, 2006: 20). Our work links with research in motivation and self-esteem and seeks to address the disengagement of students with language learning. It also puts forward the premise that young people need to learn to interact with digital technology in more critical and creative ways and take more ownership over these new forms of communication (Coiro et al., 2008). We set out initially to investigate these three broad research questions:

1. What is the significance of Multilingual Digital Storytelling (MDST) for young people and their learning?
2. What is an appropriate pedagogical framework for carrying out Multilingual Digital Storytelling work in schools?
3. What are the implications for policy and teacher professional development?

We selected critical ethnography as our main research methodology as our project needed to be collaborative and take a critical stance towards language pedagogy in schools. Our research methodology embraced both the pedagogical and political, placing social justice as a core principle in relation to language-and-culture learning. Within this critical ethnographic research paradigm (qualitative, context-based, participatory, multiperspectival, interpretive, and critical) we linked our study to ecological, collaborative, and multimodal perspectives (Anderson & Macleroy, 2016). The critical ethnographer is seen as contributing to emancipatory knowledge and discourses of social justice and the research process is seen as a dialogical performance (Madison, 2005). This dialogue, negotiation, and meeting of multiple sides created a research paradigm that was responsive to the local contexts of teachers and students and flexible in its approach.

Digital technology has played a key role in collecting research data from a range of sources: video recordings and photographs of the MDST process in schools; videoed interviews with students, teachers, parents, community members; audio-recordings of team meetings; online comments on VoiceThread; documents/schemes of work on Kannu platform; videoed film festivals; and digital stories on the project website. As the project has expanded the digital stories themselves have become increasingly significant as "embodied objects" of study (Alexandra, 2017) and provide a lens for an expanded view of literacy and language (Escott & Pahl, 2017).

5 General Research Findings: The First Phase of the Critical Connections Project (2012–2014) and ongoing

Data were collected from video recordings and photographs (observing the making of digital stories in schools; presenting digital stories at film festivals; interviews with students, teachers, parents, and community members) and documentary materials (school policies; teaching plans and materials; students' work including notes, storyboards; field notes; digital stories in draft and final versions). Data from these various data streams were collated and analyzed "to provide a collective answer to a research question" (Cohen, Manion, & Morrison, 2017: 662). The following eight key research strands were identified in our data analysis and discussed in full in our book (Anderson & Macleroy, 2016):

1. Language learning, multilingual repertoires, and identity
2. Multilingual composition and creativity
3. Culture, international partnerships, and active citizenship
4. Learner autonomy, critical thinking, and student voice
5. Engagement and motivation
6. Sites of learning: school, home, and online
7. Transformative pedagogy
8. Curriculum policy, planning, and professional development.

Lead language teachers in schools (20 teachers initially) were involved in co-constructing the project from the outset (2012) and key in making decisions about the pedagogical approach. As researchers and teacher educators (English, English as an Additional Language, Modern Languages) we had established links with language teachers in local London schools and these strong relationships formed the base of our project (Anderson & Macleroy, 2016: 133). Challenging institutional boundaries, the focus on storytelling offered a valuable means of facilitating dialogue between teachers of foreign and heritage languages, EAL and English Mother Tongue working in both mainstream and complementary contexts (6 mainstream schools; 7 complementary schools; and 3 schools in Algeria, Palestine, and Taiwan). The shift in teacher role towards becoming a facilitator was both challenging and transformative for project teachers:

> Definitely for me it has completely changed. It's not a quantum leap and it's not all of a sudden. Definitely throughout the months I've noticed a change even in the way that I'm thinking and the way I'm planning the lessons and putting the curriculum together. (Teacher, Ealing Arabic School, London)

Lead project teachers have also played an active role, in collaboration with researchers, in interrogating the MDST data collected in their different school contexts and from a range of perspectives. This collaborative and dialogic way of approaching the research project has allowed space for the "social processing of knowledge" (Louis, 2006: 3), and a deeper, more nuanced understanding of how and why MDST motivates and engages young people in language learning.

Students became integrated into our collaborative research approach and building on the work of a team member on a student participant-researcher (SPR) model *Illuminate*, we adapted and integrated this model into our project (Carlile, 2016). Two student co-researchers from each lead complementary and mainstream project school (in 2014, 2016, 2017) attended research methods training at Goldsmiths in collecting research data through interviewing, video recordings, and photographs. We provided a research brief for the students and space and time for student co-researchers to present their research findings:

> My girls felt really responsible … and after every session they went back to the form and they were interviewing the other girls … so there are all of those different research skills having to record what people are saying, and different methods which were available. It's brilliant. (Teacher, St Michael's Grammar School, London)

The project supported students' critical thinking in relation to digital literacy and they became more confident in problem-solving, decision-making, and evaluating their own bilingual digital stories and the stories of others in a wide range of languages:

> When I started making the film I thought it was going to be easy by putting a bunch of pictures together, however, I had multiple challenges while making this film such as finding the right music and fitting the film in the time frame with just pictures. However, my biggest challenge was recording my voice. This was when I needed some help because there were some words I didn't know the translation to and whether or not they made sense … I also managed to improve my Croatian and become more confident in speaking. (Student, Croatian Supplementary School, London)

A collaborative research approach where different voices are listened to and acted upon has helped to embed the pedagogical model in schools and transform practice. It also creates a space where students can support each other with camera and editing work and understanding new digital technology. As teacher educators we recognize the key role of training in the construction and sustainability of the project. Lead teachers participated in workshops led by media and drama educators on the digital storytelling process and workshops were conducted in schools for students. The close collaboration that digital storytelling work requires over time has led to a "methodology of friendship" (Tillman-Healy, 2003: 724):

> It built such a nice friendship, but respectful friendship and you don't see yourself any more like the leader in front of the class … you know your students more. It's very friendly and they're learning a lot. (Teacher, Sarah Bonnell School, London)

The project has also opened up funds of knowledge from parents, grandparents, and community members supporting young people's stories, languages, and digital technology skills. The main research findings from the project (2012–present) demonstrate that MDST involves authentic content and tasks and draws on digital media creatively and critically:

> Digital storytelling gave me a way of expressing my creativity and imagination. If you give me a camera and a laptop, anything is possible. (Student, Peace School, London)

Our Critical Connections model for multilingual digital storytelling will be illustrated in the vignettes below to demonstrate the significance of MDST to young people's experiences of language learning (Chinese, English as an Additional Language, English as a Foreign Language, Greek, Hungarian, and Portuguese) in these particular school contexts.

5.1 Introduction to Vignettes Showing Multilingual Digital Storytelling within PBLL

The next part focuses on three vignettes from mainstream project schools across this age range (10–15 years). This section analyses how MDST has been implemented in specific project schools and how teachers and students have responded to combining digital technology with a project-based approach in learning languages. The first school (Broomfield Secondary School, London) and the second school (International School in London) were involved in the project for the second phase (2015–2017); and the third school (Fengshan Senior High School, Taiwan) was involved in all three phases of the project (2012–2014; 2015–2017; 2018–2020). These project schools are particularly representative of how MDST was set up in interdisciplinary and collaborative ways and teachers and students were creative and experimental with their use of digital technology. The British Film Institute (BFI), a key project partner (2015–2017), enabled us to run advanced media workshops on green screen, stop motion animation, and editing for lead teachers at Goldsmiths and for students in schools and at the BFI and in Taiwan. Ongoing support for teachers and students in schools from members of the project team (BFI educator; drama educator; and IT technician) played a crucial part in the use of more advanced digital technology in MDST. These professional development resources can be accessed on the project website (https://goldsmithsmdst.com/professional-development/). Each of the vignettes focuses on the process of creating one particular digital story and the young filmmakers of those stories (see Table 10.2).

Table 10.2. Context of the Project Schools and Filmmakers Who Created the Three Digital Stories

Secondary Schools	Lead Project Teachers	Student Film-makers	Languages in the Digital Story	Selected Digital Stories
Broomfield Secondary School, London	EAL Teacher, Pantelis Iakovou Drama Educator, Chryso Charalambous	2 EAL learners (13–14 years old)	Greek EAL	Greek-English digital story: *Migration*
International School in London	Language Teacher, Mirela Dumić Art Teacher, Marc Smith	5 EAL learners (10–15 years old)	Hungarian Portuguese EAL	Hungarian-Portuguese-English digital story: *The B.A.D. Robot*
Fengshan Senior High School, Taiwan	EFL Teacher, Peter Lo Citizenship Teacher, Li-chen Chu	6 EFL learners (15–16 years old)	Chinese EFL	Chinese-English digital story: *How Weird is Weird?*

5.2 Broomfield Secondary School (London, UK) – *Migration*

The lead project teacher in this mainstream secondary school, who was a teacher for English as an Additional Language (EAL), became increasingly confident and interested in using digital technology to develop students' language skills and engage them in PBLL (October 2015–June 2016). He worked with a group of 12 advanced bilingual learners (12–14 years old) who had migrated to England (2013–2014) from Albania, Bulgaria, France, Greece, Italy, and Poland. The EAL teacher and our project drama educator were both Greek-English bilingual speakers and, in partnership, devised six drama sessions as part of the pedagogical approach to using digital technology in the classroom. Students were able to use elements of theatre and performance in their digital storytelling to explore questions of identity (Alrutz, 2015).

5.2.1 Pre-production: Learning empathy and transcultural skills

The overarching project theme (2015–2016) was "fairness" and the EAL teacher and drama educator decided to explore "fairness around migration" collaboratively with the EAL students. In this school, the project fostered active citizenship connecting with Personal, Social, Health, and Economic education (PSHE) and helped students to learn empathy and transcultural skills. The EAL teacher, drama educator, and EAL students were migrants themselves with specific histories, knowledge, and languages and our project sought to build on this and construct a classroom environment where multilingualism was supported and developed. During the first phase of the project work (pre-production phase), the drama educator conducted two 3-hour workshops to allow students to explore perceptions and arguments around pre-migration, migration, and post-migration as well as thinking about representation. Drama activities allowed students to experiment with different stances of the narrator (voice, facial expressions, bodily gestures) and different ways of telling stories including role play, documentaries, news presentations. Alongside the drama work, the BFI media educator conducted two digital media workshops on camera shots and angles, stop motion animation, green screen and editing.

5.2.2 Production: Using green screen to design a Greek-English digital story

Students were required to work collaboratively in the project and the EAL teacher decided to group students according to their languages. Students were then able to work across their languages in producing drafts in their mother tongue and English before an adult (parent or teacher) looked at their work. During the second phase (production phase), students began working on their digital stories (storyboarding, rehearsing, filming, subtitling, and editing). The focus here was on a digital story produced by two recently arrived students from Greece who decided to make a documentary using green screen – a technique to digitally replace the background in a video image by shooting it against a green screen (see Figure 10.2). These students were supported by the drama educator in four additional sessions to develop their roles as presenters, both in front of and behind the camera, and learn how to use drama and digital technology to create a well-structured and meaningful digital story.

The affordances of digital media enhanced the creative, affective, and dialogic elements of PBLL and the students became confident to voice their opinions in Greek and English.

Figure 10.2. Using Green Screen to Film the Greek-English Digital Story *Migration*

5.2.3 Post-production: Widening perspectives on migration and learning translation skills

During the final stage (post-production phase) these two students presented their digital story at the BFI and reflected on the project.

> I speak Greek … the drama workshops helped me gain ideas about my monologue and I personally felt I knew many things. They helped me gain a more spherical view of migration and I simply learned a lot of things … it helps us this project to make an opinion for ourselves. (Student 1)

> The way we translated the poem and the way we tried to make it sound good to an English speaker … we tried to make it in this way … it helped me in translating texts … the teacher helped me write my text better so that it sounds better to an audience. (Student 2)

These students were developing their language skills in Greek and English; learning how to make meaning in combining the affordances of different modes; and making use of digital technology to project powerful images on the screen behind them as they presented their digital story (see Figure 10.2). Student 1 created a monologue framing the digital story with questions to be interrogated:

> Migration. What does it actually mean? Is this really the simple move from one country to another? (Student 1)

whilst Student 2 wrote a personal and emotive poem interspersed into the monologue and interrogating migration:

> I wonder who is to blame. Is it my fault? Searching, searching, always searching. In my heart lies grief and pain. (Student 2)

Combining language in this way enabled these two students to create a powerful digital story drawing on their multilingual repertoire whilst interrogating questions of identity and citizenship. Their Greek-English digital story *Migration* can be viewed here:
https://vimeo.com/channels/mdstawards16/168321455

5.3 International School in London (London, UK) – *The B.A.D. Robot*

The project was implemented in this school (October 2016–June 2017) in an after-school club for EAL students to support their language development. Working collaboratively, the lead language teacher together with the art teacher set up the project in the form of workshops held in the school art space. The interdisciplinary collaboration was key to fostering an experimental and open space for multilingualism and demanding more creative engagement with digital technology. The language teacher, Mirela, had been part of an interview team conducting research on multilingual childhoods (Thomas, 2017) and she was keen to engage with innovative pedagogies to support multilingual children in schools. The art teacher, Marc, had engaged in improvisation workshops (2014–2017) and he was fascinated by the creative power of animation and how it allows students to "play with stuff, problem solve, talk to each other, focus and that is what I want from a classroom." Combining visual art with digital and linguistic strands in PBLL shifted our focus to interactions between people, artifacts, and space and how language and cognition are produced in these "material webs of human and non-human assemblages" (Pennycook, 2019: 85).

5.3.1 Pre-production: Working with objects and learning Stop Motion animation skills

The two innovative teachers worked with a group of five EAL learners that included three Brazilian students (14–15 years old) and two Hungarian students (14- and 10-year-old brothers). The Hungarian siblings had arrived in England at the start of the school year (2016) and the younger one had only a few words of English. This project allowed him to work alongside his older brother (developing ideas, interpreting, translating) in a school setting supported by teachers. The students were supported at different stages in the project by mother tongue teachers of Portuguese and Hungarian. The main project theme (2016–2017) was "belonging" and the pre-production phase of the project (supported by the media and drama educator) involved watching and analyzing short films on the theme and working with objects of personal and cultural significance to tell stories. The students explored the effects of bringing objects to life in imaginative ways (using iPads) and the brothers made a short animation of their object, showing sophistication in representing upward movement, sound effects, and comic graphics (crash, boom, pow). The older Hungarian student engaged confidently with digital technology and quickly developed skills in Stop Motion animation whilst his younger brother, a skillful musician, became adept at adding sound effects to the digital story. In this experimentation phase of the project, the five students engaged with objects as "vibrant matter" (Bennett, 2010) and learnt to make meaning in and beyond language.

The lead project teachers and student co-researcher in this school documented each stage of the process through samples of work, photographs, and video recordings uploaded onto a shared project site. A core aim of the project was to promote online communication and interaction between schools and we trialed a new online creative platform called Kannu (2015–2017). We created the following three sites: School Course Area (private area for each school); Inter-School Global Network (all project school students and teachers for sharing and discussion of digital stories); Teacher Course Area (all lead project teachers to enable sharing of ideas and resources). All sites had a connect forum area where students and teachers could comment on digital stories and create discussion threads. The art teacher created a documentary drawing on film footage across the process and shared this as an online resource (*B.A.D. Reflections* by Marc Smith: https://goldsmithsmdst.wordpress.com/other-resources/).

5.3.2 Production: Improvising and creating a digital storyboard across three languages

During the production stage of the project, the students came up with the idea of robots and artificial intelligence and a key question: "What would happen if robots could feel emotions?" The students learned through engaging with materials and the art teacher filled the classroom space with robotic materials, electronic junk, and disused computer parts. The youngest student constructed a "fantastic robot out of some wooden stuff I'd left lying around" and was credited as the chief robot designer for the digital story. This was a breakthrough and the student moved from speaking only a few words in English at the start of the project to writing a detailed back story in English for his robot. The students were working across three languages and had the challenge of creating a trilingual script. These students were not interested in traditional storyboarding and instead created a "digital storyboard" with digital sketches of each scene they could replay, watch, and comment on together (eee Figure 10.3). The narrative script came out of this process of improvising, revisioning, and recreating.

Figure 10.3. Filming the Hungarian-Portuguese-English Digital Story *The B.A.D. Robot*

The students experimented with different voices and accents in their languages and made the decision that the central robot character, B.A.D., would speak in Hungarian.

5.3.3 Post-production: Translating and collaborating across three languages

The Hungarian students worked together on the Hungarian script for the oldest robot, whilst the Brazilian students collaborated on the Portuguese script for the newer robots, and they then worked together across languages and the narration in English. Their inventiveness and linguistic sophistication were striking and the teacher noted: "These skills would not have happened in any other part of the curriculum." *The B.A.D. Robot* was scripted, animated, and narrated by all five students.Their trilingual animation was a highly collaborative process and these young people recognized the communicative power and meaning-making potential of using their full linguistic repertoire. Their Hungarian-Portuguese-English digital story *The B.A.D. Robot* can be viewed here: https://vimeo.com/220581681.

5.4 Fengshan Senior High School (Taiwan) – *How Weird is Weird?*

This mainstream secondary school in Taiwan was a key project school from the outset (2012). The lead teachers for English as a Foreign Language (EFL) implemented MDST with the support of our lead research assistant who built on personal relationships with the teachers and led digital storytelling workshops in Taiwan with the support of BFI media educators. The language teacher at Fengshan Senior High School reflected on implementing MDST in her English lessons: "None of us had made digital stories before … I learned how to use Moviemaker and all the digital and editing programs. As a teacher I also had to learn how to help students learn the basic techniques and motivate them to willingly create their own digital stories." Motivation and engagement were key in this process as the students dedicated lunchtime and after-school time to working on the project beyond the classroom. The language teacher at the end of the first year of the project commented that besides improving their English some of the students had "learned to manage their time; conquered their fear of computers and English; re-examined their life; learned how to work as a team; built confidence through overcoming difficulties; and shared digital stories with students from different parts of the world and interacted with them on the amazing *VoiceThread*" (see Figure 10.4).

One of the critical processes involved with MDST is peer assessment and this was enabled across project schools using an online tool, VoiceThread. The digital stories were embedded into VoiceThread and viewers could comment on any point of the video by typing a response and/or recording an audio or video comment. Communication using VoiceThread was restricted to project schools but facilitated across project countries as participants could post commentary from anywhere at any time. This online tool helped students to uncover common interests and perspectives across languages and countries:

> I am very excited that my work would be seen by students in the UK and I am very happy that they made comments on my film. It was also very interesting to see their films and get to know how creative the other students are. (Student, Fengshan Senior High School)

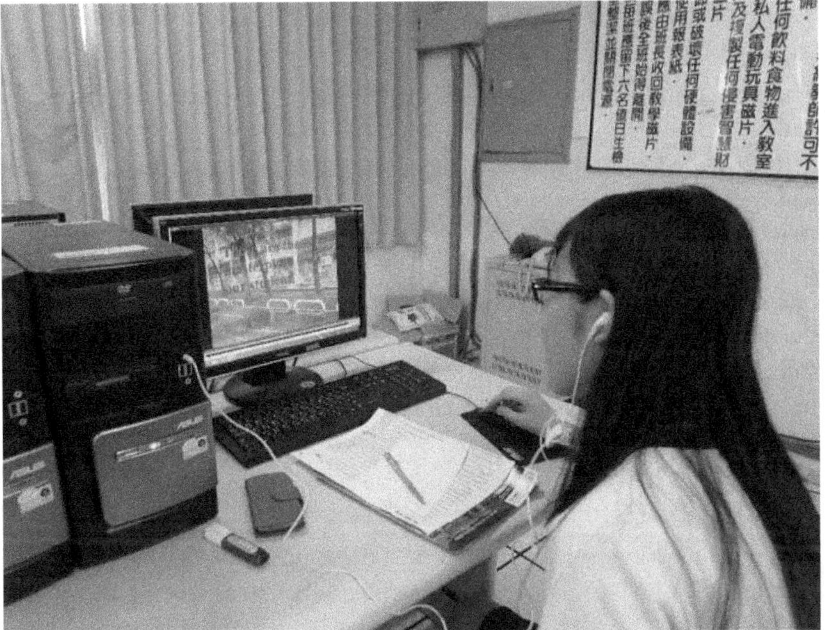

Figure 10.4. Editing a Chinese-English Digital Story at Fengshan Senior High School

5.4.1 Pre-production: Learning a foreign language through critical thinking and active citizenship

The Taiwanese students worked on the theme of "fairness" for their digital stories (October 2015–June 2016) with the lead project teacher. Their language teacher viewed the project as an opportunity for his students to develop critical thinking in their learning of English and his students chose to explore the Taiwanese educational system; appearances; school policies; the wealth gap; and gender identity. Our student co-researcher lead on the project conducted a Skype workshop for these students on designing interview questions and exploring issues that mattered to them. The digital story on gender identity is focused on here and was created by a group of six Taiwanese students (14–15 years old) learning English. The students' digital story *How Weird is Weird* shows the power of combining PBLL with digital technology and using these tools critically to produce an alternative viewpoint. Digital storytelling allows students to produce these alternative narratives of hope, justice, and compassion connected with "social engagement, participation, activism and change" (Hartley, 2017: 220).

5.4.2 Production: Exploring identity and learning to use digital technology creatively

The digital story *How Weird is Weird* is based on the true story of a teenager called "the Rose Boy" who died in their school restroom. The students show versatility and adeptness in their use of digital technology and languages and shift the focus of the story to the mother's perspective. The opening narrative of the boy's death is told in black and white with English subtitles and narrative voiceover in English, and then the story shifts to colorful moving images of his mother riding her motorbike to work in the fields. This part of the digital story is told in Chinese with Chinese and English subtitles. The students' questions to the mother give her a chance to speak warmly about her son and express her anger about what happened.

5.4.3 Post-production: Learning to make meaning across different modes of communication

The students include live footage of the mother speaking out at a Pride march and end with English subtitles about the mother making a stand for her son and others being stereotyped. The Chinese-English digital story itself becomes an affective assemblage of meaning-making across a bricolage of photos, moving images, live footage, and signs. These young people were able to combine learning English as a foreign language with active citizenship and learn to use English and Chinese together in meaningful contexts. Their Chinese-English digital story *How Weird is Weird?*can be viewed here: https://vimeo.com/channels/mdstawards16/169446882.

6 Reflections and Implications for Future Work

At the start of the Critical Connections project in 2012, we set out to investigate the significance of multilingual digital storytelling for young people and their learning. Initially, we had to convince the educational community that students could learn languages in this way, but over the past 8 years we have shown that digital storytelling is a meaningful and authentic way to apply digital technology to PBLL. We have drawn on the success of our project (implemented in over 50 schools in the UK and 15 partnership schools in other countries) and, in this chapter, focused on specific ways (Green Screen, Stop Motion animation, documentary) that digital technology enhanced language learning for students in the three vignettes. The students were engaged in authentic content and tasks and were motivated to learn new language and media skills to produce their digital story.

It was a major challenge to move away from the usual narrow, instrumental focus on testing in foreign language learning (Slater, Beckett, & Aufderhaar, 2006) to an approach which encouraged translingual-transcultural processes and genuinely valued student ideas and peer and self-assessment. We have developed an approach to assessment whereby students evaluate digital stories at the start of each project year and create their own success criteria covering language use, skills, and content. The Critical Connections website (https://goldsmithsmdst.com/) now hosts over 250 digital stories for students to choose from, created by more than 1,500 young people and curated on a MDST Vimeo channel.

However, one of the most significant challenges we still have in implementing MDST is to encourage students to interact with their peers in different schools beyond the annual film festivals and enter a critical dialogue around the digital stories. We have experimented with VoiceThread and Kannu but these platforms were difficult to install in schools and hard for project teachers and students to navigate. We believe that creating an online community of multilingual digital storytellers is key to the sustainability of this approach to PBLL.

In collaboration with lead project teachers, we created a Critical Connections Pedagogical Framework for carrying out MDST work in schools (see Appendix). This framework emphasizes the importance of building learning communities, learner autonomy, and critical digital literacy. Film literacy is known to develop life skills such as "communication, creativity, collaboration, innovation, conflict management, decision-making and critical thinking" (Donaghy, 2019: 5). Herrero (2019) in discussing future directions for film in language teaching cites our project and the importance of young language learners engaging with film as producers, curators, and critics. This shift to make language pedagogy more responsive to "accessing, analyzing, interpreting, understanding and creating visual messages in multimedia environments … is still an underdeveloped area in the language curriculum" (Herrero, 2019: 189).

The Critical Connections project has major implications for teacher professional development as the multilingual digital storytelling project can only be sustained in schools where teachers are supported to develop digital technology skills and given the confidence, motivation, and creativity to shift their pedagogical approach. In reflecting upon bringing together digital storytelling and PBLL, we recognize the importance of pushing schools to adopt a more integrated and interdisciplinary policy towards language and literacy incorporating digital technology, the arts, drama, and citizenship.

Appendix

Summary of Critical Connections Pedagogical Framework (Anderson & Macleroy, 2016: 232)

1.	**Integrated and inclusive approach to language and literacy and to the broader curriculum**	• Foreign and community languages as well as English and English as an Additional Language • Cross-curricular, thematic links
2.	**Plurilingual, multicompetency goal**	• Repertoire approach, validating bilingual/plurilingual skills • Linguistic competence viewed holistically • Intentional "translanguaging"
3.	**Building learning communities in school and out-of-school**	• Collaboration and sharing of work within and across schools locally and globally • Situated learning drawing on "funds of knowledge" in the home and community, including galleries and museums
4.	**Learner autonomy and voice**	• Agency, self-regulation, ownership • Metacognitive and language learner strategies • Presentation to a local and global audience • Active citizenship skills
5.	**Meaningful contexts (content and tasks)**	• Relevant intercultural/cross-curricular/literature content • Authentic tasks • Problem-solving • Critical thinking
6.	**Interactive, process oriented co-construction**	• Links made to prior knowledge and experience • Collaboration and peer assessment • Scaffolded learning
7.	**Critical digital literacy**	• Multimodal composition/storying • Online resources and communication • Youth culture
8.	**Intercultural orientation**	• Investigative, experiential, multiperspectival • Identity texts (including the re-imagining and re-mediating of traditional culture) • Building partnerships between students, teachers and schools locally and globally • Critical cosmopolitanism
9.	**Creativity for learning**	• Thinking outside the box • Self-expression involving personal/emotional as well as cognitive dimensions • Drawing on links between language, culture and the arts • Aesthetic appreciation
10.	**Knowledge about language (KAL)/Critical Language Awareness**	• Focus on form within a communicative context • Appreciation of commonalities and differences between languages • Critical interrogation of texts • Understanding power relationships between languages/dialects in the classroom and community

References

Abdelhadi, R., Hameed, L., Khaled, F., & Anderson, J. (2019). Creative interactions with art works: An engaging approach to Arabic language-and-culture learning. *Innovation in Language Learning and Teaching*, 13. https://doi.org/10.1080/17501229.2019.1579219

Alexandra, D. (2017). Reconceptualizing digital storytelling: Thinking through audiovisual inquiry. In M. Dunford & T. Jenkins (Eds.), *Digital storytelling: Form and content* (pp. 167–182). London: Palgrave Macmillan. https://doi.org/10.1057/978-1-137-59152-4_14

Alrutz, M. (2015). *Digital storytelling, applied theatre, & youth: Performing possibility*. Oxford: Routledge. https://doi.org/10.4324/9780203500606

Anderson, J., & Chung, Y.-C. (2011). Finding a voice: Arts based creativity in the community languages classroom. *International Journal of Bilingual Education and Bilingualism*, 14(5), 551–569. https://doi.org/10.1080/13670050.2010.537742

Anderson, J., Chung, Y.-C., & Macleroy, V. (2018). Creative and critical approaches to language learning and digital technology: Findings from a multilingual digital storytelling project. *Language and Education*, 32(3), 195–211. https://doi.org/10.1080/09500782.2018.1430151

Anderson, J., & Macleroy, V. (Eds.). (2016). *Multilingual digital storytelling: Engaging creatively and critically with literacy*. Oxford: Routledge. https://doi.org/10.4324/9781315758220

Anderson, J., Macleroy, V., & Chung, Y.-C. (2014). *Critical connections: Multilingual digital storytelling project. Handbook for teachers*. London: Goldsmiths, University of London.

Anderson, J., & Obied/Macleroy, V. (2011). Languages, literacies and learning: from monocultural to intercultural perspectives. *NALDIC Quarterly*, 8(3), 16–26.

Beckett, G., & Miller, P. (Eds.). (2006). *Project-based second and foreign language education: Past, present, and future*. Charlotte, NC: Information Age Publishing.

Beckett, G., & Slater, T. (Eds.). (2019). *Global perspectives on project-based language learning, teaching, and assessment: Key approaches, technology tools, and frameworks*. New York: Routledge.

Bennett, J. (2010). *Vibrant matter: A political ecology of things*. Durham, NC: Duke University Press Books. https://doi.org/10.1215/9780822391623

Brown, K., & Brown, M. (1998). *Changing places: Cross-curricular approaches to teaching languages*. London: CILT.

Brown, K., & Brown, M. (Eds.). (2003). *Reflections on citizenship in a multilingual world*. London: CILT.

Bustamente, C., Hurlbut, S., & Moeller, A. (2012). Web 2.0 and language learners: Moving from consumers to creators. In T. Sildus (Ed.), *Touch the world: Selected papers from the 2012 central states conference on the teaching of foreign languages* (pp. 109–131). Richmond, VA: Robert M. Terry.

Bygate, M. (2016). Sources, developments and directions of task-based language teaching. *Language Learning Journal*, 44(4), 381–400. https://doi.org/10.1002/9781405198431.wbeal1467

Byram, M. (1997). *Teaching and assessing intercultural communicative competence*. Clevedon: Multilingual Matters Ltd.

Byram, M., & Fleming, M. (1998). *Language learning in intercultural perspective: Approaches through drama and ethnography*. Cambridge: Cambridge University Press.

Carlile, A. (2016). Student participant researchers: Learner agency and creative engagement. In J. Anderson & V. Macleroy (Eds.), *Multilingual digital storytelling: Engaging creatively and critically with literacy* (pp. 87–105). Oxford: Routledge. https://doi.org/10.4324/9781315758220-5

Cohen, L., Manion, L., & Morrison, K. (2017). *Research methods in education*. Oxford: Routledge. https://doi.org/10.4324/9781315456539

Coiro, J., Knobel, M., Lankshear, C., & Leu, D. (2008). *Handbook of research on new literacies*. London: Routledge.

Cope, B., & Kalantzis, M. (2013). "Multilteracies": New literacies, new learning. In Margaret Hawkins (Ed.), *Framing Languages and Literacies* (pp. 105–135). London: Routledge. https://doi.org/10.1017/CBO9781139196581

Coyle, D., Hood, P., & Marsh, D. (2010). *CLIL: Content and language integrated learning*. Cambridge: Cambridge University Press.

Craft, A. (2012). Childhood in a digital age: Creative challenges for educational futures. *London Review of Education*, 10(2), 173–190. https://doi.org/10.1080/14748460.2012.691282

Cummins, J., Brown, K., & Sayers, D. (2007). *Literacy, technology and diversity: Teaching for success in changing times*. Boston, MA: Pearson.

Cummins, J., & Early, M. (Eds.). (2011). *Identity texts: The collaborative creation of power in multilingual schools*. Stoke on Trent, UK: Trentham Books.

Curtain, H., & Dahlberg, C. A. (2015). *Languages and children: Making the match, new languages for young learners, grades K-8*, 5th edition. New York: Pearson.

Darvin, R., & Norton, B. (2014). Transnational identity and migrant language learners: The promise of digital storytelling. *Education Matters*, 2(1), 55–66.

Donaghy, K. (2019). Using film to teach languages in a world of screens. In C. Herrero & I. Vanderschelden (Eds.), *Using film and media in the language classroom* (pp. 3–18). Bristol: Multilingual Matters. https://doi.org/10.21832/9781788924498-004

Dooly, M. (2017). Telecollaboration. In C. Chapelle & S. Sauro (Eds). *The handbook of technology and second language teaching and learning* (pp. 169–183). Chichester, West Sussex: Wiley Blackwell. https://doi.org/10.1002/9781118914069.ch12

Escott, H., & Pahl, K. (2017). Learning from Ninjas: Young people's films as a lens for a expanded view of literacy and language. *Discourse: Studies in the Cultural Politics of Education*, 40(6), 803–815.

Gonzales, N., Moll, L., & Amanti, C. (2005). *Funds of knowledge: Theorizing practices in households, communities, and classrooms*. Mahwah, NJ: Lawrence Erlbaum. https://doi.org/10.4324/9781410613462

Grenfell, M. (Ed.). (2002). *Modern languages across the curriculum*. London: Routledge and Falmer.

Hartley, J. (2017). Smiling or smiting? – Selves, states and stories in the constitution of politics. In M. Dunford & T. Jenkins (Eds.), *Digital storytelling: Form and content* (pp. 167–182). London: Palgrave Macmillan. https://doi.org/10.1057/978-1-137-59152-4_16

Herrero, C. (2019). Conclusion: Present and future directions for video, film and audiovisual media in language teaching. In C. Herrero & I. Vanderschelden (Eds.), *Using film and media in the language classroom* (pp. 188–197). Bristol: Multilingual Matters. https://doi.org/10.21832/9781788924498-016

Herrero, C., & Vanderschelden, I. (Eds.). (2019). *Using film and media in the language classroom*. Bristol: Multilingual Matters.

Kirsch, Claudine. (2016). Using storytelling to teach vocabulary in language lessons: Does it work? *Language Learning Journal*, 44(1), 33–51.

Kramsch, C. (2009). *The multilingual subject*. Oxford: Oxford University Press.

Kramsch, C. (2014). Teaching foreign languages in an era of globalisation: Introduction. *The Modern Language Journal*, 98(1), 286–301. https://doi.org/10.1111/j.1540-4781.2014.12057.x

Legutke, M., & Thomas, H. (1991). *Process and experience in the language classroom*. Harlow: Longman.

Long, M. H., & Crookes, G. (1992). Three approaches to task-based syllabus design. *TESOL Quarterly*, 26(1), 27–56. https://doi.org/10.2307/3587368

Louis, K. S. (2006). *Organizing for school change*. New York: Routledge.

Lucarevschi, C. (2016). The role of storytelling in language learning: A literature review. *Working Papers of the Linguistics Circle of the University of Victoria*, 26(1), 24–44.

Madison, S. (2005). *Critical ethnography: Method, ethics, and performance*. London: Sage.

McGarry, D. (1995). *Learner autonomy 4: The role of authentic texts*. Dublin: Authentik.

Meyer, O., Coyle, D., Halbach, A., Schuck, K., & Tinge, T. (2015). A pluriliteracies approach to content and language integrated learning – Mapping learner progressions in knowledge construction and meaning-making. *Language, Culture and Curriculum*, 28(1), 41–57. https://doi.org/10.1080/07908318.2014.1000924

Miller, S., & McVee, M. (2012). *Multimodal composing in classrooms: Learning and teaching for the digital world*. New York: Routledge. https://doi.org/10.4324/9780203804032

Mills, K. (2015). *Literacy theories for the digital age: Social, critical, multimodal, spatial, material and sensory lenses*. Bristol: Multilingual Matters. https://doi.org/10.21832/9781783094639

Mills, K., & Levido, A. (2011). iPed: Pedagogy for digital text production. *The Reading Teacher*, 65(1), 89–91.

Morgan, M., & Rinvolucri, M. (1983). *Once upon a time: Using stories in the language classroom*. New York: Cambridge University Press.

New London Group (1996). A pedagogy of multiliteracies: Designing social futures. *Harvard Educational Review*, 66, 60–92. https://doi.org/10.17763/haer.66.1.17370n67v22j160u

Parmaxi, A., & Zaphiris, P. (2017). Web 2.0 in computer-assisted language learning: A research synthesis and implications for instructional design and educational practice. *Interactive Learning Environments*, 25(6), 704–716.

Paul Hamlyn Foundation and the Innovation Unit (2010). *Learning futures: The engaging school: Principles and practices*. London: Paul Hamlyn Foundation.

Pennycook, A. (1997). Cultural alternatives and autonomy. In P. Benson & P. Voller (Eds.), *Autonomy and independence in language learning* (pp. 35–53). London: Longman.

Pennycook, A. (2019). Linguistic landscapes and semiotic assemblages. In M. Pűtz & N. Mundt (Eds.), *Expanding the linguistic landscape* (pp. 75–88). Bristol: Multilingual Matters. https://doi.org/10.21832/9781788922166-007

Phipps, A., & Gonzalez, M. (2004). *Modern languages: Learning and teaching in an intercultural field*. London: Sage.

Psaltou-Joycey, A., Agathopoulou, E., & Mattheoudakis, M. (Eds.). (2014). *Cross-curricular approaches to language education*. Newcastle upon Tyne: Cambridge Scholars Publishing.

Reinders, H., & Hubbard, P. (2013). CALL and learner autonomy: Affordances and constraints. In M. Thomas, H. Reinders, & M. Warschauer (Eds.), *Contemporary computer-assisted language learning* (pp. 359–375). London: Bloomsbury.

Rosi Solé, C. (2016). *The personal world of the language learner*. London: Palgrave Macmillan. https://doi.org/10.1057/978-1-137-52853-7

Slater, T., Beckett. G., & Aufderhaar, C. (2006). Assessing projects as second language and content learning. In G. Beckett & P. Miller (Eds), *Project-based second and foreign language education* (pp. 241–262). Greenwich, CT: Information Age Publishing.

Sneddon, R. (2009). *Bilingual books – biliterate children: Learning to read through dual language Books*. Stoke on Trent: Trentham.

Stoller, F. (2006). Establishing a theoretical foundation for project-based learning in second and foreign language contexts. In G. Beckett & P. Miller (Eds.), *Project-based second and foreign language education* (pp. 19–40). Greenwich, CT: Information Age Publishing.

Thomas, M. (2017). *Project-based language learning with technology: Learner collaboration in an EFL classroom in Japan*. London: Routledge. https://doi.org/10.4324/9781315225418

Thomas, M., Reinders, H., & Warschauer, M. (Eds.). (2013). *Contemporary computer-assisted language learning*. London: Bloomsbury.

Thorne, S. (2013). Digital literacies. In M. Hawkins (Ed.), *Framing languages and literacies: Socially situated views and perspectives* (pp. 192–218). New York: Routledge.

Tillman-Healy, L. M. (2003). Friendship as method. *Qualitative Inquiry*, 9(5), 729–749. https://doi.org/10.1177/1077800403254894

Tsuchiya, K., & Pérez Murillo, M. D. (Eds.). (2019). *Content and language integrated learning in Spanish and Japanese contexts: Policy, practice and pedagogy*. London: Palgrave Macmillan.
Van Lier, L. (2006). Foreword. In G. Beckett & P. Miller (Eds.), *Project-based second and foreign language education: Past, present and future* (xi–xvi). Charlotte, NC: Information Age Publishing.
Van Lier, L. (2007). Action-based teaching, autonomy and identity. *Innovation in Language Learning and Teaching*, 1(1), 46–65. https://doi.org/10.2167/illt42.0
Van Lier, L. (2010). The ecology of language learning: Practice to theory, theory to practice. *Procedia Social and Behavioral Sciences*, 3, 2–6. https://doi.org/10.1016/j.sbspro.2010.07.005
Vu, V., Warschauer, M., & Yim, S. (2019). Digital storytelling: A district initiative for academic literacy improvement. *Journal of Adolescent & Adult Literacy*, 63(3), 257–267.
Wang, S., & Vasquez, C. (2012). Web 2.0 and second language learning: What does the research tell us? *CALICO Journal*, 29(3), 412–430. https://doi.org/10.11139/cj.29.3.412-430
Wegerif, R. (2013). *Dialogic: Education for the internet age*. London: Routledge. https://doi.org/10.4324/9780203111222
Wen, Z., & Ahmadian, M. (2019). *Researching L2 task performance and pedagogy: In honour of Peter Skehan*. Amsterdam: John Benjamins Publishing Company. https://doi.org/10.1075/tblt.13

About the Authors

Jim Anderson is Visiting Research Fellow in the Department of Educational Studies at Goldsmiths, University of London. His work focuses on: theories and methods of second language learning and bilingualism, including Content and Language Integrated Learning (CLIL); multilingualism and new literacies; and language policy. Underlying this is a commitment to an integrated and inclusive approach to language and literacy education incorporating the areas of foreign and community/heritage language learning as well as English as an Additional Language and English Mother Tongue. Jim is co-director of the Critical Connections: Multilingual Digital Storytelling Project (2012–ongoing).

Vicky Macleroy is a Reader in Education and Head of the Research Centre for Language, Culture and Learning at Goldsmiths, University of London. Her work focuses on language development and multilingualism; creative writing practices and poetry; multiliteracies and digital storytelling; and transformative pedagogy. Underpinning her research is a commitment to research methodologies that embrace collaborative and creative ways of researching. Vicky is co-director with Jim Anderson of the Critical Connections: Multilingual Digital Storytelling Project (2012–ongoing) that uses digital storytelling to support engagement with language learning and digital literacy.

11 Epilogue: Critical Project-Based Learning and Moving Forwards in the Post-Pandemic University

Michael Thomas

1 Introduction

While teaching a foreign language is typically a stressful task at the best of times, the appearance of COVID-19 in 2020 has multiplied many teachers' already heavy workloads and job-related pressures (Macintyre, Gregersen, & Mercer, 2020). The swift transition to remote online delivery and/or blended learning has complicated an already challenging situation, with many teachers faced with having to balance work, life, and family commitments alongside teaching and administrative burdens and the requirement to learn new digital skillsets, almost overnight. Over a billion children and young people in education around the world have been affected by the transition to remote learning, as a consequence of many school, college, and university closures. While educational institutions have increasingly invested in digital education products, processes, and professional development over the last decade, it has often been the "digital champions" who have been more able to deal with the disruption most easily, leaving many other teachers to learn new technical skills (Bilyalova, Salimova, & Zelenina, 2020). The transition to online forms of education has already been a massive exercise in teacher and student resilience and adaptability and it will remain so for the foreseeable future. Across all sectors, language teaching was already a stressful existence for many teachers affected by increasing casualization, lack of autonomy, the burden of administration and ever greater systems of accountability, quality control, and evaluation (Bernstein et al., 2020; Williamson, 2017). Add to this the professional stresses and strains that accompany the role of language teaching itself, such as controlling large classes, dealing with imposter syndrome, integrating learners from different language proficiency levels, and the precarious nature of many language teaching jobs.

Of course, precarity for language teachers has been an increasingly pressing concern long before COVID-19. In the UK, for example, there have been significant decreases in language learning across all levels:

> Despite the Government's aim for 90% of pupils in England to take a language (modern or ancient) at GCSE by 2025, fewer than half of them do. Across the UK, the number of undergraduates in modern languages fell by 54% between 2008–9 and 2017–18. With fewer students applying, at least 10 modern languages departments have closed in the last decade, and a further nine significantly downsized. (Universities UK, 2020)

COVID-19 has amplified these stresses and reinforced the vulnerability of language courses, programs and teachers who do not have access to appropriate resources or IT support; however, the roots lie deeper in a shift to a marketized and competitive system of higher education (Gray, 2019).

2 Disrupting Education

In terms of the pandemic, language teachers have also felt the full effects of isolated learners who may have limited opportunities for face-to-face interaction, or had to deal with parents who are confused and burdened as a result of dramatic changes in their own social and working lives. Through all of this, teachers have had to deal with questions about how to manage positive student-teacher relationships in a profoundly disrupted educational landscape. Strategies for coping with global pandemics are not normally part of teacher training courses or language syllabi, but it is clear that teachers and learners need to be better prepared to cope with the disruption and uncertainty that such events have caused, and to have opportunities to reflect on and understand the course of action adopted, to resist avoiding difficult challenges, and to examine how best to resolve complex technical and pedagogical problems. Working in so-called "challenging" or "difficult" circumstances is not new to foreign language teachers, as this work is often conducted across the developing world in low-resource and low-tech contexts, particularly in the Middle East or Sub-Saharan Africa (Motteram, Dawson, & Al-Masri, 2020). Indeed, as COVID-19 has spread around the globe, displaced teachers and learners have been confronted with equally dramatic challenges in 2020 in the shape of unprecedented wildfires and storms in the United States, to name but one example, which have disrupted formal education. Such events seem to appear with increasing regularity each year and call into question the sustainability of current approaches to language learning and teaching in the broader context of educational provision (Akbari, 2008).

Surveying the period during lockdown has led some researchers to identify the wastage of a COVID-19 generation, disadvantaged due to a disruption that has prevented or curtailed their access to school or the digital tools now required for this form of flexible learning (Collis & Moonen, 2004; Casey & Wilson, 2005). For others, the pandemic presents both a crisis and an opportunity to reconsider language learning strategy (Zhao, 2020). In the UK context, confronted with turbulent changes following BREXIT, Kenny (Universities UK, 2020) has argued that language learning plays a key role in socioeconomic change:

> With the COVID-19 pandemic plunging the UK into its worst recession in living memory and exacerbating disparities in educational opportunity, and with the changing relationship to Europe necessitating the development of wider commercial and diplomatic relationships and the recalibration of existing ones, there has never been a more pressing need to take a strategic approach to language learning.

If the combination of BREXIT and a deep economic recession does not lead to reconsideration of what education (and in particular language education) is for, what events will precipitate such reflection? Given that forecasters have estimated that the UK's poor performance in languages may account for up to 3.5% of GDP in terms of lost investment and trading opportunities, Kenny's argument is both strategic and economic, pitching the business case for language learning in terms of its contribution to culture and society:

> If Government and civil society together succeed in reversing the persistent decline in take up of languages throughout the education pipeline, the UK could become a linguistic powerhouse: more prosperous, productive, influential, innovative, knowledgeable, culturally richer, healthier and more socially cohesive. Languages should not just be for the socially advantaged, but for everyone. We must act soon to make this a reality. (Universities UK, 2020)

Likewise, Stern (Universities UK 2020) argues that the recovery required from a post-COVID-19 world will be in need of the types of collaboration and skillsets learned by language learners:

> We're proposing a national languages strategy at a time when the UK is most in need of graduates with the skills to form invaluable international partnerships. International collaboration has been a

> vital part of the UK's response to Covid-19, and will be a cornerstone of its recovery. If the UK government is serious about their ambitions for a Global Britain, we must upskill our graduates with the linguistic and cultural understanding to shape an outward-looking, post-Covid and post-Brexit UK.

Arguments for the economic benefit of language learning have been driven by globalization and flexible labor markets, as well as mobile devices and platforms that enable anywhere, anytime learning, and apply to many other contexts, not just the UK (Nedungadi, Mulki, & Raman, 2017). Flexible pricing structures have promoted autonomous language learning during lockdown and provided employees working from home with opportunities to learn new languages. Market research suggests that the global market for online language learning is due to grow by an estimated 18.7% from 2020 to 2027 to reach over US$21 billion by 2027 (Meticulous Research, 2020). A significant driver in this growth is artificial intelligence and analytics. Language learning and the study of languages is not marginal during crises of this kind but central to how we understand them through a multidisciplinary lens.

On a practical level teachers and learners have experienced unreliable challenges of both a technical and pedagogical nature depending on the national context. While in the developing world we assume access to wifi as if it is a human right or utility like water or energy, language teachers in the developing world or low-tech contexts often lack basic resources. Although these countries may be growing in access to smartphones, access alone to such technologies does not guarantee the pedagogical literacy to use them effectively for learning (Motteram, Al-Masri et al., 2020). In low-tech foreign language contexts, internet connections can be disrupted depending on the frequency and scale of use, teachers and learners may struggle to locate necessary resources, digital skills are not uniformly present in all learning contexts, learners may lack important competencies and the ability to self-motivate or adapt to the changing learning environments, and simply adapting face-to-face content for remote online instruction without considering the importance of social presence and interaction may severely compromise the effectiveness of the learning taking place (Nedungadi, Mulki, & Raman, 2017). As such challenging circumstances become more commonplace for foreign language educators, they need to consider using simple and reliable technical solutions that do not multiply the number of applications or platforms. As such, the ability to combine opportunities for synchronous and asynchronous learning that is "in-class" and/or "autonomous" through the use of social networks for language learning could be key to enabling collaboration and social interaction, and it is important to consider if e-resources are relevant by examining their ease of use, as well as cultural sensitivity and level of content difficulty. Above all, a range of teaching strategies should be considered, including open-ended opportunities for discovery-based learning, as well as experiential approaches and case studies (Qi & Yuping, 2017).

While encouraging students to "think critically" lies at the heart of hegemonic constructivist approaches to pedagogy, the same encouragement to think critically about the role of educational institutions in the age of neoliberalism is not always as enthusiastically encouraged in teaching faculty. The marketization of education has led to competition between schools and universities through national and international rankings and the search for new markets and new customers has become an increasingly routine part of being a teacher. Digital technologies have often been at the forefront of this new understanding of education, but they have often been presented rather too simplistically via uncontested catch-phrases – "technology-enhanced learning," "personalized learning environments," "computer-assisted learning" – as if they were politically neutral and emptied of all context and interests (Player-Koro, Rensfeldt, & Selwyn, 2017). The market for online language learning has grown dramatically in recent years, particularly in the APAC, European, and North and South American markets, as a result of products in three main areas: courses, solutions, and mobile apps. Principally, growth has focused more on English, Mandarin, and Spanish, with several leading companies fragmenting the market (Cengage, Duolingo, EF Education, McGraw-Hill Education, New Oriental Education and Technology, Pearson, Rosetta Stone Inc., and Sanako). Their main competitor is the growth in open access and open source solutions such as, e.g., European Commission or UNESCO (Meticulous Research, 2020).

While the number of students studying foreign languages at GCSE, A-level, and university in the UK has steadily declined over the last decade, the defense has often been an economic-related one aimed at proving how much languages can contribute to the global economy or what percentage of graduates enter graduate-level jobs, as we have seen above. The same applies to the position of the Arts and Humanities more broadly which have been under threat around the world over the last 30 years, unable to compete with the lure of business schools, science, technology, and engineering.

The Covid-19 pandemic has forced many educators to consider what post-pandemic education in our schools and universities will be like (Williamson, 2020a, 2020b). Previous pandemics from the middle ages to the current day have had significant effects on the operation of universities in particular. Research suggests, and the events of the pandemic confirm, that there is a clear relationship between inequalities in wealth and income, educational attainment, and access to information and communication technologies required for online learning (Cauchemez et al., 2014). Indeed, wealthier groups are more likely to be powerful advocates for their own position and to promote changes to the law that benefit their interests in health and education.

Likewise, the turn towards even greater online learning has led to a renewed surge in interest in educational technology start-ups, a now highly profitable market, particularly in Asia through online tutoring. The commodification of education has produced competition rather than collaboration between universities, and a managerial corporatism which attacks their critical function has spread in place of a mission based on public service (Williamson, 2020a).

There is no guarantee after much soul-searching that the pandemic will change education for the better. However, it has raised several important socioeconomic issues: the inequalities between people in health, education, and wealth; underlying disadvantages related to lack of ICT infrastructure or access to laptops and wifi or even space to engage in undistracted online learning; the importance of a decolonized curriculum; the depth of the digital divide in different regions; and inequalities within the home, not just between homes, depending on the availability of childcare or working arrangements. In sum, debunking myths associated with the digital age has also been a consequence of the pandemic, as it is clearer than ever before that not all so-called "digital natives" have equal access, or the time, space, support, or skills to engage in online classes.

3 Moving Forwards?

While digital technologies have been central to enabling education to continue to function throughout the COVID-19 pandemic, their widespread usage has underlined once again that the key questions we face as students, teachers, and researchers are not solely technical but above all *pedagogical* (Selwyn et al., 2020). During periods of disruption and change, as students, teachers, and researchers, we need to restate what our underlying principles and values are.

The preceding chapters have sought to explore different aspects of technology-mediated project-based language learning, mapping studies on telecollaboration and virtual exchange, several case studies on PBL in a variety of languages and contexts, and looking to the future with work on social justice and civic engagement (Hernández Alvarado and Brinckwirth; Anderson and Macleroy). The chapters have explored the research context and the rise of telecollaboration and virtual exchange and the opportunities and challenges PBL faces in immersive and collaborative virtual spaces (Benini and Thomas). The potential for gains in cross-cultural understanding, motivation, learning autonomy (Morgana), digital storytelling (Xie), and peer collaboration (Chism and Faidley) seem clear in different cultural and educational contexts, but more research is needed on longitudinal projects from a mixed-methods perspective (Bangun and Alfaifi) to explore learner and teacher resilience over longer periods of time to compensate for any short term "wow factor." PBL has much to offer specific skills development, such as writing (Nami) and other languages in addition to English (Xie; Chism and Faidley), as well as new forms of "pluriliteracy" and technology-mediated approaches such as CLIL (Cinganotto). In particular, Hernández Alvarado and Brinckwirth's study on cinema and social justice projects in teletandem classrooms in Mexico and the United States and Anderson and Macleroy's iterative research on multilingual digital storytelling use innovative methodologies such as critical ethnography and dialogic, student-led, inquiry-based models to examine creative language learning experiences. These two studies both point towards rich further veins of enquiry for PBL and CALL in that they engage learners within and beyond their classrooms, within and beyond their countries, to underline the significance of language learning to explore social and political challenges that matter across disciplines, from environmentalism and citizenship to sustainability and social justice (Gras-Velazquez, 2019).

Several key findings emerge collectively from the studies contained in the volume. While digital skillsets are inevitably important, we need to consider the pedagogical approaches we adopt above all. As technologies change rapidly, technical mastery remains secondary to developing in teachers a mindset that promotes flexibility and adaptability but above all criticality (Huang, Chen, Yang, & Loewen, 2013), encouraging teachers to be less "facilitator" and more "difficultator" with respect to normalized assumptions, and moving language classrooms from the margins of the humanities to a multidisciplinary project-based approach to solving problems and connecting learners.

As this book is submitted to the publisher, the new and very uncertain academic year is beginning for pupils and students around the world. It will be some time before this book is published in 2021, and traditional book and scholarly publishing cannot hope to keep pace with the dramatic socio-economic changes happening all around us. While language teachers are being called upon to champion digital innovation and computer-assisted learning, encouraging experimentation in autonomous as well as group teaching contexts, Black Lives Matter and related social movements have highlighted the need to interrogate the assumptions of received approaches, to champion working with students and key stakeholders to address social justice, following inclusive and equal educational principles, to decolonize the curriculum, and to prepare them for an uncertain future.

While digital educational technologies have been central to continuing education throughout the pandemic, then, their widespread usage has underlined that the key questions we face are primarily pedagogical and related to our underpinning principles. In the "new normal" of the post-pandemic university:

- How will our language classrooms be changed by blended, online, or socially-distanced forms of teaching and learning?
- How would we like our teaching and learning to change?
- While remote forms of teaching have now become commonplace, how do we rationalize and justify their use and normalization?
- How will language learning affect the traditional pedagogical spaces?
- How will language educators respond to the inclusivity and equality agenda with respect to issues of class, race, gender, and sexuality?
- How will we respond to questions of sustainability and educational technology?
- What national and international role does the university have in a world affected by restrictions on travel?
- While educational technology is increasingly driven by commercial and corporate interests, what is the public mission of the school and the university?
- What are the implications of increasingly digital tracing built into educational institutions to help track students and teachers?
- What are the implications for relationships between teachers, researchers, students, and managers during these restrictions?
- How might health and safety for teachers and researchers be balanced against the increasingly corporate agenda of educational institutions?
- How does the pandemic reinforce or justify the students-as-customers approach?
- Is education only something that can be bought and a service to be provided?
- Can we make the argument that it is a public good and right?

The pandemic has brought to a head discussion about what educational institutions are for, calling into question what Freire (2000) called the banking model of education. In place of "customers" and economic metaphors, a coaching metaphor may be more appropriate, in that this requires effort from both sides, teacher/coach and student/learner. The coach is more appropriate than the facilitator which has become synonymous with constructivist approaches as we do not simply facilitate content and dialogue; whether online or offline, we have a responsibility to work *with* students to problematize accepted ideas.

Traditional language teacher training programs teach a staple of content-based skills and knowledge. We are not aware of any offering crisis management or how to teach or research during periods of extreme disruption. Given the high turnover in language teachers worldwide, particularly those in term-time, non-tenured positions in the public or private sector, it is important to consider the future training of teachers, with an emphasis on enhancing their psychological health, and reducing burnout and the number of teachers quitting the profession. The current pandemic has caused numerous challenges for language educators as a result of the swift emergence of online forms of instruction, which has deconstructed previously distinct areas of their roles. Working from home or from COVID-ready workplaces has generated new uncertainties. Faced with an increasing form of "Edflix" (education + Netflix) which "delivers" content on demand in much the same way educational institutions deliver catering, sports, or entertainment, the growing influence of educational technology has been central to this service-led approach. The problem is that content may lead to entertainment, but content alone does not lead to a meaningful learning experience, as this depends on a myriad of unpredictable types of interaction over time, which is not always immediate like fast-food or satisfying like a buying a new product.

Project-based learning offers a potential alternative to this scenario, as we have seen in many of the chapters in this volume. Connecting learners within and beyond the walls of any single classroom either face-to-face and/or through virtual exchange, what I am calling "critical project-based learning," is rooted in a form or enquiry that is collaborative and values-based, and prepares citizens, not merely consumers, for the challenges they will face in an increasingly multidisciplinary and multimodal world. Learning in projects is not only "delivered" by an institution, nor is it always particularly "satisfying"; it requires effort and failure and dissatisfaction. Indeed, it is typically more disorientating and may require reflection over a significant period of time before some of it sinks in. So, the feeling of "being all at sea" is the feeling of learning, or its possibility, and not its absence.

The pandemic has certainly been a curse; if it has any positive aspect at all, it may be that it forces us to reconsider many of our normalized assumptions. As language educators and researchers, we also need to take this opportunity to rethink what is an appropriate form of sustainable pedagogy for an age of disruption.

References

Akbari, R. (2008). Transforming lives: Introducing critical pedagogy into ELT classrooms. *ELT Journal*, 62(3), 276–283. https://doi.org/10.1093/elt/ccn025

Bernstein, K. A., Katznelson, N., Amerzcua, A., Mohamed, S., & Alvarado, S. (2020). Equity/social justice, instrumentalism/neoliberalism: Dueling discourses of dual language in principals' talk about their programs. *TESOL Quarterly*, 54(3), 652–684. https://doi.org/10.1002/tesq.582

Bilyalova A., Salimova D., & Zelenina T. (2020). Digital transformation in education. In T. Antipova (Eds.), *Integrated science in digital age. ICIS 2019. Lecture Notes in Networks and Systems*, 78. Springer, Cham. Retrieved from https://doi.org/10.1007/978-3-030-22493-6_24

Casey, J., & Wilson, P. (2005). A practical guide to providing flexible learning in further and higher education. Retrieved from http://qmwww.enhancementthemes.ac.uk/docs/publications/a-practical-guide-to-providing-flexible-learning-in-further-and-higher-education.pdf

Cauchemez, S., Van Kerkhove, M. D., Archer, B. N., Cetron, M., Cowling, B. J., Grove, P., Hunt, D., Kojouharova, M., Kon, P., et al. (2014). School closures during the 2009 influenza pandemic: national and local experiences. *BMC infectious diseases*, 14, 207. https://doi.org/10.1186/1471-2334-14-207

Collis, B., & Moonen, J. (2004). *Flexible learning in a digital world*, 2nd edition. London: Routledge and Falmer.

Freire, P. (2000). *Pedagogy of the oppressed*, 30th anniversary edition. Trans. M. B. Ramos. New York: Continuum.

Gras-Velazquez, A. (Ed.). (2019). *Project-based learning in second language acquisition: Building communities of practice in higher education*. London & New York: Routledge. https://doi.org/10.4324/9780429457432

Gray, J. (2019). Critical language teacher education? In S. Walsh & S. Mann (Eds.), *The Routledge handbook of English language teacher education*. Abingdon: Routledge. https://doi.org/10.4324/9781315659824-6

Huang, R., Chen, G., Yang, J., & Loewen, J. (2013). The new shape of learning: Adapting to social changes in the information society. In R. Huang & J. M. Spector (Eds.), *Reshaping learning SE – 1* (pp. 3–42). Berlin: Springer. https://doi.org/10.1007/978-3-642-32301-0_1

Macintyre, P. D., Gregersen, T., & Mercer, S. (2020). Language teachers' coping strategies during the Covid-19 conversion to online teaching: Correlations with stress, wellbeing and negative emotions, *System*, 94. Retrieved from https://www.sciencedirect.com/science/article/pii/S0346251X20307120. https://doi.org/10.1016/j.system.2020.102352

Meticulous Research (2020). Online language learning market: Global opportunity analysis and forecast (2020–27). Retrieved from https://www.meticulousresearch.com/product/online-language-learning-market-5025/

Motteram, G., Al-Masri, N., Hamouda, H., & Omarali, S. (2020). Exploring mobile support for English language teachers in a context of conflict: Syrian refugee teachers in Jordan. In G. Fassetta, N. Al-Masri, & A. Phipps (Eds.). *Multilingual online academic collaborations as resistance: Crossing impassable borders*. Bristol: Multilingual Matters.

Motteram, G., Dawson, S., & Al-Masri, N. (2020). WhatsApp supported language teacher development: A case study in the Zataari refugee camp. *Education and Information Technologies*. Retrieved from https://doi.org/10.1007/s10639-020-10233-0

Nedungadi, P., Mulki, K., & Raman, R. (2017). Improving educational outcomes & reducing absenteeism at remote villages with mobile technology and WhatsApp: Findings from rural India. *Education and Information Technologies*, 23, 113–127. https://doi.org/10.1007/s10639-017-9588-z

Player-Koro, C., Rensfeldt, A. B., & Selwyn, N. (2017). Selling tech to teachers: Education trade shows as policy events. *Journal of Education Policy*, 33, 682–703. https://doi.org/10.1080/02680939.2017.1380232

Qi, G. Y., & Yuping, W. (2017). Investigating the building of a WeChat based community of practice for language teachers' professional development. *Innovation in Language Learning and Teaching*, 12(1), 72–88. https://doi.org/10.1080/17501229.2018.1418635

Selwyn, N., Hillman, T., Eynon, R., Ferreira, G., Knox, J., Macgilchrist, F., & Sancho-Gilet, J. M. (2020). What's next for Ed-Tech? Critical hopes and concerns for the 2020s. *Learning, Media and Technology*, 45(1), 1–6. https://doi.org/10.1080/17439884.2020.1694945

Universities UK (2020). Language learning vital to pandemic recovery. Retrieved from https://www.universitiesuk.ac.uk/news/Pages/Language-learning-vital-to-pandemic-recovery.aspx

Williamson, B. (2017). *Big data in education: The digital future of learning, policy and practice*. London: Sage. https://doi.org/10.4135/9781529714920

Williamson, B. (2020a). Pandemic politics, pedagogies and practices: Digital technologies and distance education during the coronavirus emergency. *Learning, Media and Technology*, 45, 107–114. https://doi.org/10.1080/17439884.2020.1761641

Williamson, B. (2020b). *The datafication of teaching in higher education: Critical issues and perspectives. Teaching in Higher Education*, 25, 351–365. https://doi.org/10.1080/13562517.2020.1748811

Zhao, Y. (2020). COVID-19 as a catalyst for educational change. *Prospects*. Retrieved from https://link.springer.com/article/10.1007%2Fs11125-020-09477-y. https://doi.org/10.1007/s11125-020-09477-y

About the Author

Michael Thomas is Professor of Education and Chair of the Centre for Educational Research (CERES) at Liverpool John Moores University in the UK. He is the author or editor of over thirty books and peer-reviewed special editions and founding editor of four book series, including Advances in Digital Language Learning and Teaching (Bloomsbury), Digital Education and Learning (Palgrave), and Global Policy and Critical Futures in Education (Palgrave). Among his other books on CALL are *Project-Based Language Learning with Technology* (Routledge 2017) and *Language Teaching with Video-Based Technologies* (Routledge 2020).

Index

www.ingramcontent.com/pod-product-compliance
Lightning Source LLC
LaVergne TN
LVHW010444080826
844660LV00026B/1209
9781800500242